DAHOMEY AND
ITS NEIGHBOURS
1708–1818

Portrait of Agaja, reproduced from A. Dalzel, *The History of Dahomey,*
published in 1793

# DAHOMEY AND ITS NEIGHBOURS 1708-1818

I.A.AKINJOGBIN

*Senior Lecturer in History and Acting Director*
*Institute of African Studies, University of Ife, Ile–Ife*

CAMBRIDGE
AT THE UNIVERSITY PRESS
1967

Published by the Syndics of the Cambridge University Press
Bentley House, 200 Euston Road, London, N.W. 1
American Branch, 32 East 57th Street, New York, N.Y. 10022

Library of Congress Catalogue Card Number: 67–12323

Printed in Great Britain
at the University Printing House, Cambridge
(Brooke Crutchley, University Printer)

# Contents

*To my mother*

BERNICE ADETOUN AKINJOGBIN
ARẸMU ERIN, ARA IWERE
ỌMỌ AJIGALỌRUN BI IYAWO.

# Abbreviations

ABNJ. Archivo Bibliotheca Nacional de Rio de Janeiro.
Adm. Admiralty.
ADN. Archives Departmentales, Nantes.
ADR. Archives Departmentales, La Rochelle.
African Committee: Committee of Merchants Trading to Africa.
AHU. Archivo Historico Ultramarino, Lisbon.
AN. Archives Nationales, Paris.
APB. Archivo Publico dos Bahia.
CCR. Chambre du Commerce et d'Industries de La Rochelle.
CMS. Church Missionary Society.
CO. Colonial Office.
*E.D.* *Etudes Dahoméennes.*
EUL. Edinburgh University Library.
FO. Foreign Office.
MMA. Methodist Missionary Archives.
PRO. Public Record Office, London.

¹ In the footnotes, for the sake of brevity, only the serial number (e.g. T 70/1475) of PRO documents is given.

# Preface

This book grew out of a Ph.D. thesis submitted to the University of London in October 1963. Its aim is to trace, with the aid of hitherto unused documents, the eighteenth century political developments in Dahomey, the well-known West African kingdom which occupied approximately the southern third of the modern Republic of Dahomey, and whose capital was at Abomey. Its central theme is Dahomey's attempt to create a politically stable and economically viable state. Economic questions are therefore important, but they have been treated mainly as contributory factors to the main question of political development.

The introduction of the trans-Atlantic slave trade into the Aja country had, by the end of the seventeenth century, weakened the Aja institutions and created a political vacuum. Before the process had reached an incurable stage, however, a group of Aja had founded a new state, later called Dahomey, designed to withstand the corrosive influences of the new economic system.

By the beginning of the eighteenth century, Dahomey had grown sufficiently strong to fill the political vacuum being created by the decay of the traditional system. Between 1724 and 1727, Agaja, king of Dahomey, conquered and incorporated all the ancient Aja states. The Oyo immediately rose up in defence of the traditional system and the Europeans in defence of their economic activities. In 1730 Agaja submitted to Oyo and agreed to co-operate with the slave traders.

After that Dahomey was forced to concentrate on economic and administrative reconstruction, rendered necessary by the Oyo ravages and practicable by the peace imposed by Oyo. By 1751 the reconstruction was virtually completed.

After a brief period of prosperity, the inadequacies of the slave-trade economy started to appear. Neither the European ships nor the supply of slaves were available in sufficiently large numbers. A deep economic depression started from about 1767 and despite all efforts remained incurable in 1818, producing a

widespread dissatisfaction which finally led to the deposition of
Adandozan in 1818 and the replacement of the Tegbesu line
by another headed by Gezo.

I am indebted to a great number of persons who have all
helped me in the course of my research. In England all the
archivists, librarians and attendants at the Public Record
Office, Church Missionary Society, Methodist Missionary
Society, the Edinburgh University Library and the British
Museum; in France, all the archivists and attendants at the
Archives Nationales in Paris, the Archives Departmentales in
Nantes, La Rochelle and Le Havre and at the Chambre de
Commerce et d'Industries at La Rochelle, have all been very
kind and co-operative, as has M. R. Cornevin, Chef du Centre
d'Etudes et de Documentation d'Afrique et d'Outre-Mer.

My stay in France was made both fruitful and enjoyable by
M. Fatumbi P. Verger, M. P. Mercier of the Sorbonne, Dr
Gilbert Rouget of the Musée de l'Homme as well as by my
fellow Nigerian student at the Sorbonne, Abiola Irele.

To M. Verger I must express my special gratitude, for it was
he who collected and translated for me all the Portuguese documents I have used in this work. Just how kind he has been will
be appreciated when it is realised that these documents are
deposited as far apart as Lisbon, Bahia and Rio de Janeiro.

In many special ways, I owe a huge debt of gratitude to
Professor John Hargreaves, Burnett-Fletcher Professor of
History at the University of Aberdeen, who for many years
has given me constant encouragement and advice; to Professor
G. S. Graham, Rhodes Professor of Imperial History at King's
College, London, whose kindness and fatherly counsel are now
proverbial among those who have been privileged to come
very close to him; and to Christopher Fyfe, Reader in African
History at the University of Edinburgh, who has been a true
friend and adviser to more than one generation of West African
historians.

While I was at the School of Oriental and African Studies in
London, Professor Roland Oliver, Professor John Fage and
Mr Douglas Jones gave me the benefit of their academic experience. Both Professor Fage and Professor Oliver have been
of tremendous help in seeing that this work is published.

Without the generous grant made to me by the British

Commonwealth and Scholarship Commission, and the kindness of the officers of the British Council who administer the fund, this work could not have been attempted.

Finally, I must express my gratitude to my wife, who not only shared with me the depressions and the elations of a research student, but also read the whole manuscript through with me more than once.

I.A.A.

*July 1966*

# Introduction

Compared with other ancient West African kingdoms, Dahomey has been well served with travel accounts and scholarly
works. This is not surprising for the kingdom was, in many
ways, remarkable and has never lost its attraction for academic
and non-academic writers. To anyone who is fairly familiar
with the area, there might seem, at first sight, nothing new
to be gained from a study of its history in the eighteenth
century. Such a view, though erroneous, might seem to be
borne out by the long list of books that have appeared on the
kingdom.

In the seventeenth century, long before Dahomey became
famous, the region featured in the works of Dapper, a Dutchman, whose work was translated into English by John Ogilby
and given the very cumbersome title of *Africa, being an accurate
description of the regions of Aegypt, Barbary, Lybia and Billedul-
gerid, the land of Negroes, Guinea, Aethiopia and the Abyssines.*
William Bosman, also a Dutchman, wrote *A New and Accurate
Description of the Coast of Guinea* which was published early in
1705. In 1732 John Barbot, a Frenchman settled in England,
published *A Description of the Coasts of the North and South
Guinea.*

In the eighteenth century, when Dahomey had become the
dominant power in Aja, various Englishmen who had visited
the kingdom left accounts of their experiences behind.
Among them were William Snelgrave, who in 1734 wrote *A New
Account of some parts of Guinea and the Slave Trade*; John
Atkins, who wrote *A Voyage to Guinea, Brazil and the West
Indies*, published in 1735; William Smith, whose work *A New
Voyage to Guinea* was published posthumously in 1744. Towards
the end of the century, Archibald Dalzel published *The
History of Dahomey, An Inland Kingdom of Africa*, which was
a compilation of select passages from previous works and has
remained the history of Dahomey in the eighteenth century.
Other eminent writers, whose work will be listed in the biblio-

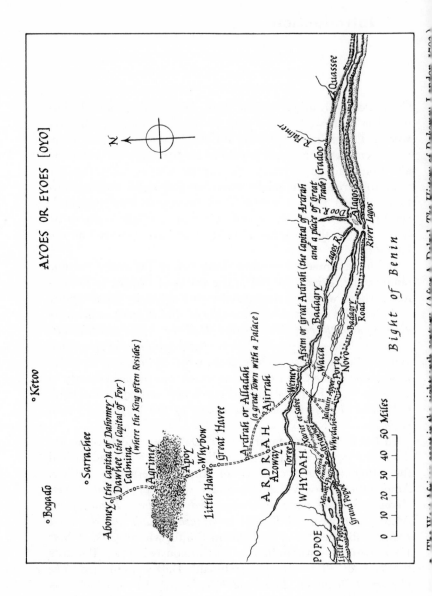

2. The West African coast in the eighteenth century. (After A. Dalzel, *The History of Dahomey*, London, 1793.)

graphy, also wrote on Dahomey in the nineteenth and in the twentieth centuries.

If all that is needed is just enough background knowledge for a detailed study of the colonial period, all the above sources may indeed be regarded as sufficiently satisfactory. If, however, what is wanted is an understanding of the historical development of the people themselves, their actions, their reaction to external stimuli, and the process of growth which made Dahomey the strong kingdom it was in the nineteenth century, in short if what is wanted is an objective history of the African kingdom of Dahomey, then these sources cannot be taken as adequate in themselves.

A close study of all of them reveals certain attitudes which may in fact make it impossible, without a new study of this type, to arrive at an accurate historical interpretation of Dahomey in the eighteenth century. Not all the travel accounts were written out of a healthy regard for Dahomey, but to satisfy a demand, or to contribute to an argument current in the country of the author at the time of writing. No one will seriously doubt that Norris's account of the reign of Tegbesu was intended primarily as a contribution towards the controversy about the abolition of the slave trade, a project which Norris opposed, or that everything that Burton wrote on Dahomey was deeply coloured by his blind belief that Africans were inferior beings. A good example of just how much Burton cared for the history of Dahomey can be illustrated by a historical 'fact' he related. On one page, he said that Agaja died in 1727, and on the very next page, he went on blithely reporting what the same Agaja did in 1732.

Even Dalzel, whose venerable work remains the only 'history' of eighteenth-century Dahomey, did not write for the edification of Dahomey. He, or his editor, was mainly interested in showing, despite the many incidents in his work which proved the contrary, that Dahomey was one of those 'savage nations' which were 'under little controul [*sic*] than that of their own will' and by that to extol the British civilisation. The commonest epithets which he used for Dahomey were 'barbarous' and 'savage'. His explanation for the wars of Dahomey were the 'insatiable thirst after blood, the barbarous vanity of being considered the scourge of mankind, the savage pomp of dwelling in a house garnished with skulls and stained with human gore'. Most serious historians no longer regard such supercilious attitudes as a valid basis of historical judgement.

Moreover, an examination of these accounts will reveal that in fact only two decades of the eighteenth-century Dahomey, 1724–34, and 1770–80, were actually covered by published eyewitness accounts. In Dalzel, the remaining decades have been filled in as best as the author could.

Equally inadequate as histories in themselves are the oral traditions. The historian's distrust of anything that is not written has largely prevented, until recently, an objective attitude towards this source. Consequently there has been no uniform approach to its use.

My own experience during two years of collecting different kinds of oral traditions among the Yoruba, a people closely related in history and culture to the Dahomeans, has convinced me that most writers on West Africa have not clearly distinguished between different kinds of traditions. They do not seem to be aware that certain kinds of traditions are 'documentary' in character and that others are largely 'interpretative', and that both have differet 'evidential' values. For Dahomey, the 'interpretative' kind of oral traditions have been mostly collected and largely presented as the 'history' of Dahomey. The danger here is that the 'interpretative' class of oral traditions almost always serves the interests of the narrator.

Our knowledge of eighteenth-century Dahomey up to date therefore is a mixture of facts, fables and prejudices, sanctioned by usage and rendered acceptable by a general lack of interest in genuine African history except as an aspect of European imperial activities. In other words, there has been no scholarly historical work, devoted mainly to a study of the political developments in Dahomey in the eighteenth century. There is therefore something yet to be learnt from a study of this type.

In the nineteenth century, Dahomey was obviously an important West African kingdom, an oasis of internal order and sound administration in a sea of surrounding chaos. The basis of this unique position was laid in the eighteenth century. What then was the process of its political growth, what were the factors governing that process, and why did Dahomey succeed where other neighbouring kingdoms apparently failed?

The only contemporary documents to which the historian can turn for answers to these questions are the records of the different European African companies, five of which were established at Allada and Whydah at different times during the seventeenth and eighteenth centuries. They were the Brandenburgers, the Dutch, the English, the French and the Portuguese. The Brandenburgers, established in 1684, did not operate for more than a few years and had left the country before 1700. The Dutch too were gone by 1730, driven away by Agaja. For the greater part of the eighteenth century therefore the English, the French and the Portuguese, the last of which established at Whydah in 1721, were the most permanent European traders in Aja. Accordingly, their records have mostly been used.

The records of the English Royal African Company, or after 1751 the Committee of Merchants Trading to Africa, are chronologically the fullest, though they are far from being complete. They are now part of the Treasury Papers (T 70) in the Public Record Office. Usually the few surviving private papers of the local officers are much more helpful for this work than their public dispatches, particularly in the case of Whydah.

The records of the successive French Companies, from 1712 to about 1791, are lodged in the Archives Nationales in Paris, as part of the Colonial Office Papers under the index C. 6: *Senegal Ancien*. They do not contain as many items as the English records, but usually they have been better preserved. The French officers' practice of writing separate dispatches at the same time, one on the trade and the other on current affairs, and of keeping full diaries of their interviews with the kings of Dahomey, have made their surviving documents very full and useful.

A most unexpected and invaluable French source are the records of the Provincial traders deposited in the Archives Departmentales, particularly at Nantes and La Rochelle. The B. and C. series in both places, and especially at Nantes, are very useful. The series contain the short reports of all the captains who made round voyages from Nantes or La Rochelle to West Africa, America or the West Indies and back. Usually, each account gives the date of departure, the description of the articles of trade carried away, different ports of call in West Africa and the length of stay in each port, events in the ports during the captain's stay, the number of slaves carried away and date of departure from West Africa to the West Indies. It also contains similar notice of the captain's activities in the West Indies. These sources of information are sometimes supplemented by similar ones at the local Chamber of Commerce of which the papers at La Rochelle have been most useful.

In Paris, I was able to secure the private papers of an eighteenth-century slave trader, M. Proa, from one of his descendants, M. Marchand, through the kind introduction of M. Delafosse, the Archivist at La Rochelle.

In Paris also, I was fortunate enough to meet the surviving head of the Wegbaja family, Prince Justin Aho, who, if Dahomey were not now a Republic, would presumably be king, and who still keeps court and performs court ceremonials as his ancestors had done. The four different interviews I had with him were very helpful towards my understanding of certain place-names, and certain names of the kings of Dahomey.

I was not able to consult the Portuguese sources myself. Those that have been used in this work have been collected and translated for me by M. Fatumbi Pierre Verger. They are mainly the official correspondences between the kings of Dahomey, the Viceroy (later Governor) of Brazil and the kings of Portugal. In the Archives at Bahia, they are kept under the title *Ordens Regiais* (OR) or simply under 'Correspondence'. At Rio de Janeiro, they are numbered serially. At Lisbon, they are usually kept in boxes (*Caixa*) and stamped with names that do not at first sight suggest their connection with the Aja country, for example, São Thome.

For the last thirty years of this study, the Companies' records are either non-existent or are very thin. To fill in the gap, Admiralty (Adm. I), Foreign Office (FO.) and Colonial Office (CO.) records have been consulted, as have parliamentary papers, and the letters of certain agents of the Church Missionary Society (CA 2), and Methodist Missionary Society (MMA.), who are known to have been in Dahomey within the first sixty years of the nineteenth century.

Although these documents were not mainly concerned with Dahomean affairs, and are by no means as complete as could be wished, they have repaid patient search. They have been used to correct a few but important opinions, currently but mistakenly held, on certain aspects of the history of Dahomey, have brought precision where our knowledge was only hazy and have served as a check on the oral traditions. This last function may have an important bearing on the future evaluation and use of oral traditions for serious historical purposes.

With the passing of the colonial era and the re-emergence of African states whose relation with the outside world is almost exactly similar to those of their predecessors of the eighteenth century, such a study as this should have more than academic interest.

# 1

## The political decline in Aja

The great political consequences of the slave trade on the West African states have been more repeated than studied. It has been credibly implied that the Europeans brought with them an experience of political activities different from those existing in contemporary West Africa, and that the economic activities in which they engaged were either completely new or had never been practised on such a vast scale. It has also been granted that the new situation arising from their presence ultimately gave rise to new political formations. Yet the growth of those states, the factors governing their growth and the part played by the Africans in that process have not been sufficiently studied in the different parts of West Africa where the European activities were concentrated.

Among those who had to make institutional and political adjustments as a result of the European activities in their country were the Aja people of the later kingdom of Dahomey. The strains and stresses of the new ideas and practices on their ancient institutions became apparent from about the middle of the seventeenth century. By the beginning of the eighteenth century those institutions had become clearly inadequate. Their struggle in the eighteenth century to create a new, politically stable and economically viable state, called Dahomey, is the subject of this book. Whatever happened in Aja affected all their neighbours, particularly the Yoruba, whose reaction formed an integral part of the Aja struggle.

The area lying roughly between the mouth of the Niger and longitude 1° east, and between the sea coast and latitude 9° north, could be regarded as a country, and perhaps might have been so delineated if a political map of West Africa had existed, say, at the beginning of the fifteenth century. It might also have been, and henceforth will be, called the Yoruba-Aja country. Its coastline was later called the 'slave coast' by the Europeans from about the end of the seventeenth century onwards.[1] Early in 1826, when Clapperton asked an Oyo man for the boundary of the Yoruba country, he was given virtually the above description.[2]

Beyond a low-lying coastal belt, the land gently rises towards the north, where it flattens out into a kind of table land, which nowhere rises higher than three thousand feet above sea level. The land formation makes the rivers flow from north to south and the area is well drained. Lagoon systems, which have now silted up at many points, ran along the whole coastline. Rainfall is heavy in the south and east but is lighter towards the north and west, making the north and west a more open country than the south and east. In many places the conditions are suitable for agriculture and the rearing of livestock. In the eighteenth century, for example, travellers reported the presence on the coast of an abundance of maize, which was harvested twice a year, and of animals such as sheep, goats, cattle, pigs, dogs, and poultry of all kinds including muscovy ducks.[3] Another observer at the beginning of the nineteenth century reported that a few miles inland, millet was grown in large quantities.

The Yoruba kingdoms, numbering about fourteen major and many minor ones at the beginning of the eighteenth century, occupied mainly the eastern portion of this area. The major kingdoms were Benin (or Ibini), Ekiti (or Efon), Egba, Egbado (or Awori), Ife Igbomina, Ijamo, Ijebu including Idoko, Ijesha, Ketu, Ondo, Owu, Oyo and Shabe. The smaller ones were scattered all over modern Dahomey and Togo republics.

Their oral traditions have not been exhaustively collected, nor have those collected been definitively analysed. Such of them as have been collected are, however, remarkably in agreement that the rulers of all their major kingdoms migrated from Ife though they differ on exactly the number of these major kingdoms.[4] The Oyo tradition, collected by the Reverend Samuel Johnson towards the end of the nineteenth century, relates that there were seven, while current Ife traditions maintain that there were sixteen. The tradition of Oyo goes further to say that Ife itself was

[1] See map 1.
[2] Hugh Clapperton, *Journal of a Second Expedition into the Interior of Africa* (London, 1829), p. 57.
[3] A. Dalzel, *The History of Dahomey* (London, 1793), p. 3.
[4] S. Johnson (ed. O. Johnson), *The History of the Yorubas* (Lagos, 1956), pp. 17–18.

9

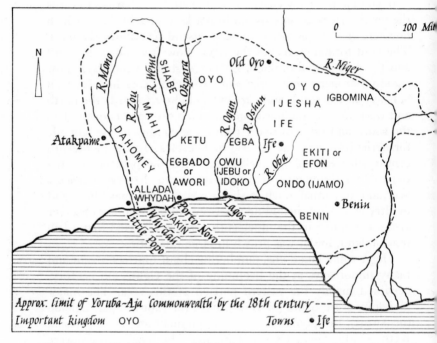

0       100 Mil

N

R. Mono

R. Zou

R. Wème

SHABE

R. Okpara

Old Oyo ●

R. Niger

OYO

OYO

IGBOMINA

IJESHA

MAHI

R. Ogun

R. Oshun

IFE

DAHOMEY

KETU

EGBA

Ife ●

EKITI or
EFON

Atakpame ●

EGBADO
or
AWORI

OWU
IJEBU or
IDOKO

R. Oba

ONDO (IJAMO)

ALLADA
WHYDAH ●

● Benin

Porto-Novo

Lagos

BENIN

Whydah

JAKIN

Little Popo

Approx. limit of Yoruba-Aja 'Commonwealth' by the 18th century ---
Important kingdom    OYO           Towns   ● Ife

2. The Yoruba-Aja 'Commonwealth' in the seventeenth and eighteenth centuries.

founded by the emigrants from Arabia,[1] but the Ife tradition maintains that the whole world originated from Ile Ife.

Until further evidence comes to light therefore, the date of the foundation of Ife and of most of the major kingdoms cannot be stated with certainty. Guesses about the probable date of the foundation of Ife range from 2000 B.C. to between A.D. 600 and 1000. It can however be said with some degree of confidence that most of the Yoruba kingdoms known to be existing in the eighteenth century had been founded by the beginning of the fourteenth century.

The Aja occupied the western portion of the Yoruba-Aja country. At the beginning of the eighteenth century, the most important of their kingdoms were Allada, Whydah, Popo, Jakin and Dahomey.

It may well be true that before these kingdoms were founded, the Aja lived in autonomous villages.[2] However, oral traditions would suggest that from the time they came into contact with the Yoruba, probably before the fourteenth century, they started to adopt the Yoruba institutions and to live in kingdoms.

These traditions, collected in Togo and among the Ewe in Ghana, would suggest that the Aja were gradually pushed westwards as the Yoruba expanded until they gathered around Tado, from where they dispersed in various directions. Some went to Nuatja or Watchi, which later became the centre of Ewe dispersal, and others returned eastwards as a result of dynastic quarrels and settled at Allada, from where they founded the kingdoms whose names are quoted above. It has been suggested, and may well be true, that the stories of the migration of the Yoruba and the Aja peoples constitute a single series of migration with Ife, Ketu, Tado and Nuatja as the four main stopping and dispersal points.[3]

The date of the foundation of Allada is uncertain but all the earliest events connected with it would suggest a period towards the end of the sixteenth century, probably about 1575. First there is a curious Oyo tradition which relates that 'Sabigana' emigrated from Sabe to the Yoruba country during the reign of Obalokun, the Alafin of Oyo,[4] which can be dated to the last

[1] S. Johnson, *History*, p. 3.
[2] M. J. Herskovits, *Dahomey, An Ancient West African Kingdom* (New York, 1938), vol. II, p. 3.
[3] Jacques Bertho, 'La Parente des Yoruba aux peuplades de Dahomey et Togo', in *Africa* (1949), pp. 121–32.     [4] S. Johnson, *History*, p. 168.

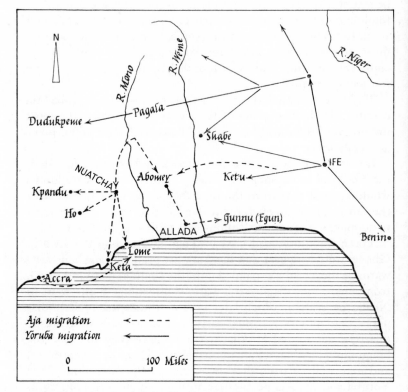

3. The migrations of the Yoruba and Aja peoples. (After J. Bertho, *Africa*, 1949, pp. 121–32.)

decades of the sixteenth century. This tradition would seem to be referring to the last stage in the eastward movement of the Aja from Tado to Allada because the suffix '-gan' (gana) was used for Aja titles and because the 'Shabe' in question would not appear to have been that founded by a descendant of Oduduwa, the ruler of which was called 'Onisabe'. It would seem to be the capital of the old Whydah kingdom written as 'Savi' or 'Xavier' by the Europeans but which may have been pronounced 'Sabwe' with the 'bw' sounding like the 'w' in modern Ewe.

Then there is the Dahomean tradition which relates that two reigns after the foundation of Allada by the Tado emigrants certain Aja princes left there as a result of dynastic quarrels to found Abomey. Dahomey was most probably founded about the beginning of the seventeenth century, about 1620,[1] and the reigns of two kings at such an unsettled time could not have extended for more than fifty years. At all events, the first known European notice of 'Ardra' appeared in the map of Arnold de Langum published in 1596.[2]

The dominant cultural influence in the whole area were the Yoruba, who, judging from the large area of land which they are said to have occupied in the different oral traditions, were obviously by far the more numerous of the two groups.[3] Travellers in the early seventeenth century noticed, for instance, that the lingua franca there was 'Alkomysh', the language of the Olukumi, the name by which the Yoruba of the area were known.[4] Modern anthropologists have also recorded[5] that most

---

[1] J. D. Fage, *An Introduction to the History of West Africa* (Cambridge, 1956), p. 93; C. W. Newbury, *The Western Slave Coast and its Rulers* (Oxford, 1961), p. 10; R. Cornevin, *Histoire du Dahomey* (Paris, 1962), p. 92.

[2] R. Cornevin, *Histoire du Dahomey*, p. 24.

[3] All the oral traditions relating to the foundation of Dahomey agree that the Abomey plateau belonged to the Yoruba people of Igede (Gedevi) before the Aja came. Le Herisse, *L'Ancien Royaume du Dahomey* (Paris, 1911), ch. XII.

[4] John Ogilby, *Africa, Being an Accurate Description of the Aegypt, Barbary, Lybia, etc.* (London, 1670), p. 647. The words *Oluku mi* mean 'my friend'. Early Yoruba from modern Dahomey to the Benin region seem to have borne the name. Some people in Haiti are still called 'Lukumi', and they speak recognisable Yoruba. Others in the Ibo area of Nigeria are still called Onukumi; they also speak recognisable Yoruba.

[5] Jacques Bertho, 'La Parente de Yoruba aux peuplades de Dahomey et Togo', in *Africa* (1949), pp. 121–32; P. Hazoume, *Le Pact de sang au Dahomey* (Paris, 1937), p. 139; Le Herisse, *L'Ancien Royaume*, pp. 92–155, enumerates many of the gods though his spelling of their names may sometimes make them at first sight unrecognisable.

of the religious beliefs in the whole area tend to originate from Ife, or some other part of the Yoruba region.

Religious beliefs and language are agents which generally modify social institutions and we may assume that the Aja borrowed a great many of the Yoruba institutions as well. Common institutions freely borrowed or imposed, common religious beliefs and a common language made the unity of the Yoruba-Aja country a reality. Yet within this unity, the Aja retained their distinct identity even though there were, and still are, areas where distinctions were blurred.

Before the arrival of the Europeans, the Yoruba-Aja peoples lived under a monarchical form of government. Each of the major kingdoms both in Yoruba and Aja had a principal town and a number of subject towns, villages, hamlets and markets. Each king had, as his helpers, a number of hereditary chiefs charged with specific duties. Within his territory, the king, with the help of his chiefs, ruled with a large measure of independence. He could install his own sub-kings and head men, he could levy his own taxes and spend it the way he liked. All serious criminal cases ended with him. He could wage wars within his own kingdom and even against a neighbouring kingdom without anybody's interference.

Within each state, the people had specific ideas about which authority was legitimate and which was not, and expressed relationships, social and governmental, according to a single accepted 'social theory'. This social theory was never written. It was probably more practised than theorised about, but was nevertheless generally known and accepted, and was woven into the social fabric of the people's lives so thoroughly that even today, particularly in areas which have been hardly affected by modern European civilisation, traces of it are still discernible among them. It is this persisting relic, together with the recorded examples since the seventeenth century of certain specific acts of state, such as coronation ceremonies, declaration of wars, celebration of festivals, etc., that has made possible the attempt to reconstruct the theory as the basis underlying the traditional political organisation of the Yoruba-Aja kingdoms.

What held all the various Yoruba and Aja kingdoms together derived from the claims and acceptances that all the kings of the major kingdoms were descendants of the same great ancestor.

The Yoruba mention seven or sixteen kingdoms and the Aja mention three, sometimes four, kingdoms as forming part of their respective countries. In the Yoruba country, for instance, all the kings claim to have descended directly or indirectly from Oduduwa. And the Aja kings of Allada, Whydah and Dahomey all claim to be the descendants of a Nuatcha prince, who had unsuccessfully contested the throne at home and had migrated to Allada. In all the Yoruba and Aja kingdoms, the person occupying the throne of the original ancestor was regarded as 'father' of all the other kings and all the other kings regarded one another as 'brothers'.

This father–son relationship between the person occupying the throne of the original ancestor and the major kings was the basis of the constitution of the Yoruba-Aja country. The 'father' had the duty to give the final sanctions to the appointments of any of the kings, who in turn took an oath never to attack his territory. In the Yoruba country, for instance, the elections of the kings of all the most important kingdoms were sanctioned at Ife with the presentation of different symbolic objects, among which swords and cutlasses feature prominently. In Aja, the kings were either crowned in Allada or by agents sent out from Allada.

From the way in which the relationships between kingdoms have been practised since before the seventeenth century and are today explained in the whole of the Yoruba-Aja country, it is clear that the people regarded the state as a larger version of the family,[1] with the king standing in the same relation to his subjects as a father to his children. Among the appellations which the Yoruba give to all their kings is the word *baba* (father) and Dahomeans call their kings *Dada* which means father.

In other words, each 'father-king' of each 'family-state' looked on his neighbour in a particular family relationship, and all the 'father-kings' of all the 'family-states' looked on one particular king as 'Father' who in turn regarded all the other kings as 'sons'.[2] This way of looking at the state and country

[1] In the Yoruba country, for example, great care is taken to connect all the most important kingdoms to Ife and regard their founders as 'sons' of Oduduwa, the ancestor of the Yoruba. In Aja all the kings equally descended from one common 'father'.

[2] The situation still obtains in western Nigeria today. The Ooni of Ife is still regarded as 'father' by the most important western Nigerian Obas. Dahomey no longer has kings.

will be called the '*Ebi*' social theory,[1] and the country thus formed will be called, for lack of a better expression, an '*Ebi* Commonwealth'. The Yoruba-Aja country was therefore not a 'national' state, but an '*Ebi* Commonwealth'.

The first corollary that must be noted therefore is the belief that the relationship was not forced, but natural. The 'father kingdom' did not take its title from conquest but from descent. Its authority therefore did not depend on force but on natural obedience freely given. No kingdom could be correctly described as dependent on another. Just as in a family, all the kingdoms were interdependent. Each kingdom had its duties to the father-kingdom, and the 'father-kingdom' owed duties to all the others. These duties, which were regarded as sacred, were largely well defined. It was believed that the non-performance of them would offend the souls of the departed ancestors and bring both temporal and spiritual disasters reverberating throughout the whole country.

The second corollary is that the bond of society was blood relationship, not security or common economic interests. A man was a citizen of a kingdom because his family was a unit within the kingdom and he was a citizen of the whole country through his kingdom. Nobody could assume citizenship without being born into it, and once born into it, no one could opt out.

The smallest unit within the state was not the individual, but the family, which included dead and unborn generations, and to which belonged such things as state offices, agricultural lands, industries, priesthood and the like. A foreigner could join the society through intermarriage with any of the 'citizens' but only the issues of such a marriage who could later claim blood relationship were regarded as citizens.

This form of political organisation had many advantages. For example, it simplified local administration in an age when transport was difficult and it devolved social service commitments on small family units. It had many faults, however, the greatest of which was its weak central authority. By emphasising that obedience was based on natural allegiance, the 'father' of the '*Ebi* Commonwealth' was left without his own army to defend the overall interests of the 'Commonwealth' either against a recalcitrant member or against an outside intruder.

---

[1] *Ebi* means family, but will be used in preference to the English word to avoid the idea of English family which is different from the African one.

This fault was all the more serious because the emphasis on 'family' and 'blood relationship' made the overall interests of the 'Commonwealth' a secondary and often a remote concern for the citizens. In the face of an external pressure, their first instinct would be to defend their own immediate 'family' interests, which might easily lead to fragmentation.

This great fault notwithstanding, the Yoruba-Aja peoples had reached a degree of political stability under this system by the beginning of the sixteenth century. Each kingdom had had its relationship to all the others fixed. None of the 'son-kingdoms' could simply march an army on the 'father-kingdom' and hope to become head of the country by conquest without widespread repercussions. Even when they migrated in large numbers, relationships in their new places of abode were easily re-established.

It is not suggested that life then went on in perfect harmony, without quarrels and without friction. It is not even suggested that the model worked perfectly. No political model ever does. What is suggested is that within the country, certain rules had been established, which if broken would incur a general censure.

This made for stability. As it is well known, however, political developments, constitutional amendments and reinterpretations, can and do occur within already generally accepted standards and norms without necessarily upsetting such standards or norms. In other words, stability need not create, and must not be confused with, static conditions. It is not necessary to have a complete destruction of the old before conditions are created for progress. It must therefore not be imagined that static conditions prevailed from the moment this stability was created until the Europeans came to destroy the old ways. From our little knowledge of Yoruba politics, it can be shown that there were developments within the accepted *Ebi* social theory. Ife and Oyo applied the theory differently. In the heyday of expansion, Ife insisted on installing its own prince at the head of every 'new' (which may have been conquered) kingdom in order to maintain the 'family' link. Oyo, in its own time of ascendancy, did not always insist on an Oyo prince. Instead, it maintained the existing arrangement, and only installed an *Ajele* who was theoretically lower in rank than the king, but in fact possessed greater powers. Despite this difference, there is no mistaking the fact that both Ife and Oyo were applying the same principles.

The economic activities in which the Aja engaged at Allada were probably quite similar to those in which they had long engaged, and which the Europeans reported in the seventeenth and eighteenth centuries. Agriculture was the main occupation.[1] The Allada region, like most of the Yoruba-Aja region, was a good agricultural land, and the Aja people were reported to be so industrious that they planted every available space.[2]

Industries included cotton spinning, cloth weaving, calabash and wood carving, iron works, beer brewing and salt making. Exchange was stimulated by a series of markets established in different parts of the country. One such market was situated in a place called 'Ba', where 'every four days they have a free market of salt brought from Jojo in great quantities by canoes and from thence carried to the territory of Ulkama'.[3] At another spot 'four or five miles from Ba by a great tree, a free market is kept every day where the inhabitants sometimes to the number of three or four thousand, come with all sorts of commodities'.[4]

Commerce consisted of the exchange of agricultural and manufactured goods. There was a common currency in cowrie shells, which, with the existence of a lagoon system and a common language, encouraged long-distance trading between all parts of the country and perhaps beyond.

It would seem that the slave trade was not a significant part of the economic activities of the Yoruba-Aja peoples before the European introduced it. The first piece of evidence for this assertion is a negative one. Although the earliest Europeans to visit the Aja coast reported seeing markets where many things were bought and sold, none reported actually seeing a slave market, which interested them most, and for which they earnestly inquired as they reported having heard of such markets eight hundred miles inland, that is far beyond the limits of the Yoruba-Aja country.[5]

The second piece of evidence is more positive. An English traveller writing of the eighteenth-century Aja said that 'the discerning natives account it their greatest unhappiness that

---

[1] John Ogilby, *Africa*, p. 396.
[2] W. Bosman, *A New and Accurate Description of the Coast of Guinea* (London, 1705), pp. 342–3.
[3] John Ogilby, *Africa*, p. 367. Ulkama probably means Olukumi, that is Yoruba. [4] *Ibid.* p. 367.
[5] John Barbot, *A Description of the Coasts of North and South Guinea* (London, 1732), p. 327.

they were ever visited by the Europeans. They say that we christians introduced the traffick [*sic*] in slaves and that before our coming they lived in peace'.[1]

The arrival of the Europeans and the introduction of the 'traffick in slaves' on an unprecedented scale brought new factors into the politics of the Aja. European exploratory activities along the Western coast of Africa started around the middle of the fifteenth century under Portuguese initiative. Between 1461 and 1471, the Yoruba-Aja coast had become well known.[2] For a long time, the Portuguese maintained the monopoly of the advantages accruing from their discovery, but from about 1530 onwards, they were gradually but increasingly challenged. First came the French from about 1530, then the English from about 1553,[3] and finally the Dutch from 1595.[4]

Dutch attacks on the Portuguese possessions in West Africa were particularly vehement, because the Dutch had since 1568 been fighting a war of independence against Spain. When Portugal became an integral part of the Spanish monarchy in 1580, all the former Portuguese possessions came under Dutch attack. In 1637 the Dutch captured St George d'Elmina, the Portuguese headquarters in West Africa, and by 1642, had practically driven the Portuguese away from the Gold Coast region.

Arguments about the economic advantages, which these European explorations conferred on West Africa, are still going on. It has been suggested that the Portuguese introduced maize to West Africa, but the latest evidence on this controversy would seem to contradict the suggestion.[5]

For the purpose of future political developments, it is important to bear in mind first that the arrival of the Europeans increased social insecurity. The earliest Europeans were not particularly friendly to the Africans, whom they often seized as objects of curiosity to be shown to the kings and nobles in Europe,[6] or to be sold. The Portuguese sent armed galleys

---

[1] W. Smith, *A New Voyage to Guinea* (London, 1744), pp. 266–7.

[2] John Barbot, *A Description*, p. 11.

[3] J. W. Blake, *European Beginnings in West Africa, 1454–1578* (London, 1937), pp. 106–60.

[4] A. W. Cardinal, *The Gold Coast*, 1931 (Accra, 1932), p. 19.

[5] D. W. Jeffreys, 'How Ancient is West African Maize?' in *Africa*, vol. XXXIII, no. 2 (1963), pp. 115–29.

[6] Elizabeth Donnan, *Documents Illustrative of the History of the Slave Trade to America* (4 vols. Washington, D.C. 1930–34), vol. I, pp. 18–19.

along the coast to burn the houses and canoes of the natives for alleged 'recalcitrance'.[1]

The slaves that were being exported from West Africa to the West Indies, from the early years of the sixteenth century until the joint-stock companies were formed in the seventeenth century, were not all bought from the African sellers. A great many of them were secured by violence committed by the European captains. Towerson reported that when he visited Elmina in 1555, the natives would not come near him because a Mr Gainish had stolen natives the previous year and carried them off while pretending to buy gold from them.[2] John Hawkins, who went on three slave-trading voyages to Sierra Leone between 1562 and 1568, surprised dancers at night and burned whole villages to obtain his cargo.[3]

Secondly, the arrival of the Europeans in West Africa sharpened political upheavals. This was most apparent on the Gold Coast where the European activities were at first almost entirely concentrated. The Europeans brought their rivalry from Europe to their new settlements and they fought there as they were used to doing in Europe. During these local wars, they all hired African allies to fight their fellow Europeans. Such African allies became enemies of one another as they became of the Europeans against whom they were hired to fight. Such enmity would become a fruitful source of quarrel and wars between the African kingdoms.

When the Europeans had become well established, they all took part in local African politics.[4] In this again the Dutch probably excelled every other European nation. They tried to subject African kingdoms to their own authority and hired natives in one kingdom to fight against another kingdom, particularly when trade was dull.[5] Taking part in local African politics was not, however, confined to the Dutch. The English and the Brandenburgers practised it. Sir Dalby Thomas was an implacable enemy of the Fetu (in modern Ghana) over whom he imposed a woman ruler in 1704, contrary to their tradition.[6]

The European activities on the Aja coast in the sixteenth

---

[1] W. Blake, *European Beginnings in West Africa* (Hakluyt Society Series, vol. I, 1942), p. 55.
[2] E. Donnan, *Documents*, vol. I, p. 43.  [3] *Ibid.* pp. 18–19.
[4] H. A. Wyndham, *The Atlantic and Slavery* (London, 1935), pp. 15–16; Sir Dalby Thomas to R.A.C., 1 Jan. 1706 (T 70/6).
[5] *Ibid.*  [6] *Ibid.*

century are not as well documented, or at least they have not been as well studied, as their activities farther west on the Gold Coast. The Portuguese built no forts there as they had done on the Gold Coast, and they did not seem to have come into contact with any powerful rulers as they had encountered at Benin or Ijebu. One explanation for this might be that the Aja were still living largely in Tado and did not move eastwards until about the 1570s. Another might be that the Portuguese were not particularly attracted to the region because they were predominantly engaged in exporting gold and pepper, neither of which was available in large quantities in Aja.

With the arrival of the Dutch on the West African scene from about 1595, the Aja region could not have remained neglected for long. The Dutch were, at least, as much interested in human traffic as they were in gold, and it was they who first formed a joint-stock company devoted to a systematic exploitation of the slave trade. In West Africa, the region which the Aja came to inhabit from the end of the sixteenth century onwards was reputed to be thickly populated even before the arrival of the Aja and as such would attract the attention of the Dutch early. The Aja therefore could not have been more than a few decades old in their new habitation at Allada when the Dutch arrived in their midst. What happened immediately after and its effects on the new migrants is not quite clear, but there can be no doubt that once established among the Aja, the Dutch would apply the same policy and practices as they were doing on the Gold Coast.

What can be said with some degree of confidence is that soon after the arrival of the Dutch in the Aja country, the first serious attack was made on the traditional political organisation of the Aja. This attack was the foundation of Dahomey. This important event might not have been entirely unconnected with the activities of the Dutch in Aja, though exactly how much the Dutch were directly involved is uncertain.

According to the traditions of Abomey, a succession dispute arose after the death of Kokpon, the second Aja king to reign at Allada, between Te-Agbalin his elder son and Dogbagrigenu (Dako) his younger son. The latter was elected but was later deposed, whereupon his supporters went northwards to the Igede (Gede or Guede) kingdom where they later founded Abomey.[1] The Ajase Ipo (Porto Novo) version of the same

[1] Le Herisse, *L'Ancien Royaume*, p. 279.

tradition relates that Te-Agbalin also left Allada at the same time and went eastwards to found Ajase Ipo.[1] This latter version is, however, a rationalisation of later events as it will be seen that Ajase was founded in 1730.[2] It seems probable that it was Te-Agbalin who procured the means to oust his brother from the throne and who later ascended the throne.

There can be no doubt that this incident, which led to the foundation of the kingdom of Dahomey, ought to be dated to the early years of the seventeenth century, perhaps around 1620.[3] It has been pointed out that Leo Africanus mentioned a kingdom named 'Dauma' early in the sixteenth century, that in 1575 Thevet mentioned a kingdom of 'Dauma' in his Universal Cosmography which appeared in Mercator's atlas of 1560 and that of Ortelius in 1570,[4] and that a map of Guinea published in 1627 located Dauma in almost the exact position of modern Abomey.[5] It must, however, be borne in mind that Allada itself was not founded until late in the sixteenth century. Moreover, and this is the decisive point, the earliest Dahomey king-list given by Agaja in 1728 makes it improbable that any names could have been left out of the king-list now existing. In 1728 Agaja made it clear that he was the fourth leader of the Aja in the Igede region, coming after his grandfather, his father and his brother.[6] This would make him the third king (for his grandfather was not regarded as king) and the second generation after the formal inauguration of the kingdom. The relative longevity of the Wegbaja kings notwithstanding, it would be extraordinary if two Dahomean kings covered more than a hundred years before 1708.

If the location of a kingdom called 'Dauma' was correctly sited in the sixteenth century in the area where Abomey later grew, it would pose the problem as to whether there was a previous kingdom, an idea that cannot be entirely ruled out in the present

---

[1] A. Akindele and C. Aguessy: *Contribution à l'étude de l'ancien Royaume de Porto Novo* (IFAN, Dakar, 1953), pp. 20–8.

[2] See chapter 3.

[3] J. D. Fage, *History of West Africa*, p. 93.

[4] R. Cornevin, *Histoire du Dahomey*, p. 96.

[5] Adande, 'Notes and Comments' (unpublished), kindly shown to me by Mr D. H. Jones.

[6] Delisle, 'Extrait du Registre', 26 Aug. 1728 (AN. C. 6/25). Later traditions, accepted by Newbury and others, would tend to stretch the list further back and thus increase the genealogy. C. W. Newbury, *The Western Slave Coast*, p. 10.

state of our knowledge of the area. Did Aho (Wegbaja) take over the name? Is the traditional meaning given for the word Dahomey (in Dan's belly) a rationalisation of a word strange to the Egun (Gun) language? There would seem to be little doubt that the Dahomey kingdom over which the descendants of Dako and Wegbaja ruled was founded in the early years of the seventeenth century, after the establishment of the Dutch activities among the Aja at Allada.

It would seem very probable that the foundation of Abomey was the first reaction of the Aja to the Dutch activities among them. Before the Aja settled at Allada from Tado, they would already have been familiar with the European activities on the Gold Coast and with the social insecurity and political upheavals arising from them. Their own migration from Tado to Allada may have been partly due to their desire to seek security from the chaos in the west. When therefore the Dutch came among them in the early years of the seventeenth century they would be faced with a very difficult choice.

This may have been the basic cause of the contention between the princes of Allada after the death of Kokpon. Their dilemma would be that the Dutch possessed superior firearms, and if not befriended, might give those arms to an unfriendly neighbouring kingdom. In their new insecure position, they could not afford to make enemies. To allow them into the country, however, was to start the same process as had caused chaos on the Gold Coast and had contributed to their own migration. One section among the princes of Allada would appear to have favoured an outright expulsion of the Europeans and another championed their being welcomed under strict control. It appears that Dogbagri-Genu, leader of the anti-Europeans first won but was later driven out by the pro-Europeans.

Three things at any rate seem clear from such evidence as we now have at our disposal. First, whatever forced Dogbagri-Genu and his supporters out of Allada also caused them to harbour an inveterate hatred for the Dutch. For, when Agaja, king of Dahomey, conquered Allada and Whydah in 1724 and 1727, he chased out the Dutch, not only from Dahomey but also from all the neighbouring territories from Badagry in the east to Little Popo in the west. Nor did he rest even at the risk of incurring the displeasure of Oyo until Hertog, the last Dutch representative at Badagry, had been killed in war about June 1737. These actions of Agaja would suggest that the Dutch probably played a part in deposing Dogbagri-Genu, Agaja's grandfather, and he was taking his revenge.

Secondly, it is clear that the same reasons that drove the Dahomeans away from Allada also made them oppose the slave trade. Although before 1727, references to Dahomey (or Foin, Fon) were few and far between, yet it is known that in 1670–71,[1] and again in 1687–8,[2] they barred the way to the Allada slave raiders who were going into the interior to procure captives. There was no suggestion that the Dahomeans wanted to act as middlemen. On each occasion, the raiders came back without slaves, bought or caught.

The proposition that the foundation of Dahomey was 'initially stimulated by the need to resist attacks from Oyo'[3] does not seem to be supported by any evidence yet known. First it should be noted that Igede, where the migrant Aja settled after leaving Allada, was already a Yoruba kingdom[4] and not a new frontier open to constant Oyo raids. Secondly, it does not appear that Oyo had yet enthusiastically embraced the slave trade by the early seventeenth century. In fact Oyo's enthusiasm for making any contact with the Europeans cooled greatly, when, according to oral traditions, eight hundred Oyo messengers sent by Obalokun, the king of Oyo, to a king in Europe, failed to return.[5] Thirdly the number of the Aja who migrated from Allada northwards does not appear to be large. They occupied about two villages under their first leader,[6] and were probably not more than six hundred persons in all. These obviously could not resist an Oyo army at that time.

Thirdly, it is clear that whatever forced Dogbagri-Genu and his supporters out of Allada also caused them to reject the traditional social theory and the political system based on it. The most important development that followed the expulsion of Dogbagri-Genu was that he and his followers rejected the '*Ebi*'

---

[1] J. Barbot, *A Description*, p. 120.
[2] P. Roussier, *L'Etablissement d'Issigny, 1687–1702* (Paris, 1935), pp. 14–15.
[3] D. H. Jones, 'The Kingdom of Dahomey', in *History and Archaeology in Africa* (London, 1955), p. 63; R. Oliver and J. D. Fage, *A Short History of Africa* (1962), p. 123.
[4] Le Herisse, *L'Ancien Royaume*, pp. 277–8.
[5] S. Johnson, *History*, p. 168.
[6] Delisle, 'Extrait du Registre', 26 Aug. 1728 (AN. C. 6/25).

social theory and the political organisation founded on it. They decided to found a new kingdom based on a completely new concept. They represented a state as a pot perforated all over and a king as water which must be made to stay in that pot. Before that could be done, however, there must be a group of people prepared to put a finger each in each hole, and such persons represented the subjects.[1]

A comparison of this symbolism with that of a state as a family written large, would at once reveal startling and ominous differences. In a dry place like the Abomey plateau, water was uncommon and precious; and not as ubiquitous as fathers were. Secondly, the qualification required for citizenship was not blood relationship, but simply a willingness and ability to serve the king. Anybody at all from any part of the world could be a citizen. Emphasis was on individuals, as signified by 'one finger' and not on families. Thirdly the relationship between the king (Dada or 'father') and his subjects was not interdependent as in a family. On the contrary, every citizen must serve and be subservient to the king, the precious article that must be maintained in place by all.

From the way in which the Dahomean oral traditions explain how Dahomey came to possess any piece of land, the founders of Dahomey also believed that the only sure source and guardian of a right was no longer blood descent, but might. For although as refugees they were received by kind hosts, they did not take their title from gifts. On one pretext or another, they killed their hosts and gradually possessed their kingdom,[2] a possession that they then realised could only be held by force. Nothing in the new Dahomey resembled the immutable natural law of relationship laid down by departed ancestors whose wishes were sacred.

In certain respects, this principle ran very close indeed to the modern European idea of a national state. It certainly made it possible for several people, seeking adventure or security, to come to Dahomey and become citizens. Many Portuguese

---

[1] My attention was first drawn to this tradition, which was first articulated by Gezo, by M. Pierre Verger, who has spent many years collecting oral evidence in Dahomey. M. P. Mercier confirmed it when I met him in Paris, as did Prince Justin Aho, the oldest surviving representative of the ancient kings of Dahomey, whom I met in Paris in 1962. None, however, seems to have realised the revolutionary nature of this symbolism.

[2] Le Herisse, *L'Ancien Royaume*, p. 279.

mulattoes and at least one Englishman became Dahomeans in
the eighteenth century. It is no accident that the population of
Abomey, as far as it has been examined, is cosmopolitan.[1] The
principle made it possible for the Dahomean army to be quickly
replenished in the troubled times of the early eighteenth century, whenever it appeared to have been almost completely
annihilated.

It was however a dangerously revolutionary principle for the
time and place. Its most dangerous implication was that a determined section of the Aja had rejected the Aja constitution and
had formulated an alternative which had a strong central direction, the very element which the traditional system had lacked.
Unless the European activities were successfully grafted into the
traditional system, this new principle would eventually challenge
the old one.

Te-Agbalin and his supporters who had thought that the
European economic activities could, without damage, be accom-
modated under strict control, formulated their policies in the
light of their knowledge of the contemporary events. First they
decided that the Europeans would not be allowed to build forts
in Aja. Tezifon, king of Allada, enunciated this policy fully in
1670 when the French asked him for permission to construct
a fort in his territory.

...With regard to the factory at Ardra, he would give directions to
the prince and the two great captains to go in person there and aug-
ment the buildings, but that he could not allow them to build a
factory in their manner. 'You will,' says the king, 'make a house in
which you will put at first two little pieces of cannon, the next year
you will mount four, and in a little time your factory will be meta-
morphosed into a fort that will make you master of my dominions
and enable you to give laws to me.'[2]

Secondly, they decided that all the European activities in Aja
must be concentrated at the capital, Assim (Allada), to which
place all the Aja would be free to go. This would avoid the risk
of European diffusion, prevent rivalries and quarrels amongst the
Aja, and enable uniform actions to be taken as new issues arose.

These policies of centralisation and control reckoned without
two factors. The first was the reaction of the other Aja, whose

[1] C. W. Newbury, *The Western Slave Coast*, p. 6.
[2] T. Astley, *A New and General Collection of Voyages and Travels* (London,
1745–7), vol. III, pp. 69–70.

kingdoms were thus closed to the Europeans, though they themselves were free to trade at Allada. Their rulers failed to see why they should be deprived of a greater share of the ill-gotten wealth which the slave trade brought. However much Allada might stress the security aspect of its policies, there could be no doubt that the slave trade brought wealth[1] which had not been part of the traditional perquisites of the Allada monarchy, and it was this aspect which the other kingdoms saw and resented.

The second factor with which Allada did not reckon was the European reaction. With the establishment of the European colonies in the New World, each European nation wanted its own exclusive source of African labour with which to work the plantations, and a European power already established in one place in West Africa would not encourage another power to establish in the same place. As the Aja country was populous, and therefore most inviting for the slave traders, and as the Dutch were already established in Allada, the other European powers would like to establish themselves in the other Aja kingdoms. They would tend to resent the restriction imposed on their 'freedom of movement' by the king of Allada.

These two factors were significant because if the Europeans and the other Aja kingdoms decided not to co-operate with Allada in carrying out its policies, there was practically nothing that Allada could do. Obedience to Allada having never been based on force could not be maintained by force without Allada seeming to break the Aja constitution. Indeed Allada did not have the force with which to coerce the Europeans.

With the Europeans wanting to establish factories in the other Aja kingdoms, which wanted them to come, it is not surprising that Allada's policy of centralisation and control eventually failed.

This failure was not due to lack of exertion on the part of Allada which, in the thirty years between 1640 and 1670, did all it could to achieve success. Twice during this period, the kings of Allada sent embassies to the European monarchs in an attempt to persuade them to concentrate at Allada all the activities of their subjects in the Aja country.

The first embassy was sent by Toxonu (Toshonu) in 1658 to Philip IV of Spain, who was probably regarded in Aja as the

---

[1] J. Ogilby, *Africa*, pp. 465–7, gives an indication of the likely revenue from sales tax.

## Dahomey and its Neighbours

most powerful European monarch. It was provoked by the abortive attempt in 1644 of certain French missionaries to establish a post in Whydah[1] which Allada had seen as a breach in its policy. Toshonu was determined to prevent a recurrence of this kind of threat. Toshonu sent an Aja man, called Bans, to ask that the Spanish subjects be sent to establish both trading and missionary posts at Allada, and probably meant by that to convince the other Europeans that Allada could serve as a convenient centre for whatever activities they wished to engage in in Aja. It is doubtful whether he ever wanted to change his religion or encourage his subjects to change theirs. It is even probable that he was not particularly eager to increase Allada's slave trade.

Spain, debarred by the papal bull from trading in West Africa, took the missionary aspect very seriously. With the help of Bans, a booklet entitled *Doctrina Christiana* was prepared. It was a catechism written in Spanish and Egun (Gun), the language of Allada and was designed to teach the rudiments of the Roman Catholic beliefs in a simple form. Armed with these, eleven Capuchin missionaries left Spain on 15 November 1659 and reached Allada on 14 January 1660.[2]

The mission, however, failed. Toshonu did not show the expected enthusiasm to change his religion. In fact he declared, after many prevarications, that he had no intention of doing so. Nor did he readily allow his subjects to change theirs. When nine of the eleven missionaries had died of various causes, the remaining two left Allada in 1661.[2]

The main success of the venture was that the Allada people learned enthusiastically to read and write. In 1670 d'Elbee reported that the king had been trained in São Thome and that he, his eldest son and most of the chiefs in Allada spoke Portuguese to perfection.[3]

By the time the Capuchin missionaries left, the resentment of the other Aja kingdoms against Allada at being deprived of European establishments had become alarmingly pronounced. The division which Allada had sought to prevent by centralisation had been created. Dissatisfaction of Whydah with Allada

[1] J. Barbot, *A Description*, p. 120.
[2] H. A. Wyndham, *The Atlantic and Slavery*, p. 35; H. Labouret and P. Rivet, *Le Royaume d'Ardra et son Evangelisation au XVIIᵉ Siècle* (Paris, 1929), pp. 6–30.
[3] T. Astley, *Collection*, vol. III, pp. 68–72.

28

was almost the first thing that the missionaries heard about when they landed at Allada in January 1660; and their presence at Allada, while Whydah as yet had no European post, could only sharpen the disagreement.

The second Allada embassy to Europe in the interest of the Allada policy was dispatched to France in 1670 by Tezifon, Toshonu's successor and was directly caused by the arrival of the French in the Aja country in that year.

The French West India Company was formed in 1664.[1] In 1666 it sent out a mission to West Africa to reconnoitre and recommend places where French forts and factories ought to be built. In November 1669 it sent out two ships under d'Elbee to establish a French factory at Allada. In January 1670 d'Elbee reached Allada where he met Tezifon, probably the son of Toshonu.

It was clear almost from the moment the French arrived that Tezifon was going to find it difficult to retain the French in Allada. The first problem was the supply of the slaves, which was not very large in Allada and which Tezifon was not particularly eager to expand. When Dubourg, who was in charge of the trade side of the expedition, promised that the French would build a factory at Offra and would send four ships annually for the slave trade, Tezifon replied that he already had more ships than he could load with slaves. 'Last year some had been forced to go away without cargoes, that there were then six on the coast and four at Elmina who only waited advice from their factory to come here. So that he wanted neither ships nor merchandise.'[2]

It was in the interest of the policy of Allada, however, to let them stay and not go to Whydah. So, after the French had bestowed handsome presents on all who mattered in the capital and had raised the price of slaves, Tezifon allowed himself to be persuaded. He issued a proclamation on 8 January 1670 that the French were allowed to trade and he gave them a house as he had given the Dutch.

The second problem arose immediately. Neither the Dutch nor the French wished to settle down and trade peacefully together. The Dutch strongly objected to the French being allowed to trade at Allada and asked Tezifon for a treaty that

[1] T. Astley, *Collection*, vol. III, pp. 65–76; J. Barbot, *A Description*, pp. 325–50.　　　　[2] *Ibid.*

would confer the exclusive trade of Allada on them, but Tezifon refused to sign such a treaty. Then, as soon as the French were given the freedom to trade, they started to outdo the Dutch and to ask for conditions which would have made them 'the most favoured nation' at Allada, but the king again refused, saying that he regarded all the foreigners in his territory as being of equal standing.

Unable to obtain the right of exclusive trade or precedence at Allada from Tezifon, the French and the Dutch turned on each other. They started disputing about which of their national flags was more important, and resorted to a free fight to settle the issue. Tezifon's officers stopped them and warned 'both parties how much his master would be offended at such proceedings, adding that he would never suffer such disputes in his dominions, but would banish the aggressors'.[1] The contending parties therefore referred their dispute to the king for decision, which in effect would have enabled one of them to claim precedence over the others in Allada, but Tezifon emphasised that he regarded them as equals in his territory. He advised them to ask for the verdict about which of their flags was more important from their countries, and ordered that until the verdict was known no more flags must be displayed.

It was after this incident that Tezifon, either on his own initiative or at the instigation of the French, decided to send an embassy to France. If successful the move might induce the French to remain at Allada and not seek other posts, at least in the Aja country. Matteo Lopez, whom he sent, spoke Portuguese very well like most of the rulling class at Allada during that period. He reached France on 3 December 1670 and in the following two weeks was given a truly royal welcome, which he reciprocated with a dignity, grace and due deference characteristic of his own people.

Below the glittering surface, things did not move as either the French or Lopez wanted. The French traders attributed to Lopez a speech which they read to the French king but which Lopez neither composed nor wished to make. Lopez would not sign the treaty proposed by the French because he objected to the first and the fifth clauses, which went against the policy of Allada and would have given the French preference over all the other Europeans and allowed them to cover their

[1] J. Barbot, *A Description*, p. 325.

factories at Allada with tiles. Probably because of the winter cold, to which he was not accustomed, Lopez asked to be taken back as quickly as possible.

He left Paris in the middle of January 1671,[1] and ought to have reached Allada, latest, by the following March. For some unexplained reason, he did not reach Allada until October.[2] In the interval, he and Carolof,[3] the French-employed Danish 'gentleman of fortune' who accompanied him, quarrelled, about what is not known, and Carolof refused to hand over to Lopez, as he ought, the presents which the king of France had sent to Tezifon in return for the ones which Tezifon had sent him.

The embassy was therefore largely a failure like the previous one. Neither the French nor the Allada had any cause to be particularly fond of each other after it. To worsen matters, Carolof could not see Tezifon for a long time after his arrival as Tezifon was engaged in pacifying the Dahomeans who had, for the first recorded time, barred the way to the Allada raiders.

The failure of this embassy pricked the bubble of Allada's policy of centralisation and control. Boredom at Allada or a preconceived plan, induced Carolof to wander westwards. First, he went to Great Popo, where the king, who probably shared Whydah's disgust for Allada's centralisation policy, offered to take much lower duties from Carolof than those taken at Allada. From Great Popo, he went to Whydah. There the king again lured him with all kinds of promises and inducements unobtainable at Allada. For this reason, Carolof established a French factory at Whydah in 1671. Probably as a result of Carolof's establishment, which the king of Allada could not prevent, ships started to go to Great Popo whose people therefore started trading in their own port.[4] With Whydah and Great Popo ports opened, Allada's policy was defeated and the stage set for the internecine rivalry which Allada had wanted to prevent.

For the next thirty years, Whydah, Allada and Great Popo vied with each other for the greater share of the slave trade in the Aja country. Whydah won the contest because it threw itself wholeheartedly into the trade and offered the Europeans every

[1] T. Astley, *Collection*, vol. III, p. 79.
[2] J. Barbot, *A Description*, p. 120.
[3] For the career of Henry Carolof, variously spelt Carloff, Karloff, Carloof, etc., see E. Donnan, *Documents*, vol. I, pp. 77–8, 98–9.
[4] J. Barbot, *A Description*, p. 325.

alluring condition which they sought. The English, who had established at Allada in 1674,[1] started sending ships to Whydah in 1681[2] and finally removed their headquarters thither in 1683.[3] The Dutch settled a factory at Whydah in 1682, and the Brandenburgers in 1684.[4] The Portuguese too were back, for they were reported to be taking part in Whydah politics between 1670 and 1680.[5] Whydah's victory was complete in 1704, when in a six-clause convention all the European traders agreed that Whydah port should be regarded as an international neutral port, and that the ships in harbour or in sight of it should not be molested, even if there was war in Europe.[6]

Fundamentally the cause of the failure of Allada's policy was the inadequacy of the Aja institutions to cope with the new situations arising out of the European activities. Allada lacked and did not devise the machinery for the equitable distribution among the Aja states of the new wealth accruing from the European trade. Because of this, it could not successfully persuade all the other Aja kingdoms to acquiesce in its policy. These latter therefore continued to feel cheated. The longer this feeling continued, the less respect they had for the authority of the 'father' and the weaker the bond between the 'father-kingdom' and the 'son-kingdom' grew.

Moreover, Allada lacked the force with which to make the Europeans obey its orders. The Europeans did not have the same respect for the authority of the 'father' as the Aja had, and they were not bound by any fear of religious sanction if they disobeyed him. The only thing that could make them respect the wishes of the Allada authority was force, which the traditional constitution did not give to the king of Allada. Therefore Allada could not effectively stop any lawlessness if the Europeans decided to indulge in it, nor could it stop them from establishing anywhere else in the Aja country when they finally decided to do so. This lack of adequate force also finally made it impossible for Allada to stop the chaotic consequences that followed the failure of its policy.

---

[1] K. G. Davies, *The Royal African Company, 1672–1713* (London, 1957), p. 228.  [2] William Cross to R.A.C., 13 June 1681 (T 70/1).
[3] K. G. Davies, *op. cit.*
[4] J. Barbot, *A Description*, p. 453.
[5] W. Bosman, *A New and Accurate Description*, pp. 365–6; J. Barbot, *A Description*, p. 334.
[6] P. Labat, *Voyage du Chevalier des Marchais* (Paris, 1735), vol. 2, p. 109.

The result was a further weakening of the already inadequate Aja institutions, a process that dealt a great blow at the preservation of the traditional political system. Whydah's success at attracting the Europeans led to a general scramble for the slave trade and the least attempt by Allada to hinder any of the kingdoms was regarded as a sufficient reason for estrangement. Between 1671 and 1682 relations were so strained that the *Ebi* social theory was proving no longer adequate to hold the country together. European visitors talked of Great Popo as being 'independent' of both Allada and Whydah,[1] of Whydah and Tori as being 'separate' kingdoms (meaning they were independent of each other and of Allada), and even of Offra, Allada's port, as 'rebelling' against the authority of Allada.[1]

Allada tried to restore its own authority by force, but was under the disadvantage of never having been a military kingdom, and therefore never having an adequate force. To repair the inadequacy, it hired other people to do its fighting. In 1680 it secured the services of the Little Popo-Accra, who, having been driven out of their kingdom in 1677 by the Akwamu,[2] were likely to be sympathetic to traditional authority. Ofori, their king, conquered Offra, but ran out of ammunition when he attacked Whydah and had to retreat.[3] His retreat therefore left the strongest of the rebels untamed.

If Allada could hire mercenaries, so could the other Aja kingdoms. Agbangla, the new king of Whydah, hired the crew of a French ship in 1682 and sent them against the Great Popo, but the French crew lost.[4] He did not rely solely on European alliances, which were too transitory, but made an alliance with the Akwamu, the enemy of the Little Popo-Accra. Thus Allada using the displaced Accras, and Whydah using the freebooting Akwamu, fought inconclusive wars in the years immediately after 1680.

It may be pointed out that this was the basis of the relationship between Whydah and Akwamu. The Whydah–Akwamu alliance was something like the solidarity of bandits against the traditional legalism of the Allada–Little-Popo–Accra. The

---

[1] W. Bosman, *A New and Accurate Description*, pp. 335–6; J. Barbot, *A Description*, p. 323.
[2] Ivor Wilks, 'The Rise of Akwamu Empire 1650–1710', in *Transactions of the Historical Society of Ghana* (THSG), vol. III, pp. 100–28.
[3] J. Barbot, *op. cit.*
[4] W. Bosman, *op. cit.*

alliance was in all essentials completely ineffective, but it was remarkably enduring. Whydah's invitation in 1702 to the Akwamu army after its victory over Little Popo, Allada's ally, was in effect a demonstration of their solidarity and did not constitute Akwamu's conquest of Whydah.[1] We shall see Akwamu supporting Whydah again in 1728 when the latter had been conquered by Dahomey.[2]

In the 1680s the lack of decisive victory by either party and the weakening of all the accepted values created a power vacuum, which in turn brought lawlessness. With the new enthusiasm for the slave trade, man-stealing was widespread. Slave raids, sanctioned by the authorities, became the new fashionable occupation. Everyone sought slaves and no one seems to have questioned any slave owner how he got them. For example, the people of Tori kingdom, hitherto farmers, took to man-stealing.[3] The Whydah people stole their Great Popo neighbours in such great numbers that within ten years even a casual European visitor noticed a sharp decrease in the population of Great Popo.[4]

It is not surprising therefore that the number of slaves exported out of the Aja country in the decades immediately after 1671 increased at a great rate. Up to about 1671, an estimated annual average of only about three thousand slaves were carried away from the whole of the Aja country.[4] In the 1680s, Great Popo alone could fill a whole ship in a few days. Whydah exported about a thousand a month, that is about twelve thousand a year, and Allada had increased its own annual quota. In 1678 an English factory at Offra, the port of Allada, estimated that Allada exported between six and seven thousand slaves per annum.[5]

While the social insecurity was increasing and the traditional bonds between the Aja kingdoms were being slowly destroyed, the basis of the internal administration within each kingdom was also being slowly dismantled by the desecrating hands of the European factors. For, once they had settled in a kingdom, their desire for pre-eminence for their individual nations and their building up of parties of native supporters that could be

---

[1] Ivor Wilks, in the article cited above, erroneously thought it did.
[2] See chapter 3.
[3] J. Barbot, *A Description*, pp. 345–6.
[4] *Ibid.* pp. 323–7, 350.
[5] K. G. Davies, *The Royal African Company*, p. 228.

used to back their pretensions, became a fruitful source of friction that could mean unending civil wars. Moreover, the factors made sure that the ruling classes were in favour of the activities in which they wanted to engage.

What this could mean was soon plain. The king who had brought the French into Whydah died soon after 1671. His eldest son ought to have succeeded him after performing the traditional rites at Allada, and no native opposition to him seems to have arisen. The European traders, however, thought that he was not sufficiently pro-European, so the Dutch, the French and the Portuguese drove him out and forcibly installed his younger brother, who took the name Agbangla.[1]

This was a complete breach of the constitution and the conservative chiefs may have refused completely to recognise his authority. It seems in fact that he relied for most of his reign on European support, for which reason he always gave them whatever concession they sought.

This blatant European intervention was not an isolated case. When Agbangla died in August 1703,[2] the same process was repeated. By then the several European factors had each had the support of a faction within the Whydah state. Peter Duffield, the director of the English fort, supported by his own faction, put Aisan[3] or Amat, Agbangla's second son, on the throne of Whydah before the death of Agbangla was publicly announced and before the eldest son knew of it. This latter asserted his right, and a civil war broke out, but Duffield and his faction won,[4] and for the second time in thirty years, a king had been illegally installed on the Whydah throne by the Europeans and the ceremonies according to the *Ebi* theory omitted.

Allada could not be expected to countenance any Whydah king so unconstitutionally installed. There was, however, nothing much the king could do to stop the process. For there appears to have been no traditional machinery by which he could divest an illegally installed 'son' of his possession. The only course

---

[1] W. Bosman, *A New and Accurate Description*, pp. 355–6; J. Barbot, *A Description*, p. 323.

[2] P. Duffield to R.A.C., 25 Aug. 1703, 7 Oct. 1703; John Carter to R.A.C., 26 Aug. 1703 (T 70/13).

[3] E. Dunglas in *E.D.* vol. XIX, p. 34 has written the name 'Hayehouin' but I shall keep the spelling Aisan, because it seems to me nearer the original.

[4] Peter Duffield to R.A.C., 5 Aug., 7 Oct. 1703; John Carter to R.A.C., 26 Aug. 1703 (T 70/13).

open was to deprive Whydah of the economic advantage that had enabled it to be so contemptuous of the traditional system.

This proved impossible for many years because the chaos caused by the man-stealing and the lack of effective authority in Aja brought the Oyo army down twice against Allada in the last twenty years of the seventeenth century.

Oyo, as we have noticed, was one of the major kingdoms of the Yoruba-Aja country. Its reputed founder was a prince from Ile-Ife, called Oranyan, who was also the founder of the present Benin dynasty. Because of its geographical position Oyo quickly became the richest of the Yoruba kingdoms and was able to build up a strong cavalry army. By the middle of the sixteenth century it had become the strongest kingdom in the Yoruba–Aja country.

Its first expedition against Allada was between 1680 and 1682.[1] The immediate cause is unknown, but was probably not Oyo's desire to clear a way to the coast, for the Oyo traders seem to have had access to the coast long before then.[2] It may have been that certain Oyo traders had been affected by the Aja raids, which the Alafin sent his army down to avenge. Over half of Allada was destroyed during this campaign and the mere mention of the name of Oyo afterwards created panic among the Aja.[3]

The second invasion occurred in 1698 and was directly caused by certain Aja people sending to the Oyo authorities for protection. The latter sent to the king of Allada to advise him to govern more justly, but the king of Allada injudiciously killed Oyo's messengers. So once again a great part of Allada kingdom was destroyed, but the king, who was particularly wanted, escaped.[4]

These two attacks greatly weakened Allada and rendered it incapable of maintaining its rivalry with, let alone checking, Whydah, but it did not solve the problem of the disintegration of the Aja society. Whydah could not take the leadership simply because its wealth had increased, and Oyo, though an acknowledged overlord, could not pry too much into the family affairs of the Aja.

In 1705, when Allada had recovered sufficiently from the

[1] J. Barbot, *A Description*, pp. 351–2.
[2] J. Ogilby, *Africa*, p. 480.     [3] J. Barbot, *A Description*, pp. 351-2.
[4] W. Bosman, *A New and Accurate Description*, p. 397.

ravages of the Oyo, the king promptly declared all the Allada roads leading to Whydah closed.[1] Aisan, however, behaved reasonably, pacified the king of Allada, performed the traditional ceremonies and had himself crowned by the traditional messenger from Allada.[2] About the time of his coronation, an agreement seems to have been reached between Allada and Whydah by which each agreed not to molest the trade of the other. It seemed that the new economic activities could, after all, be grafted into the old order. Then suddenly in 1708 Aisan died, leaving a minor of thirteen years as a successor, a minority which allowed the forces of disintegration to flourish.

By the end of the seventeenth century therefore, it had become quite clear that the European activities in Aja could neither be concentrated in one place nor controlled by the Aja authorities. It has also become apparent that those activities had started to weaken the traditional institutions which were meant to contain them. The whole process had justified the stand which the founders of Dahomey had taken at the beginning of the century. The increasing realisation that they were right, the increasing social insecurity and the chaos into which the traditional institutions were falling would lead more and more Aja to join the supporters of Dogbagri-Genu in the Igede region.

All that can safely be said about this earliest phase of Dahomey's growth is that the descendants of Dogbagri-Genu built their state quietly but surely. Dogbagri-Genu himself was not made king in his new home, there being no territory over which he could rule. When his son, Aho, had conquered a few more villages, he was made king and took the name Wegbaja. By the time of his death around 1680, he had added eighteen more towns and villages to the nascent kingdom.[3]

Akaba ascended the throne after Wegbaja, and soon the little kingdom was attacked and almost completely destroyed by Weme. Akaba, however, recovered and was able to continue the Dahomean expansion. By the end of his reign in 1708

[1] Richard Willis to Sir Dalby Thomas, 25 July 1705 (T 70/5).
[2] T. Astley, *Collection*, vol. III, pp. 41–3; Labat reported this as having taken place in 1725, but there is an error in his dating: first, because the king he mentioned was Aisan or Amat, who reigned between 1703 and 1708, and secondly, because in 1725 there was no Allada to perform the ceremony, it having been destroyed by Dahomey in 1724.
[3] Delisle, 'Extrait du Registre', 26 Aug. 1728 (AN. C. 6/25).

the Dahomey kingdom consisted of at least forty towns and villages.[1]

The oral traditions do not give the names of all these earliest conquests, but the location of the few of them that are remembered is significant. They lay directly southwards and south-eastwards of Abomey, across the region which the Allada people would have to cross if they were going to raid for slaves. Probably Dahomey sought to control this area not to engross the trade but to stop it, as the attempts of 1670 and 1687 already cited would seem to suggest.

Apart from this bare outline of the Dahomean expansion, nothing is known of the growth of its internal administration. It will be reasonable to suppose, however, that such organisations would be directly controlled by the king and would not be hereditary, that every important citizen would be personally required to do obeisance to the king to symbolise his 'putting a finger in the perforated pot' and that the state had a standing army. The emigrants, who had been forced to seek safety under Wegbaja as a result of the increase in the social insecurity that had followed the unrestricted slave trade after 1671, probably constituted the element which replenished the Dahomean army after it had almost completely been wiped out by Weme. By the time that Akaba and Aisan died in 1708, Dahomey had gained tremendously, not only in territory and men, but also in military experience and in confidence, and was ready to reimpose order on the Aja if the process of disintegration continued unchecked.

---

[1] E. Dunglas, 'Contribution à l'histoire du Moyen Dahomey', in *Etudes Dahoméennes*, vol. XIX, p. 96. Delisle, 'Extrait du Registre', 26 Aug. 1728 (AN. C. 6/25).

# 2

## The End of a System, 1708-24

In 1708 the crisis provoked by the impact of the slave trade on the traditional Aja political system entered its final phase. Huffon, the king of Whydah,[1] and Agaja, the king of Dahomey,[2] both ascended the throne in that year. They were to be the protagonists in this final act of the drama that saw the imposition of the Dahomean rule on the old Aja country.

Between 1708 and 1724 constitutional issues in Aja were no longer solved according to the traditional practice. This caused a breakdown in the internal administration of both Whydah and Allada and contributed to a war, precipitated by the Dutch factor at Whydah, which went on for eight years before it petered out. This breakdown was both the sign and the cause of a power-vacuum in Aja. In 1724 Agaja was invited to Allada to use means that were other than traditional to settle a traditional issue and he destroyed Allada in the process.

Two main constitutional issues during this period show that important ruling sections among the Aja of Whydah were increasingly disregarding the traditional precepts in the early eighteenth century. The first and much the more important was the question of the accession of Huffon, who was a minor when his father died. The Whydah traditional constitution provided that whenever a king died without a successor, the Gogan of Sahe[3]

[1] Du Coulombier, 'Relation envoyer à la Compagnie Royale de l'Asciente', 29 May 1714 (AN. C. 6/25).
[2] No authority for this date before Dalzel has been found, but there is no need to doubt its accuracy, for Dalzel may have had access to information now lost, and all writers on Dahomey have followed the dating. A. Dalzel, *History of Dahomey*, p. 7; M. J. Herskovits, *Dahomey*, vol. I, p. 13; E. Dunglas: 'Contribution à l'histoire du Moyen Dahomey', in *Etudes Dahoméennes (E.D.)*, vol. XIX, p. 101; C. W. Newbury, *The Western Slave Coast*, p. 14.
[3] This is the spelling used by the present Whydah descendants for the ancient capital of the old kingdom of Whydah. See Casimir Agbo, *Histoire de Ouidah du XVIᵉ au XXᵉ siècle* (Avignon, 1959), *passim*.

was to succeed.[1] A minor who could not perform all the traditional ceremonies was not a suitable successor, and there was no provision for a regency.

The Gogan therefore put in his claim and was supported by a party headed by chief Carter, the general superintendent of Whydah trade, and a pro-English chief.[2] If the traditional practice had been followed, he would have succeeded without any serious opposition. Those who had supported Aisan's accession in 1703 under the leadership of chief Assu, however, backed Aisan's young son, Huffon. Two factions therefore emerged in 1708, probably along the same lines as in 1703, and both were prepared to use non-traditional means to settle the issue.

Chief Carter gathered an army of between twelve and fifteen thousand soldiers to back the Gogan. Chief Assu obtained the help of about eight hundred European soldiers and marines to support Huffon,[3] and with the backing of his own followers, he quickly won the contest that ensued. Huffon, a child of about thirteen years, was forcibly enthroned king of Whydah.

The second issue occurred in 1717. On the night of 18 July the death of the reigning king of Allada was announced to Huffon in the traditional way.[4] Instead of performing his duties as prescribed by tradition on such an occasion, Huffon sought the advice of Bouchel, the director of the French fort. Bouchel told him to do nothing until a new king was elected at Allada, and then to send presents and request the new king for harmonious relations. Huffon accepted the advice.

A week later the Allada chiefs, who must have been surprised at Huffon's behaviour, came again to announce that a new Allada king had been installed. Huffon then sent presents, not as tradition prescribed, but as Bouchel advised.

Such apparently minor breaches of the tradition show that the Aja rulers, who ought to have been the jealous guardians of the established order, were themselves not unwilling to use foreign ideas to solve their problems when it suited them. By

---

[1] Du Coulombier, 'Mémoire de la suitte des affaires du pays de Juda', 14 Feb. 1715. A similar arrangement was known in ancient Ife, where, the oral tradition says, if an Obalaaye lived to see the death of three Ooni (the king of Ife), he was automatically made the next Ooni.

[2] This must not be confused with the Yovogan, a post that had not yet been created.

[3] J. Barbot, *A Description*, p. 453; Du Coulombier, 'Relation envoyer à la Compagnie...', 10 Aug. 1714 (AN. C. 6/25).

[4] 'Conseil de direction', 27 July 1717 (AN. C. 6/25).

such behaviour, they and their European accomplices were weakening the binding force of traditional belief and causing its eventual destruction.

Probably neither Huffon nor the Europeans consciously set about breaking up the Aja political organisation. They may have thought that they were merely protecting their different economic interests. Huffon to the very last believed in the traditional ways,[1] but he wanted to encourage the Europeans to send ships to his port rather than to the Allada port of Jakin. The Europeans also looked on Whydah as the greatest slaving port in West Africa in the early eighteenth century and did not wish to lose it. They opposed the succession of the Gogan because they had long regarded him as a difficult man to deal with,[2] and they may have felt moreover that a minority would offer them greater opportunities to influence the development of economic policy.

The result of Huffon's accession in 1708 was, however, a complete breakdown of the internal administration at Whydah. Huffon's tender age, which prevented him from performing all the crowning ceremonies, rendered him a king without authority until about 1726 when he was old enough to do so. As there was no constitutionally accepted regency, there was no central authority. The chiefs who had backed the rival claimants remained unreconciled with one another. Chief Carter swore never to forgive chief Assu; and chief Aplogan, who probably supported Huffon, remained an inflexible enemy of the Gogan. The chiefs who had opposed Huffon's accession were able to treat him as if he were no king at all.

Examples abound between 1710 and 1715 of the lawlessness that ensued as a result of this situation. In October 1710 an unidentified chief raised a rebellion against Huffon, but was quickly defeated with the support of the general populace.[3] Huffon, however, was not allowed to punish the rebel as good administration demanded. Instead, an extraordinary council of the elders met in which he was made to reconcile with the rebel and at which he provided a feast for all.[3]

[1] In 1722, when he could have been happy at the armed revolt against Allada's authority, he offered to help Allada. See Bouchel to La Compagnie, 30 April 1722 (AN. C. 6/25).
[2] T. Astley, *Collection*, vol. II, p. 412. Philip called the title 'Springatha', trying to render intelligible the Aja sound.
[3] Hicks to R.A.C., 18 Oct. 1710 (T 70/22); Seth Grosvenor and James Phipps to R.A.C., 3 Jan. 1711 (T 70/5).

About 1712 Huffon himself, for unknown reasons, declared war against the Gogan and asked his chiefs to aid him. The Aplogan, a sworn enemy of the Gogan, very promptly responded and did more than he was requested, by burning all the houses, farms and villages belonging to the Gogan. When Huffon and the Gogan were later reconciled, the Aplogan and the Gogan persisted in their enmity. Between 1712 and 1715 they fought private battles in Whydah which Huffon was completely unable to stop.[1]

The behaviour of the European directors increased this chaos. Once Huffon was on the throne, the same self-interest that had led them to support his candidature tended to drive them into competition for the greatest share of the Whydah slave trade. This attitude was carefully fostered by their employers in Europe. The instructions which the English Royal African Company gave to William Hicks, its representative at Whydah in 1711, was typical.

We pray you to cultivate so good an understanding with the king that upon our settlement and obligeing [*sic*] to furnish him with everything, he will yield to discharge the French from any trade in his country, and advise us your thoughts of the best methods of securing to us the sole trade of Whidah.[2]

Each European Company also wanted the largest share of the gold brought by the Portuguese traders to Whydah to buy slaves. The Dutch considered that the Portuguese traders there were under their authority by virtue of a clause in the treaty of Munster of 1648. But the Portuguese authorities in Brazil had never acknowledged the Dutch right.[3] The English wanted to

---

[1] Du Coulombier, 'Mémoire de la suitte des affaires du pays de Juda', 14 Feb. 1715 (AN. C. 6/25).

[2] R.A.C. to William Hicks, London, 13 Nov. 1711 (T 70/52).

[3] The Dutch claimed the right to impose a tax of 10 per cent of the total cargo on any Portuguese ship carrying European goods which came to trade within an area called 'Costa da Mina', which seems to have been defined as the area lying roughly between the western coastal boundary of modern Ghana and Godomey in modern Dahomey. They maintained that the right had existed since 1621, was officially acknowledged by the Portuguese in the Treaty of Truce signed between the United Provinces and Portugal in 1641 and incorporated into the treaty of Munster in 1648. See Viceroy of Brazil to King of Portugal, Bahia, 9 May 1726 (APB. OR 21 . 132), enclosing a letter from the Dutch general of Elmina Castle to the Viceroy of Brazil where the General's quotation of the exact wording of the clause of the treaty has been torn out; A. F. C. Ryder, 'The Re-establishment of the Portuguese factories on the costa da Mina to the mid-18th century', in *JHSN*, vol. I, no. 3, Dec. 1958, p. 160.

be the chief carrier of any European goods which the Portuguese might need at Whydah, so that they could monopolise the Portuguese gold.[1]

Irrespective of the Company's direction, exactly how the 'sole trade of Whydah' was to be secured depended largely on the temper of the factor on the spot. If he believed in friendly persuasion, he could follow the Company's instructions, give presents and employ intrigue to bring the authorities round to his side. Even such a method, however, tended to weaken the Whydah administration, by producing a violent reaction from the other directors who were less successful, as is clearly shown by the result of the manoeuvres that followed the accession of Huffon.

In January 1709 the English Royal African Company presented Huffon with a crown that cost thirty pounds and was requested by Hicks, its representative at Whydah, to send a 'fyne scymeter, a hat and feather and scarlet cloak for the king who is 14 years old', to secure the trade monopoly at Whydah. To achieve the same advantage, the French offered Huffon 'the Dartmouth Galley and her cargo, with the cargo of the "Joseph and Thomas"' Hicks then went a step further and placed one Charles Green at Sahe, made him a factor and charged him with the duty of cultivating the friendship of the Whydah authorities.[2]

By 1710 it was clear that Hicks had been immensely successful and the English were preferred to any other European nation at Whydah. This alarmed the French and aroused the resentment of the Dutch against both the English and Huffon. The Dutch threatened to burn the English fort and when prevented they remained unplacated and promised to take vengeance on Huffon. The good understanding existing between Hicks and Huffon prevented the Dutch design from being immediately carried out but they continued to watch for a favourable opportunity.[3]

If the use of presents ultimately threatened the Whydah administration, still more dangerous to law and order was the use of force to secure commercial advantage. Every European nation

---

[1] Thomas Pindar to R. Wills, 19 Sept. 1707 (T 70/52); R.A.C. to Ambrose Baldwyn, 14 Dec. 1720 (T 70/53).
[2] William Hicks to R.A.C., 12 Jan. 1709 (T 70/5).
[3] W. Hicks to R.A.C., 15 March 1711; S. Grosvenor and J. Phipps to R.A.C., 3 Jan. 1711 (T 70/5); R.A.C. to W. Hicks, 4 Oct. 1711 (T 70/52).

trading at Whydah had important Whydah chiefs attached to its interest. A fight between any two European directors was therefore easily transferred to their Whydah supporters and, if not quickly checked, could ultimately lead to a civil war, as Blaney's attitude in 1714 showed.

Blaney, the English director, proposed to a council of Whydah chiefs two measures for 'improving' the Whydah trade. He sought permission to construct a canal from the sea to the forts so that ships, or at least boats, could be used to discharge the European merchandise and head porterage eliminated. He further proposed that he be allowed to control the canal and charge tolls from anyone who used it.

Secondly, he proposed that he be allowed to control the Brazilian Portuguese captains because their activities were 'injurious' to the Whydah trade.[1] No doubt if these two proposals had been granted as they stood, they would have resulted in great advantages for the English trade or more probably to Blaney's personal advantage.

Du Coulombier, the director of the French fort, therefore told chief Assu that Blaney was motivated by avarice and self-interest and that his proposals would not result in the general improvement of the Whydah trade or bring any advantage whatsoever to Whydah. He further reminded chief Assu that there was a prior plan devised in 1712 by himself and the former English director, for controlling the Portuguese trade, which would be more beneficial to the trade and Whydah in general.[2] Chief Assu repeated du Coulombier's warning to the council of Whydah chiefs, whose suspicion had in fact been aroused by the 'unnatural' proposal to build a canal. The council therefore rejected Blaney's two proposals.

Blaney, however, resolved to subject the Portuguese to his own control by force. He armed eighteen Mina (perhaps Little Popo) men and asked them to break up the people assembled to trade with the Portuguese at the 'captain's trees'. The Portuguese complained to the king of the molestation and Huffon asked the Dutch to seize forty slaves belonging to Blaney as an indemnity for disturbing the market. When the Dutch carried out this assignment, Blaney armed eighty Africans, four Europeans and

[1] Du Coulombier, 'Mémoire de la suitte des affaires...', 14 Feb. 1715 (AN. C. 6/25).
[2] *Ibid.*

with himself at their head, went to the Dutch fort 'to seek an explanation'.[1]

Blaney's action created panic in the town. Chief Assu, who was then in the French fort transacting business, gave the alarm that civil war had broken out and without knowing who was fighting whom, asked the French director to send out his 'war boys' while he himself rushed home for his weapons. The French director sent twelve soldiers but by the time they reached the fort gate, the whole town was in an uproar and the Dutch director was being dragged, feet first, towards the English fort.[2] Blaney and the Dutch director were fined and Blaney was later expelled for causing a breach of the peace. But the incident, and the fact that the Assu could assume that there were permanent hostile camps into which each citizen fitted as soon as there was a commotion, was a clear illustration of the disturbed atmosphere which had come to prevail at Whydah.

Some account of the relations between Allada and Whydah during these years will further serve to illustrate the disordered condition of the Aja country and the contribution of the European traders to the situation. Allada, the 'father-state' of the Aja and the custodian of the Aja traditions, resented the breach of those traditions at Whydah. The accession of Huffon, which was carried out without any reference to Allada, strongly displeased the 'aged king of Ardra'. Huffon had refused moreover to pay certain customary gifts to the Allada chiefs and had dispensed with the services of his own traditional chiefs in the internal administration of Whydah. Those chiefs complained to the king of Allada.[3] So small, however, had the 'fatherly' authority of the king of Allada become that he was completely unable to do anything to induce Huffon to obey the traditional precepts.

This sense of frustration was doubtless increased by the realisation at Allada that the only thing that made Huffon so defiant was the prosperity of the slave trade at Whydah and that Allada's trade was not equally flourishing. In spite of the agreement in 1705 between the two kingdoms, very few references

[1] Du Coulombier, 'Mémoire de la suitte des affaires...', 14 Feb. 1715 (AN. C. 6/25).
[2] *Ibid.* Gov. and Council C.C.C. to R.A.C., 3 Sept. 1715; J. Blaney to R.A.C., 20 March 1716, 17 April 1716 (T 70/6).
[3] Du Coulombier, 'Relation envoyer à la Compagnie...', 10 Aug. 1714 (AN. C. 6/25).

are found in the documents to the trade of Allada between 1706 and 1714, a sure sign of its decline.

It was, however, the Dutch who caused Allada's suppressed anger and frustration to erupt into open hostility. The Dutch factor at Whydah still resented Huffon's friendship with Hicks and the English. As soon as Hicks died on 5 April 1712, he precipitated a war between Whydah and Allada by sending one of his company's ships to attack a Portuguese ship lying in Allada harbour.[1]

A quarrel between the Dutch and the Portuguese might, at first sight, appear unconnected with the relations between Allada and Whydah. In fact it was. Any disturbance at Allada port was a matter of great concern to the Allada authorities, for a reputation that the port could not afford protection to the shipping would drive the captains away from it. Moreover, because the agent of this particular disturbance came from Whydah, the king of Allada held Huffon responsible for the affront. He looked on it as contravening the Allada–Whydah agreement of 1705 which stipulated that neither was to harm the trade of the other. The Dutch director must have known the unpleasantness that his action would cause and he probably designed it to punish Huffon.

Allada immediately declared a war on Whydah. The king of Allada closed all the roads linking Allada and Whydah, intending this as a measure of outright economic warfare to deprive Huffon of the wealth that had made him so disobedient and bring more European ships to Allada port. On 13 February 1714 he again summoned a grand assembly of all his provincial rulers for a deliberation. The assembly agreed to continue to keep the roads shut and each of the provincial rulers promised faithfully to prevent any slaves being taken across his territory to Whydah. The blockade went on, with only a temporary lift in 1717, till 1720.[2]

Its effect on Whydah trade was immediate. As early as 15 May

---

[1] Hilliard and Green to R.A.C., 5 April 1712 (T 70/5); 10 June 1712 (T 70/2); J. Blaney to R.A.C., 22 April 1714 (T 70/5).

[2] J. Blaney, M. Hardrett and W. Rogers to R.A.C., 22 May 1714, 6 Aug. 1715 (T 70/5); J. Errington to R.A.C., 7 May 1715; Governor C.C.C. to R.A.C., Nov 1715, 18 Feb. 1716 (T 70/6); R. Mason, D. Welsh and W. Bramston to R.A.C., 10 Dec. 1715, 3 and 12 June 1716; W. Baillie to R.A.C., 20 Nov. 1716 (T 70/19); W. Baillie to ?, 31 May 1719 (T 70/1475).

1712[1] Hilliard and Green, joint acting directors of the English fort at Whydah, reported that slaves were 'scarce by means of the pallaver between the kings of Whydah and Ardrah'. All the seven ships despatched to Whydah by the Royal African Company between January 1713 and December 1714 returned with their slave cargo incomplete, and one of them had to be sent to Jakin for its slaves when there was none to be had at Whydah,[2] the trade of which continued bad until 1720 with only occasional reliefs.

This economic war was Allada's answer to the weakening of the traditional bonds in Aja, but it did not achieve the quick victory needed if authority was to be restored. Its greatest achievement was to cause inconvenience to the European traders at Whydah, to impoverish Huffon and thereby to increase the internal chaos at Whydah and to aggravate the breakdown in its own authority.

Huffon took vigorous measures to solve his kingdom's problems. Since the traditional chiefs were too involved in their own personal squabbles to help in the duty of government, he turned to 'new men' whom he styled 'king's servants'. In 1712 he formed them into a council from which he excluded all the traditional chiefs and in which he vested the final decision on every important issue. He himself accepted their decisions without question. The traditional chiefs attributed this unconstitutional step to childishness on Huffon's part. Huffon replied by declaring himself of age in 1713,[3] when he was only about eighteen years old, an action that must have alarmed even those chiefs who had remained loyal to him.

These measures did not, however, solve Whydah's administrative problems. The new men were inexperienced and were unnecessarily elated by the power vested in them. They sought

---

[1] Hilliard and Green to R.A.C., 15 May 1712 (T 70/5).
[2] S. Grosvenor and J. Phipps to R.A.C., 6 March 1713 (T 70/2); R.A.C. to Hilliard and Green, 17 March 1713 (T 70/52); Green to R.A.C., 14 Oct. 1714 (T 70/3); J. Blaney and C. Green to R.A.C., 29 Sept. 1713 (T 70/3); J. Blaney to Bate and Steward, 12 Jan. 1714 (T 70/3); R.A.C. to J. Blaney and C. Green, 8 Oct., 22 Oct. 1713 (T 70/52); J. Blaney and M. Hardrett to R.A.C., 22 April 1714 (T 70/18), 22 May 1714 (T 70/3), 5 Aug. 1714 (T 70/18); R.A.C. to J. Blaney, C. Green and M. Hardrett, 1 April 1714 (T 70/52); J. Blaney and M. Hardrett to R.A.C., 3 Nov. 1714 (T 70/3).
[3] Du Coulombier, 'Relation envoyer à la Compagnie...', 10 Aug. 1714 (AN. C. 6/25).

to bolster up their position by acquiring wealth by all means, fair and foul, and by poisoning the king's mind against his traditional chiefs. By 1714 their method of acquiring wealth was visibly harming the trade and they had so effectively maligned the traditional chiefs that even chief Carter, who seems to have become reconciled with Huffon and was one of the very few among them who continued to see the king regularly, was once seen standing in front of the palace for twenty-four hours before Huffon would consent to speak to him. All that the 'new men' had achieved by 1714 therefore was to render the European directors and captains discontented, and the traditional chiefs afraid for the safety of their persons, their property and the kingdom of Whydah.[1]

The critical stage which the hostility with Allada reached in 1714 probably caused Huffon and his traditional chiefs to patch up a truce before the end of that year. It was necessary to find a way of breaking Allada's stranglehold on Whydah economy if the Whydah were not to be impoverished. Huffon decided to fight Allada, and his chiefs probably agreed with him. He and his chiefs started to buy large quantities of guns and gunpowder. The English director and an English captain who noticed the rising demand for ammunition in 1713 wrote to England for fresh supplies. Between September 1713 and March 1714 the Royal African Company alone sent over three thousand guns of all descriptions to Whydah.[2] The French and Dutch could hardly have sent less than the English total.

With these arms, the first pitched battle was fought between Allada and Whydah about the middle of April 1714.[3] Considering the quantity of arms, the battle was a remarkably small and inconclusive affair. Whydah gained no advantage. The Europeans felt it as just one more minor inconvenience to trade and it did not even increase the stock of slaves for export.

Huffon therefore started to make alliances. First he approached Blaney, the English director, called himself 'the company's son'[4] and asked for military help against Allada. Blaney laid down

---

[1] Du Coulombier, 'Relation envoyer à Messrs de la Compagnie...', 10 Aug. 1714 (AN. C. 6/25).
[2] J. Blaney to R.A.C., 29 Sept. 1763 (T 70/22); E. Coward to R.A.C., 15 Oct. 1713 (T 70/22); R.A.C. to J. Blaney, C. Green and M. Hardrett, 25 March and 1 April 1714 (T 70/52).
[3] J. Blaney and M. Hardrett to R.A.C., 22 April 1714 (T 70/3).
[4] J. Blaney to R.A.C., 22 April 1714 (T 70/5).

impossible conditions, because he did not believe, as Hicks had done, in allying with any African king:[1]

If they will regulate the extravagant prices the Portuguese pay; if they recover the Company's debts by former agents; if they exclude all English but the Company's ships from trading in their country and demand no customs for any ships of the Company...These things he believes they'll not comply with.[2]

He would only recommend 'a silk union flag for the king to show he is English'.[3]

Disappointed by the English, Huffon turned to the Little Popo Accra and the Akwamu. Towards the end of 1714 he approached Ofori, described as the 'king of Little Popo Keta and Accra';[4] and to someone described as the 'great Captain of Accra' for military help against Allada. Ofori seems to have agreed to send a contingent by the end of January 1715.

About May 1715 Huffon approached the governors of the Cape Coast Castle and asked them 'to prevail with the king of Quamboe [i.e. Akwamu] to assist them'.[5] The governors showed no interest, but Huffon managed to contact the king of Akwamu and to continue discussions with him until 1718.[6]

On the assurance of help from Ofori, Huffon despatched an army against the Allada province of Tori. On 18 January 1715 chief Assu set out with his own contingent to join the expected Little Popo Accra army and together make for the front.[7] The Gogan also set out with his own contingent. The unanimity with which these former opponents of Huffon rallied to his call gave high hopes of success.

The expedition, however, failed to achieve its purpose. Ofori did not send enough soldiers in January 1715 and fresh negotiations had to be entered into. Finally, more of Ofori's soldiers turned up but it is not known whether they fought any battles or for how long they stayed. In September and October 1716 they were still inactively camping near the European forts at

[1] J. Blaney to R.A.C., 4 Aug. 1714 (T 70/5).
[2] J. Blaney to R.A.C., 15 July 1714 (T 70/5); J. Blaney, M. Hardrett and W. Rogers to R.A.C., 22 June 1714 (T 70/26).
[3] *Ibid.*
[4] Du Coulombier, 'Mémoire de la suitte des affaires...', 14 Feb. 1715 (AN. C. 6/25); W. Baillie to R. Bleau?, 21 May 1717 (T 70/1475).
[5] Lancelot Green to Governor C.C.C., 28 May 1715 (T 70/6).
[6] W. Baillie to ?, 21 Aug. 1718 (T 70/1475).
[7] Du Coulombier, *op. cit.* (see note 4 above).

Whydah.[1] Akwamu's intervention, if it took place, was, as usual, ineffective, and the expedition against Allada had petered out by 1717, long before the negotiation with the Akwamu was completed.[2]

Probably the most important cause of Whydah's failure was the irreconcilable enmity between the traditional chiefs. During the campaign of January 1715 the Aplogan refused to allow the Gogan's contingent to pass through his territory, which they had to do to get to Tori, the battlefront. Huffon could not coerce the Aplogan into obedience because the council of the traditional chiefs said that such a move would only result in civil war, that the Gogan's supporters would seek to revenge the insult of 1712, and the Aplogan's friends would resist them.[3]

Despite all his efforts, Huffon found himself powerless before the entrenched position of these chiefs. First, their offices belonged to their families and they could only be removed as a result of an offence against tradition, on the recommendation of their families who then had the right to nominate new candidates. As the chiefs were usually the heads of their families, and therefore the highest authorities on their family traditions, that meant virtually that they could not be removed. Nor could they be deprived of their land, which also belonged to their families and not to the king.

Secondly, Whydah, like Allada, had no central army controlled exclusively by the king. Its army was made up of the contingents contributed, armed and led by each chief to the king's wars. Only a king who had completed all the traditional rites, which Huffon had not, could summon such an army and expect an implicit obedience.

In such an arangement, a single powerful chief could easily cause the failure of a whole expedition, as the behaviour of the Aplogan has shown. As the situation worsened, many chiefs probably reserved their strength for their personal enemies rather than for the king's service. As Huffon was not yet a full king, some of the chiefs may have decided to ignore his summons altogether.

[1] 'Accounts and Journals, Cape Coast Castle', September and October 1716 (T 70/383).
[2] R. Mason, D. Welsh and W. Branston to R.A.C., 10 Dec. 1715 (T 70/19).
[3] Du Coulombier, 'Mémoire de la suitte des affaires...', 14 Feb. 1715 (AN. C. 6/25).

The way in which the slave trade was organised at Whydah actually increased the power and influence of the chiefs. Certain chiefs were originally given the duty of taking the taxes from each of the European nations who traded at Whydah and of being the immediate protectors of such nations against any injustice. Under the arrangement, chief Assu was the 'French' chief and Carter the 'English' chief. By the beginning of the eighteenth century, such chiefs had virtually become the controllers of the trade of those nations put under them. This became an important source of patronage, and some of the chiefs probably became richer and commanded more immediate respect than the king.

It would seem that Huffon realised perfectly well that the fundamental cause of his own failure was the weak position of the monarchy in the actual practice of the *Ebi* social theory. He also knew that theoretically, the king was absolute. So from 1717 onwards, he applied with increasing vehemence, what may be called 'the reserved powers of the crown'.

He resuscitated and extended the institution of the 'king's men' and created them into chiefs, each with specific duties, to replace those of the traditional chiefs. Between 1717 and 1720 he

...among them appointed whitemen's captains as he called them, or rather judges and superintendents of trade to whom all addresses must be made and by them a decision given so that a hundredth part of what was done never came to his ear or what did being delivered by them he received as from an oracle.[1]

He created a standing army of his own, which was an innovation, the nucleus of which was formed by a sergeant and twelve soldiers, all in uniform, contributed by the English fort. The French director also sought permission from his employers to contribute a similar contingent so that he might not be outdone,[2] but whether he did so is not known. To this nucleus were added the Whydah citizens whom Huffon had 'marked in the face so that everyone may know and not oppose them'.[3]

In 1718 he tried to centralise the slave trade by creating a chief and ordering 'that all slaves come to this caboceer's hands who

---

[1] W. Baillie to Governor of C.C.C., 10 May 1720 (T 70/54). 'Conseil de Marine', 16 Sept. 1717 (AN. C. 6/25).

[2] *Ibid.*

[3] W. Baillie to Governor C.C.C., ? 21 Aug. 1718 (T 70/1475).

may dispose them to whom he had a mind'[1] and at the same time ordered that all the Europeans who traded privately in Whydah must pay duties on the slaves that they sold to the ships just as all the African traders did.[2]

He tightened the internal security by ruling that the European directors must not go out of the country or visit any Whydah chief without first obtaining his permission or re-export any merchandise once landed at Whydah.[2] He also tried to raise the prestige of the crown by ruling that all his subjects must remain prostrated while talking to him and no chief must be seen going around too frequently with the Europeans without his prior permission. Wealthy subjects who might be uncontrollable were accused of some crime or the other and fined very heavily, a practice that did not exclude the European directors.[3]

None of these measures were actually beyond the constitutional powers of the king, but it had not been customary to apply them as vigorously. They therefore aroused the discontent of the people who, in 1717, made a representation to Huffon that if they were not treated more gently, they would desert the country. Huffon pacified them, but the traditional chiefs openly said that they no longer cared for the king.[4]

By 1720 the traditional chiefs had retired to their country houses and would not go to Huffon even when summoned. Baillie reported, probably without exaggeration, that

Those new customs quite disgusted the cabbasheers, so that not one of them gives a pin for him or minds any law he makes...Here I had from some of the greatest men in the country who assure me if he continues his tyranny much longer, they'll be obliged to take a violent course with him, they know that they have in him too much experienced the ill fate of a country governed by women and children and this shall never succeed him. There is not at present one of his great men that will go neare [*sic*] him when he sends for them...In short sir, these people are not without solid judgment ...The Blacks are not so abjectly slavish in what concerns themselves, if he was to meddle with any of the great men here, they would soon show their horns.[5]

---

[1] W. Baillie to Dawson, 26 Oct. 1717 (T 70/1475); W. Baillie to Phipps and Bleau, 15 April 1717 (T 70/1475), 10 May 1720 (T 70/54).
[2] W. Baillie to Phipps and Bleau, 15 April ? 1718 (T 70/1475).
[3] *Ibid.*
[4] 'Conseil de Marine', 1 Nov. 1717 (AN. C. 6/25).
[5] William Baillie to Governor C.C.C., 10 May 1720 (T 70/54).

In 1720 when Huffon made a law that the European ships must be supplied with slaves in turn, according to the order of arrival, Whydah citizens openly took their slaves to any ships they pleased as if the law had not existed. When Baillie and the French Director asked the king to enforce his order, he recanted.[1]
The European directors also reacted very unfavourably to Huffon's measures. They refused to co-operate with him in his attempt to centralise the slave trade. They resented the taxes imposed on them and the limits set on their freedom of movement, and they regarded Huffon's whole policy with distaste and himself with intense hatred. Baillie said that he was expressing the feelings of all the Europeans at Whydah when he wrote on 10 May 1720:

I have in this short time come through more difficulty than in all the forty-five months I have been at Whydah through...the insupportable villany of this insupportable tyrant, whose insolence is now grown to such a height that neither white nor blacks are able any longer to tolerate it. There is not any of our privileges he does not daily dispense with where he finds his present interest or is buzzed by his bribed D–S or wives, no customs or settled law of his country in respect of Europeans which he does not impetuously break through, no injustice robbry [*sic*] or other villany he does not encourage. In short he is a monster of a nature, appeared designed for a public plague and till he is by some extraordinary means reduced to reason, here will be no peaceable living for any European of the least spark of soul, nor any security at all for their effects in this country.[2]

It is not surprising therefore that the actions of the Europeans were completely unhelpful to Huffon in all his attempts to solve Whydah's problems. Frightened by the breakdown of Whydah administration and by the inept management of the war, they constantly attempted, between 1714 and 1720 to get out of Whydah to settle at Allada or wherever there was a prospect of slave trade between the Volta and Epe.
In 1714, after the first inconclusive battle between Whydah and Allada, Blaney the English director at Whydah decided

to settle Aguga near river Vulta and continue the settlement at Jacquine and settle a factory at Appah [Epe] by which and the help of a good sloop or long boat, they can easily have communication with the Bight and Calabar.[3]

[1] *Ibid.*    [2] W. Baillie to Governor C.C.C., 10 May 1720 (T 70/54).
[3] J. Blaney to R.A.C., 4 Aug. 1714 (T 70/5).

He thought that the settlement at Epe would be easy because an exiled prince from there who was being invited back had asked him to come and settle an English factory in his territory.[1] But his plans did not materialise.

Du Coulombier, the French director, also planned to remove the French headquarters to Allada. He instructed Bouchel, the French resident agent at Allada, to conduct the negotiations for a planned withdrawal thither. Bouchel asked the king of Allada to grant seven conditions before the French would establish their headquarters at Jakin which by that date had become Allada's chief port. First that the king of Allada would allow the French to sit on chairs; secondly that the Epe port would be closed; thirdly that as soon as a French captain reached Allada, the king would grant him audience and declare the trade open the same day; fourthly that the king would build a trading house on the coast at his own expense for the French; fifthly that the trade would henceforth be carried on at the seashore and not in the capital as hitherto; sixthly that the king would make insulting a whiteman an offence for his subjects and punish anyone offending against such law to the satisfaction of the Europeans and finally that the king and his chiefs would promise that the Allada traders would offer their slaves to the French first before offering them to any other European trader.[2] Negotiations on these points went on until April 1715 when they were called off by Bouchel.

Again, between 1717 and 1720, all the European directors planned to leave Whydah. Baillie thought of removing the English headquarters to Keta and Little Popo and started serious secret negotiations with Ofori which do not appear to have had any success.[3] In 1718 both the English and the French looked to Jakin.[4] And the Dutch headquarters at Elmina summoned the Dutch director at Whydah to recommend whether it was worthwhile keeping a fort there any longer.[5]

Soso, who ascended the throne of Allada in 1717, was as determined as his predecessor to ruin Whydah's trade and keep Huffon the 'obedient son' he ought to be. In 1717 and 1718,

---

[1] J. Blaney and M. Hardrett to R.A.C., 3 Nov. 1714 (T 70/6).
[2] 'Mémoires des negociations du Sieur Bouchel à Ardres', 2 Jan. 1715; Du Coulombier to Messrs de la Compagnie, 16 April 1715 (AN. C. 6/25).
[3] W. Baillie to R. Bleau?, 21 May 1717 (T 70/1475).
[4] W. Baillie to Phipps and R. Bleau, 15 April 1718 (T 70/1475).
[5] W. Baillie to Phipps and R. Bleau, 4 Dec. 1717 (T 70/1475).

while the Europeans were thus trying to get out of Whydah, he kept sending 'daily invitations' to all of them[1] to come and settle in his kingdom. He was on the point of success in the first quarter of 1718 when the strict measures he then enacted ended all the probability of European removal to Allada.[2] In 1721 when the Portuguese decided to build a fort in Aha, they chose Whydah rather than Allada.[3]

The failure of the Europeans to remove to Allada meant the failure of Allada's attempt to weaken Whydah trade and end the power vacuum in Aja, and can be accounted for by several reasons. The first was the general hostility of the Aja kings, for economic or security reasons, to such removals. In 1714 du Coulombier had to pay Huffon heavily before he was allowed to remove certain articles from Whydah to Jakin for trade. When the other European directors followed his example he was expelled from the country after being accused of being the cause of all the economic misfortunes of Whydah.[4] When the ruler of Jakin heard that Blaney wanted to establish at Epe, he successfully prevented it, though we are not told how.[5]

Secondly Allada did not want to give any more concessions to the Europeans than they already had, which might further weaken the authority of the Allada monarchy or cause discontent among Allada chiefs and citizens. This was partly why the negotiation between Bouchel and the king of Allada broke down in 1715. All the seven conditions demanded by Bouchel were calculated to give special privileges to the French at the expense of everyone else concerned.

Thirdly the slaves bought from Allada cost the Europeans on the average much more than the slaves bought from Whydah. The cost of porterage was higher at Allada than at Whydah,[6] probably because the Allada capital, where the trade was centred, was farther inland than the European forts at Whydah. Moreover, it had become traditional at Allada to buy slaves in lots, by which the European captains were forced to take the good

---

[1] W. Baillie to ?, 15 April 1718 (T 70/1475).
[2] W. Baillie to the Gentlemen at Cape Coast Castle, 30 April 1718 (T 70/1475).
[3] 'Etablissement d'une Comptoire Portugaise à Juda, 1721' (AN. C. 6/25); A. F. C. Ryder, 'The Re-establishment of the Portuguese...', in *JHSN*, vol. 1, no. 3 (1958), pp. 160–1.
[4] Du Coulombier to Messrs de la Compagnie, 29 May 1714 (AN. C. 6/25).
[5] J. Blaney to R.A.C., 20 March 1715 (T 70/6).
[6] W. Baillie to Governor C.C.C., 30 April 1717 (T 70/1475).

and the bad slaves together, whereas at Whydah the slaves were bought singly and the Europeans could choose the good ones and reject the bad ones. This was probably why the Portuguese, who insisted on only the healthiest slaves, 'as good as waxwork', were more fond of Whydah than of Allada. Finally, Allada traders insisted on being paid in cowries for slaves[1] while the Whydah traders, though they preferred cowries, did not mind being paid in cheap goods if the European traders told them that cowries were not available.

Soso was unwilling to change this pattern of Allada trade which was on the whole advantageous to the Allada traders. In fact he concluded, from the informations he had picked up from European captains, that the Europeans would always want slaves. He was therefore confident that no matter what measures he took, the European slave traders would always come to Allada, 'and the great prices they sold slaves at where they carry them can enable them to be at some more charge to him'.[2]

Accordingly in April 1718 he more than doubled the customs duties hitherto paid by the captains and enforced the law that all the European captains must go to Allada to trade.[3] An attempt to get him to relent by Albertus, the Dutch factor at Jakin, who was generally regarded as his friend, was unsuccessful and Albertus himself was forced to obey the new regulations.[4]

The European directors, on their own side, did not always seriously mean to remove even when they threatened. For removal involved great expenses in building and new establishment. Usually they used the threat as an instrument for securing greater concessions for themselves from either Allada or Whydah. William Baillie clearly expressed this in 1718 when Huffon's measures were making all the directors uneasy:

The French and I have had several consultations concerning this and think far more advisable to try to curb him by sending some of the first ships to slave at Jacquine whereby we can perhaps make him sensible of how far the trade of his country depends on his friendship with Cos [i.e. Company's] chiefs...[5]

---

[1] Du Coulombier, 'Relations envoyer à Messrs de la Compagnie', 10 Aug. 1714 (AN. C. 6/25).
[2] W. Baillie to Governor and Council C.C.C., ? Dec. 1718 (T 70/1475).
[3] W. Baillie to Governor and Council C.C.C., 30 April 1718 (T 70/1475).
[4] W. Baillie to Governor and Council C.C.C., 21 Aug. 1718 (T 70/1475).
[5] W. Baillie to ?, 15 April 1718 (T 70/1475).

Behind the minds of the Europeans lay the feeling that there was really nothing to choose between Whydah and Allada. In 1715 du Coulombier, concluding his despatch to the French Minister on why he had terminated the negotiation with the king of Allada, wrote:

but as up till now I see nothing stable in this coast of Ardra, I do not believe, Monseigneur, that this is the suitable time to hurry to make an establishment at Jakin and accordingly I have made no more move...[1]

In August and again December 1718 Baillie wrote: 'you see gentlemen how these kings agree and may judge thence what we may expect, this being altogether as much sett [*sic*] on his interest as the other is on his and will surely go by the ears together.'[2]

The Allada–Whydah war had therefore achieved nothing when it petered out in 1720. Whydah still kept the European forts and Allada still controlled the paths to the supply of slaves. Whydah had not been able completely to prevent the Europeans going to Allada nor had Allada been able completely to stop slaves from being brought to Whydah, the trade of which remained sufficiently encouraging for the Portuguese to decide to establish there in 1721.

Though it did not solve anything, the war however had important negative consequences. Because it was indecisive, it confirmed and indeed aggravated the power vacuum in Aja. It worsened the internal chaos in Whydah and left the Whydah chiefs contemplating a 'violent action' against Huffon, and the European directors looking for 'an extraordinary means' to reduce him to reason.

It worsened the relations between Allada and Whydah. Eight years of hostility and fratricidal wars left behind a great deal of bad blood and made it impossible for the two kingdoms to join together to recognise, much less oppose, a common danger. Harmony between the Aja kingdoms was never again completely restored under the old political system which was greatly weakened if not virtually ended by the very fact that the war lasted so long. Allada could no longer command the filial duties of Whydah as promptly as in the past.

[1] Du Coulombier to Messrs de la Compagnie, 16 April 1715 (AN. C. 6/25).
[2] W. Baillie to Governor and Council C.C.C., ? Dec. 1718 (T 70/1475).

The losses which the traditional chiefs suffered from the lack of success caused acute internal problems in both Whydah and Allada which persisted after the war had ended and which were much more dangerous to the existence of those kingdoms than any specific act of hostility undertaken during the preceding eight years of war.

With the return of peace, however precarious, trade revived at Whydah[1] and the Portuguese started building their fort there in 1721, in spite of loud protests from the Dutch, the French and the English. The revival probably eased some of the old discontent and made the European traders and the African chiefs much more friendly to Huffon than formerly. Baldwyn, the English director who had succeeded Baillie in 1721, rejected the idea of a new establishment at Jakin as being disadvantageous to trade which he said could best be carried on from Whydah.[2]

The threat to Whydah trade caused by the activities of the European pirates in 1719 and 1720 certainly produced a new community of interest between Huffon, his chiefs and the European directors.[3] Huffon summoned a grand council consisting of his chiefs and the European directors to consider positive actions against the pirates. For the first time since the beginning of Huffon's reign, they all agreed on a course of action. Whydah authorities wanted the Europeans to take their cannons to the seashore for use against the pirates. The European directors agreed on the condition that they would be allowed to build forts on the seashore. Finally the Whydah authorities agreed, though reluctantly, and everybody seemed happy.[4] Unfortunately nothing resulted from this harmony mainly because the English sent warships out to patrol the West African coast, thus rendering any effort at Whydah unnecessary.

The end of the war does not seem to have produced peace and internal stability at Allada. Exactly what went on inside Allada in the first two decades of the eighteenth century are obscure, mainly because European references to the kingdom are few. Those few references, however, tend to suggest that its internal problems were similar to those of Whydah, that the authority

---

[1] Baldwyn and Peck to R.A.C., 8 Sept. 1721, 25 Jan. 1722 (T 70/27); 27 Oct. 1722 (T 70/23).
[2] Baldwyn to Lynn, Jan. 1722 (T 70/7).
[3] J. Atkins, *A Voyage to Guinea, Brazil and the West Indies* (London, 1735), p. 18; 'Mémoire concernant la colonie de Juda, Côte de Guinée', 1722 (AN. C. 6/25).          [4] *Ibid.*

of the king was rapidly diminishing, that his chiefs were recalcitrant and that the king, though not a minor, was as incapable
of solving those problems as Huffon. In short, in Allada as in
Whydah, the old precepts no longer had a strong binding force.

The breakdown of the French–Allada negotiations of 1715
was partly caused by the inability of the king to make his chiefs
obey him. Both the Jakin and the Allada chiefs made it plain to
the French captains then trading at Allada that they would behave as they thought fit, irrespective of the king's agreement
with the French. The ruler of Epe was not prepared to close his
port to satisfy French wishes, nor could the king of Allada coerce
him to do so, even though it was recognised that the former was
under the latter.[1]

In November 1717 Soso, who had just ascended the throne of
Allada, made a law that all firearms brought into the country
must be sold to him alone.[2] In April 1718 he again ruled that the
European captains must buy his slaves before they bought any
from anyone else and that all the cowries that came into the
country must be sold to him alone. These actions suggest that
Soso was also trying hard, as Huffon was doing around the same
time, to raise the power, the prestige and the wealth of the
monarchy above those of his subjects.

Not all the Allada chiefs had scrupulously continued to observe
the king's closure of the Allada–Whydah roads for the whole
length of the Allada–Whydah war, particularly after the end of
1714. For it would appear that some slaves continued to filter
through to Whydah from Allada as from 1715. This meant that
the chiefs who obeyed the king were sacrificing the gains they
might otherwise have made and pinning their hopes on the
eventual success of their cause. When the war ended incon-
clusively, the loyal chiefs became dissatisfied and put pressure
on the king to renew the war. This came to a head in April 1722,
when Soso was forced to close the Allada–Whydah roads again.
The action, however, seemed too late and did not satisfy the
Allada chiefs who then asked Soso to abdicate or grant a list of
concessions, which has not been preserved. Soso was completely
powerless and was forced to grant all that they demanded.[3]

[1] Du Coulombier to Messrs de la Compagnie, 16 April 1717 (AN. C. 6/25).
[2] W. Baillie to Dawson, 9 Nov. 1717; W. Baillie to ?, 30 April 1718
(T 70/1475).
[3] Bouchel to Messrs de la Compagnie, 30 April 1722; Levesque to Messrs
de la Compagnie, 30 Jan. 1723 (AN. C. 6/25).

In spite of that, not all the chiefs were satisfied. A ruler of one of the provinces declared himself 'independent' of Soso's authority and got an army together to back his assertion. This in the *Ebi* social theory was not only incomprehensible but monstrous. Even Huffon was appalled and he offered all the help he could muster in guns, cowries and gunpowder, to bring back the rebellious chief.[1] It is not known how the attempt fared. About January 1724 Soso suddenly died,[2] and a succession contest ensued between two candidates. The defeated candidate, instead of acquiescing, sought the help of Agaja, king of Dahomey, and the issue took an unexpected turn.

Since 1708 Dahomey had continued to grow in strength. The succession of Agaja in that year is generally agreed to be a departure from normal usage. The traditions about his succession are confused, but there is no need to doubt the fact that he succeeded his elder brother, Akaba.[3] The general explanation given for this seems to involve some confusion with later events. The official version, related to Le Herisse, says that Akaba reigned with his twin sister Ahangbe and that the arrangement had worked well because Ahangbe had been content to remain in the background. When Akaba died, this version continues, the problem of keeping the kingdom together faced the kingmakers, because if they wanted to be strictly just they would have had to choose the sons of both Akaba and Ahangbe as joint kings.

To avoid the chaotic result that could follow such a division of authority, the tradition continues, the sons of both were pushed aside, and Dosu,[4] Akaba's younger brother, was elected under the name Agaja.

This rationalisation, however, leaves many questions unanswered. If Ahangbe had been enthroned with her twin brother, then she ought to be qualified to carry on after his death, since

---

[1] Bouchel to Messrs de la Compagnie, 30 April 1723; Levesque to Messrs de la Compagnie, 30 January 1723 (AN. C. 6/25).
[2] Tinker, Mabyn and Humphrey to R.A.C., ? Jan. 1724 (T 70/7); F. P. Mendes to V. F. Cezar de Meneses, 16 July 1724 (APB. OR. 19 Dec. 56); W. Snelgrave, *A New Account of Some Parts of Guinea and the Slave Trade* (London, 1734), pp. 6–7.
[3] Le Herisse, *L'Ancien Royaume*, pp. 15, 294–5; Sossouhountto, 'Les Anciens Rois de la Dynastie d'Abomey', in *E.D.* vol. XIII (1955), pp. 25–30; E. Dunglas in *E.D.* vol. XIX, pp. 99–100.
[4] In Dahomey, Dosu is the name given to a child born immediately after twins. In Yoruba the same name is spelt Idowu.

the traditions do not say that both died at the same time. Moreover, Dahomean society is patrilineal[1] and the sons of Ahangbe, being descendants on the female side could have no serious claims to the throne.

Anatole Coissy has sought to explain away these difficulties by postulating that Ahangbe reigned for a short time after Akaba, and that when she died Akaba's sons were too young to occupy the throne.[2] Dunglas agrees with Coissy about the probable age of the sons of Akaba and further proposes that Agaja was originally made a regent for Akaba's son, but refused to hand over when the heir was old enough.

Both Coissy and Dunglas overlook one statement in the oral tradition that Akaba was already advanced in age when he ascended the throne. He is also generally accepted to have reigned for between twenty and twenty-eight years.[3] Under normal circumstances therefore he ought to have had grown-up children when he died.

Agaja's statement to Delisle in 1728 would tend to contradict any suggestion that Ahangbe reigned between Akaba and himself and would suggest that he directly succeeded his brother. Recounting his and his ancestor's achievements to Delisle he mentioned his grandfather, his father and his brother.[4]

In short it would seem that Ahangbe did not reign in Dahomey, that her sons could not have been serious rivals to Akaba's sons, who, if they existed, are unlikely to have been too young to succeed in 1708. The puzzle as to why Agaja succeeded in 1708 remains unsettled.

A solution can be attempted from other statements in the Dahomean traditions. The full meaning of the proverb from which the name Agaja was extracted is 'no one throws into fire, a green tree which is still standing'. Le Herisse has rightly interpreted this adage as meaning that the line of Wegbaja was still able to supply a king and could not yet be jettisoned or brushed aside.[5] There is here an implication that the paternity of Akaba's sons was in doubt, that Ahangbe's children were not regarded as full-blooded *Ahovi* or princes, and that as long as

[1] M. J. Herskovits, *Dahomey*, vol. I, p. 87.
[2] Anatole Coissy, 'Une reigne de femme dans l'ancien Royaume d'Abomey', in *E.D.* vol. II (1949), pp. 5–8.
[3] Le Herisse, *L'Ancien Royaume*, pp. 14–15; E. Dunglas in *E.D.* vol. xv, p. 90.
[4] Delisle, 'Extrait du Registre', 13 Sept. 1728 (AN. C. 6/25).
[5] Le Herisse, *L'Ancien Royaume*, pp. 15–16.

there was available a candidate certainly of the true blood, he should be preferred to any with such doubtful claims.

Dunglas, from some curious tradition he had collected, has attributed infertility to Tegbesu.[1] But contemporary documents say that he had children and that he was succeeded, not by a brother, but by a son.[2] Could it be that the traditions have become confused and that it was Akaba who really had no sons of his own even though oral traditions gave names of his supposed sons? The suggestion is tempting as it would solve most of the apparent contradictions in the accepted account.

The choice of Agaja as king in 1708 had great consequences for Dahomey. He was the most minutely described and the most admired of all the eighteenth-century Dahomean kings. A French director at Whydah in 1728 described him as middling in height and full bodied, 'slightly bigger and having wider shoulders than Molière'.[3] Snelgrave who saw him in 1727 said his face was pitted with the smallpox but was nevertheless attractive and that he had a majestic bearing.[4] Estimates of his age by the European are untrustworthy, but in 1727, twenty years after he had ascended the throne, Snelgrave said that he was about forty-five. If, however, he was the brother next in age to Akaba, as tradition affirms and as his name Dosu would suggest, then Agaja could hardly be less than thirty-five in 1708 and fifty-five when Snelgrave saw him in 1727.

At his accession, the kingdom of Dahomey covered the Abomey plateau and consisted of at most between forty-two and sixty-two towns and villages. This would imply that the total area was small, since urban life was the rule rather than the exception in that part of West Africa and villages were packed very closely together. The kingdom was probably not as large as either Allada or Whydah.

What it lacked in size, it gained in efficient organisation. Its monarchy was a strongly centralised institution, controlled all the appointments and dismissals of the chiefs and had a standing army.

[1] E. Dunglas in *E.D.* vol. xx, pp. 3–4.
[2] R. Norris, *Memoirs of the Reign of Bossa Ahadee, King of Dahomey* (London, 1789), p. 105; Conseil de direction à la Compagnie, 10 July 1754; Guestard to La Compagnie, 10 July 1754 (AN. C. 6/25); Guestard to Ministre de Colonies, 7 June 1774 (AN. C. 6/26).
[3] 'Extrait du Registre', 26 Aug. 1728 (AN. C. 6/25).
[4] W. Snelgrave, *A New Account*, p. 7.

As soon as Agaja ascended the throne he took two steps which showed his political astuteness and military genius. First he instituted a system of spies, the *Agbadjigbeto*, whom he sent to any town or village he might wish to attack. They were required to present themselves in such a place as simple merchants and learn the local language. They were to study the military potentiality and the defence arrangements of such places, know their protective gods, and report these details to Agaja on their return. If possible they were to enter into a pact of mutual friendship and non-violence with the most important chiefs there. Back at Abomey they were to manufacture reasons, for propaganda purposes, why the particular places they had visited must be attacked.[1]

Secondly, Agaja instituted a military training scheme, which in time produced a highly efficient, though not wholly professional, army, by allowing 'every common soldier a boy at the public charge, in order to be trained up in hardship from the youth'.[2] The armies that conquered Allada and Whydah were trained in that way and when Snelgrave saw them during an early morning exercise in 1727, his comment was 'this sight was well worth seeing, even by us Europeans'.[3]

The details of the history of Dahomey between 1708 and 1724 are obscure, but must have consisted of successful wars against a number of the neighbouring towns and kingdoms. Agaja inherited a number of disputes from the previous reign, one of which was against Weme. Tradition remembers him as having sent an army to Aslo-Ouessa soon after his accession, and it was probably during this campaign that his army caught one 'Agazaye' whose head was one of the eight heads of 'famous kings' which Agaja showed to Delisle in 1728. Some of his successes before 1724 probably also included the taking of Didouma and of Povey (Pobe), lying north-west and south-east respectively of Abomey.[4] But the majority of them have been forgotten.

By 1714, the 'kingdom of Fouin' (i.e. Dahomey) had become a power to reckon with by Allada and very well known to the European traders through the port of Epe which the Dahomean traders used.[5]

---

[1] Le Herisse, *L'Ancien Royaume*, pp. 64–5; P. Hazoume, *Le Pact dus ang*, pp. 19–20.
[2] W. Snelgrave, *A New Account*, p. 78.          [3] *Ibid.*
[4] Le Herisse, *L'Ancien Royaume*, p. 295; A. Dalzel, *History*, p. 7.
[5] Du Coulombier to Messrs de la Compagnie, 16 April 1715. This is so important in view of future developments that I shall quote du Coulombier's

In 1717 Dahomey quietly intruded itself into the Allada–Whydah dispute in a way that showed the efficiency of Agaja's spies and Agaja's own calculation. At that time the internal disagreement at Whydah was at its height, and Allada–Whydah relations at their worst. Agaja then approached Soso to be allowed to intervene in Whydah affairs. In October 1717 both Soso and Agaja agreed that Huffon should be driven away from the Whydah throne.[1] How the booty was to be shared, we do not know, but for the next month rumours were flying around the forts at Igelefe that Soso was planning to instal his 'brother' at Whydah in place of Huffon.[2] This probably meant that Agaja had been promised the Whydah throne.

Agaja probably expected a quick military action, the kind which Soso was not used to, or which was impossible under the *Ebi* system. The project, however, had not developed beyond the stage of rumour when Allada started the *So Anubomey*[3] ceremony in December 1717. As this was expected to last for at least three months, and no military expeditions were generally undertaken during the period of the festival, Whydah residents breathed a sigh of relief.[4] Nothing resulted from the grand design. Agaja had to wait patiently for the next ten years.

No more was heard of Dahomey until 1724 when the defeated candidate to the throne of Allada appealed to him for help. Such internal division was the most helpful situation that Agaja could have hoped for in his design, revealed in 1717, to destroy the coastal kingdoms.

The new king of Allada approached Huffon and represented to him that Agaja's invasion of Allada would be dangerous to both Allada and Whydah,[5] and ought therefore to be the joint concern of both. But Huffon refused to offer any help.

words, in the eighteenth-century French in which he wrote them: 'A L'esgard de tous articles par lesquels le roy promet en pr [premier] lieu de fermer son port d'Apa...le roy n'en est pas absolumen le maitre pour le premir(?) sa province d'Apa est trop eloignee d'Arder pour obliger de force son fidalgue a luy obeyr joint a ce que les marchands des Royaume de Foin et du Benin peuvent sy rendre avec leur esclaves sans passer sur d'autres terres dependantes du Royaume.'

[1] W. Green to R.A.C., 22 Oct. 1717 (T 70/22).
[2] 'Conseil de Marine', 22 Nov. 1717 (AN. C. 6/25).
[3] The document actually says that the ceremony was 'le Sou' (the So) and that it was expected to last for three months. That suggests that the 'Customs' of Dahomey had a long ancestry.
[4] 'Conseil de Marine', 22 Nov. 1717 (AN. C. 6/25).
[5] A. Dalzel, *History*, p. 9.

Huffon may have been influenced in this attitude by private assurances from Agaja, or by his own belief that whatever rendered Allada too weak to close the trade routes was advantageous to Whydah. Certainly the bad blood caused by the previous twelve years of active and cold war left the two kingdoms open to Agaja's ambition.

On 30 March 1724 Agaja's army entered Allada[1] ostensibly in aid of the defeated candidate to the Allada throne. Apparently there was no resistance until Agaja's army got to the capital where the king's palace was the first objective. The new king resisted and there followed a battle that went on for three days and which has been described in great details by Bulfinch Lambe, the English factor who was then being detained at Allada for some alleged offence.[2]

The king's palace was taken and set on fire after the king had been killed. The houses of the most important chiefs where large contingents of troops may have been stationed were then attacked. One such house was that of a 'Captain Blanco' where Lambe had been imprisoned as soon as the alarm of the invasion was given and from where he was taken prisoner and led to the Agau, the General Commander of the Dahomean forces, who was still in the king's palace watching it burn.

The sight witnessed by Lambe when he was being led out stunned him. 'When we went out there was scarce any stirring for bodies without heads, and had it rained blood, it could not have lain thicker on the ground.'[3] After the first day's battle the war was virtually over. The next two days were spent in looting and making captives. On the third day of the invasion, the Agau invited Lambe 'to come and sit down with him and the petty captains of war while they counted the captive slaves, which they did by giving a booge to everyone. The whole amounted to upwards of two grand cabess, or above eight thousand in number'.[4]

The contestant who had sought Agaja's help was not installed. Instead he was driven out and became a fugitive en-

---

[1] F. P. Mendes to V. F. Cezar de Meneses, 16 July 1724 (APB. OR. 19 doc. 56).
[2] W. Smith, *A New Voyage*, pp. 171–89, contains a full reproduction of Lambe's letter; W. Snelgrave, *A New Account*, p. 7; F. P. Mendes to V. F. Cezar de Meneses, 16 July 1724 (APB. OR. 19 doc 56).
[3] W. Smith, *A New Voyage*, pp. 171–89.
[4] *Ibid.*

camping with all his followers somewhere on the Whydah coast.[1]
Agaja permanently and by force took possession of Allada, the
ancient capital of the Aja.

This conquest of Allada effectively ended in Aja the old
political system based on the *Ebi* social theory. The fact
that the reigning king was killed, the capital burned and the
people disbanded meant that the link with the souls of the ancestors had been cut. And although the Aja remained a people
in the Yoruba-Aja country, leadership among them could no
longer be claimed according to the traditionally accepted *Ebi*
social theory. Agaja had precipitated a revolution the end of
which was not yet in sight.

It is not surprising that Agaja turned the appeal for help into
an occasion of conquest. Dahomey, it will be remembered, had
rejected the traditional constitution and had formulated a new
one. There was therefore bound to be a clash between the 'old'
and the 'new', and Agaja, who had fully prepared for the eventual clash, seized the opportunity offered by the internal division
at Allada. In other words, the conquest was the logical culmination of the principles for which the Wegbaja dynasty had stood,
the principle of authority deriving from and backed up by force
rather than based on the order of birth.

The events of the last sixteen years would easily explain why
Allada fell so easily. Since 1708 the power vacuum in Aja had
increased. In both Allada and Whydah the authority of the kings
was increasingly challenged and weakened. Instead of helping
the king to govern, the chiefs refused to obey the king's orders
and fought private battles among themselves. A war had broken
out between Allada and Whydah which could not be stopped for
eight years and which only petered out. Nothing that Huffon did
was able to restore tranquillity at Whydah. The Europeans contributed to the lawlessness and encouraged the disunity. No one
in Aja had the power and the prestige to hold the country together any longer.

In such a situation, ancient precepts would no longer have
the binding force that they used to have and the lives and property of the ordinary citizens would be most insecure. Such
people would lack the will to defend an institution that did not
give them protection.

[1] Viceroy of Brazil to King of Portugal (encl.), 22 May 1726 (APB. OR. 19
doc. 61).

In contrast to the situation in Allada and Whydah, Dahomey was a stable kingdom where the king had the supreme authority and controlled an army. Life there was comparatively safe. Its history since 1708 had consisted of successful wars against little known Yoruba-Aja towns. Once Allada was taken the rest of the Aja country must be brought to recognise the new basis of authority.

# 3

## A New Political System, 1724-40

Having destroyed Allada, and therefore the basis of the old political system in Aja, Agaja was next faced with the problem of extending Dahomey's rule over the rest of the Aja. Between 1724 and 1727 he easily subjected all, or most of the remaining Aja kingdoms. He soon discovered, however, that it was not so easy to hold his new conquests, for the Oyo resolutely defended the traditional political system and the Europeans and a few important Dahomean subjects showed, in no uncertain terms, their dislike of Agaja's policy towards the slave trade. The result was that between 1726 and 1740 Dahomey suffered a series of external invasions and internal revolts which resulted in the loss of its independence to Oyo in 1730 and nearly led to its complete destruction between then and 1740.

It was an unexpected turn of events. In March 1724, as a result of Agaja's successes, all the other Aja kingdoms were confronted with a very delicate problem of political readjustment. They had not yet accepted force as constituting a valid basis of right. Yet Dahomey, hitherto regarded as the 'younger son' of Allada and therefore the least privileged in the *Ebi* social theory, had destroyed the 'father' and donned his mantle. Clearly they must either submit or be prepared to defend the old system.

Some of the rulers quickly decided to readjust as best they could. The ruler of Jakin, whose territory at the eastern seaboard of the Old Allada kingdom had not been touched in the sack of March 1724, suspected that it might be Agaja's next target. He, like the rest of the Aja rulers, had no adequate forces with which to resist attack. To keep his territory out of danger, he submitted to Agaja about April 1724,[1] though mainly to buy time.

The Aplogan, ruler of Gome, a province of Whydah, which adjoined the former Allada province of Tori, took a much more decisive step, which is not surprising when his record of in-

[1] W. Snelgrave, *A New Account*, pp. 20-1.

subordination is remembered. The chaotic situation in Whydah had apparently convinced him that the traditional system no longer had any future and was therefore not worth defending. In the second half of 1726, he transferred his allegiance and his territory from Huffon to the victorious Agaja.[1]

Only Huffon, still keeping the rest of Whydah kingdom, made no move. Since he was a staunch believer in the *Ebi* social theory, he could hardly have been pleased with Agaja's treatment of Allada, but he betrayed a deplorable inability to assess Agaja's strength. He seems to have believed that Whydah was in no immediate danger and was in any case strong enough to beat back any attack by Dahomey. He told Snelgrave in an interview that 'if the king of Dahomey should offer to invade him, he would not use him when taken according to their customs that is, cut off his head, but would keep him for a slave to do the vilest offices.'[2]

In spite of this boast, Huffon neither defended the traditional system nor showed a proof of his confidence by trying to bring back the Aplogan to obedience.

His attitude is all the more surprising because Agaja made no secret of his determination to incorporate the rest of the Aja country into Dahomey. As soon as he had conquered Allada, he prepared for an invasion of Whydah. About April 1724, he discussed his intentions with Bulfinch Lambe, his English prisoner of war.[3] Lambe, completely misjudging Agaja's temperament and underrating his competence, had attempted to dissuade him from the enterprise by saying that Whydah kingdom was populous, that the people knew how to use firearms and that the European forts might aid it with their artillery against an invading army.

However, Agaja had not been intimidated. Even the Oyo invasion of Dahomey in 1726, to be described below, was not sufficient to make him abandon the project. He had found out 'by his spies how much the great men and people of Whydah were divided'.[3] He probably also knew that the European direc-

---

[1] *Ibid.* p. 9; A. Dalzel, *History*, p. 17; E. Dunglas in *E.D.* vol. xix, p. 152. Contrary to Dunglas, Agaja probably did not invade Gome, because it would have been unlike him not to pursue a victory home.

[2] W. Snelgrave, *A New Account*, pp. 6–9; E. Dunglas in *E.D.* vol. xix, p. 151; A. Dalzel, *History*, p. 17.

[3] W. Snelgrave, *A New Account*, pp. 12–13, 59–61; E. Dunglas in *E.D.* vol. xix, p. 152.

tors and traders were usually inclined to scuttle out of a country rather than stay to offer help if any difficulties arose. He had, however, learned from Lambe's warning the need to plan his intended invasion more securely.

Between 1724 and 1727 he carefully sought to neutralise Whydah firearms and the European artillery which Lambe had pointed out as the two possible sources of great opposition to his forces. Oral tradition in Dahomey, which seems quite credible, relates how Agaja rendered Whydah arms useless, by asking Na Gueze, his daughter who had been married to Huffon, to pour water on all the gunpowder in Huffon's arsenal, which she did the night before Agaja's descent on Sahe, the capital of Whydah. Agaja next sought to make the Europeans neutral in the impending struggle. Through his trade representatives at Whydah, the best known of whom before the invasion was Jongla (or Zunglar), he promised them that

if they stood neuter, and were not found in arms, they should receive no damage in their persons or goods in case he proved conqueror, and that he would ease their trade and remove diverse impositions laid on it by the king of Whydah. On the contrary if they appeared in arms against him, they must expect his resentment.[1]

As soon as the European directors received this message they immediately started to think of how best they could keep neutral. At first they contemplated leaving the forts temporarily, but finally decided to remain and take no part in fighting.

All these actions portray Agaja as a complete contrast to Huffon. In place of the latter's boast and lack of plan, the former was far-sighted and purposeful. He was so tenacious that neither fear nor adversity would divert him from his original goal. Moreover, he was very thorough.

Agaja's thorough preparation paid dividends. When on 26 February 1727 his army descended on the rest of Whydah kingdom,[2] they met hardly any resistance. As soon as the first alarm was sounded, the whole population took to their heels in disorder. Huffon was conveyed away in a hammock to the safety of

---

[1] W. Snelgrave, *A New Account*, pp. 12–13, 59–61; E. Dunglas in *E.D.* vol. XIX, p. 152; Dunglas has suggested that Agaja worked entirely through Na Gueze.

[2] 'Accounts and Journals for Whydah', 28 Feb. 1727 (T 70/598); W. Smith, *A New Voyage*, p. 190; W. Snelgrave, *A New Account*, pp. 2–3; Smith says the invasion took place 'about the beginning of February', but Snelgrave is more accurate.

an island near Great Popo, just in time before his palace was set on fire. Eyewitnesses related that

> about five o'clock the same afternoon, they saw such numbers of people flying from all parts of the country towards the seaside that it was surprising, for the fields were covered with them many miles round and their black colour made them more conspicuous in a clear sunshiny day, on a fine champaign country.[1]

Faced with practically no opposition, Agaja's army subjected the major part of Whydah kingdom within five days. More than five thousand Whydah were killed and between ten and eleven thousand made prisoners. The European factories at Sahe[2] were burned and looted, with the English factory alone losing goods worth about 77 marks or about two thousand five hundred pounds sterling. More than forty Europeans, directors and traders, were taken prisoner and marched to Agaja at Allada where they were kept fifteen days before being released.[3] The occupation of Whydah kingdom was complete and the Whydah were never again able successfully to reoccupy their land, try as hard as they might afterwards.

With the conquest of Whydah, all the most important kingdoms of the old Aja had been absorbed into the new kingdom of Dahomey. In Aja, but not in Yoruba, the *Ebi* social theory had been replaced by the 'perforated pot' theory. Why was the Revolution so easy?

One reason of course was the thoroughness of Agaja's preparation, but a much more important reason was the complete weakness of the old political system. Whydah fell, like Allada before it, without striking a blow because of its internal division and its complete administrative breakdown. One might have expected that after March 1724, Huffon and his chiefs would have appreciated the urgency of the threat from Agaja and sunk their differences to meet the common danger. No such reconciliation,

---

[1] W. Snelgrave, *A New Account*, pp. 14–17; W. Smith, *A New Voyage*, p. 190.
[2] These factories at Sahe must not be confused with the forts at Igelefe. They were unfortified houses, built originally by the Whydah authorities for the convenience of the Europeans visiting the capital, and maintained subsequently by the European occupiers.
[3] 'Accounts and Journals for Whydah', 21 March 1727 (T 70/598); Viceroy of Brazil to King of Portugal, Bahia, 18 June 1727, transmitting a letter from Whydah dated 4 April 1727 (APB. OR. 22 doc. 58); A. Dalzel, *History*, p. 27.

however, took place. Instead, several incidents between 1724 and 1727 show that the same internal troubles that had been weakening the administration in Whydah since 1708 continued and perhaps increased.[1]

There seems to have been a civil war early in 1725 between Huffon and certain of his chiefs. Huffon had lost to his enemies, had been forced out of his capital and had to borrow goods to resettle there in April of that year.[2]

His authority, which had never been really strong, was never fully re-established after that event. Towards the end of 1725 and early in 1726 the Dutch were able with impunity to flout the laws and conventions of Whydah. A Dutch galley, ignoring the established neutrality of Whydah port, carried out a veritable campaign against the Portuguese shipping. In November it sank one Portuguese ship, the *Tempeste*, after a fifteen minute battle in Whydah harbour, and on 18 December ordered another Portuguese ship trading at Whydah to weigh anchor, and go to Jakin to trade.[3] In March and April 1726 the Dutch twice attempted to set the Portuguese factory at Sahe on fire but failed on both occasions. Had they succeeded, they might have burned Huffon's palace as well. Although the Portuguese complained to Huffon and pointed out the seriousness of the Dutch lawlessness, Huffon did, and probably could, not take any measure to bring the Dutch to order.[4]

The extent to which authority had completely vanished in Whydah kingdom was shown in April 1726 when a drunken brawl developed into a civil war in which all the important chiefs immediately took sides without pausing to discover the rights and wrongs of the case. There was a pitched battle between the chiefs who supported the English and the Portuguese on the one side, and those who supported the French on the other. A fire started by them burned three-quarters of Igelefe and fighting went on sporadically for more than a month,[5] without Huffon being able to stop it.

[1] W. Snelgrave, *A New Account*, p. 5.
[2] 'Accounts and Ledgers for Whydah', 31 Jan.–30 June 1725 (T 70/889); Wyatt to R.A.C., 28 April 1725 (T 70/4).
[3] Viceroy of Brazil to King of Portugal, 13 March 1726, encl. a letter from Whydah dated 3 Jan. 1726 (APB. OR. 21 doc. 131); Viceroy of Brazil to King of Portugal, 9 May 1726 (APB. OR. 21 doc. 132).
[4] F. P. Mendes, director of the Portuguese fort at Whydah to Viceroy of Portugal, 22 May 1726 (APB. OR. 21 doc. 61).
[5] *Ibid.*

In this state of lawlessness, the ordinary citizens of Whydah would lack any protection and might have no urge to fight for the preservation of their kingdom. Many of them may have joined Agaja as the Aplogan had done. In such a situation it is not surprising that Whydah fell without striking a blow.

Scholars of the history of Dahomey have suggested that Agaja invaded both Allada and Whydah because he was an enthusiastic slave trader who was shut in from direct contact with the Europeans on the coast and who therefore had to force his way through for the benefit of his own slave trade.[1]

They have been led to their conclusion largely from the evidence of such eighteenth-century writers as Snelgrave and Norris, and from the oral traditions collected later. In 1734 Snelgrave related what seems an eyewitness story of the cause of Agaja's attack on Whydah. He said that Agaja had sent an ambassador to Huffon to ask him for a free pass to the coast and to offer to pay the normal duties. When Huffon refused to grant this request, Agaja decided to invade Whydah.[2] In 1789 Norris wrote with very great emphasis and a tinge of impatient annoyance, that he

knew many of the Whydasians as well as Dahomans who were present when Trudo attacked that kingdom. They attributed his enterprize solely to the desire of extending his dominions and of enjoying at first hand those commodities which he had been used to purchase of the Whydasians who were in possession of the coast,[3]

and went on to repeat Snelgrave's story.

Le Herisse[4] and Dunglas[5] have recorded traditions which strengthen the theory that Agaja needed to be in direct contact with the European traders at Whydah to possess European manufactured goods like Huffon.

A thorough examination of these sources, however, raises doubts as to whether Agaja's motives are to be correctly inferred from them. Both Snelgrave and Norris wrote mainly to defend their vested interests in the slave trade, which they felt were being threatened. When Snelgrave wrote, Bulfinch Lambe, who

---

[1] J. D. Fage, *History of West Africa*, p. 93; C. W. Newbury, *The Western Slave Coast*, p. 23.
[2] W. Snelgrave, *A New Account*, pp. 5–6.
[3] R. Norris, *Memoirs*, pp. xiii–xiv.
[4] Le Herisse, *L'Ancien Royaume*, p. 296.
[5] E. Dunglas, in *E.D.* vol. XIX, p. 149.

had been Agaja's prisoner of war in 1724, had just brought to St James's Court a bogus prince called 'Prince Adomo Orinooko Tomo' to deliver what was probably a genuine message from Agaja to the effect that Agaja wanted other Europeans than the slave traders, 'that the natives would sell themselves to us on condition of not being carried off, that we might settle plantations'.[1]

Snelgrave, who since 1704 had been trading in slaves in all parts of the 'slave coast', and had discovered that Whydah 'was the principal port of all the Guinea Coast for the slave trade',[2] wanted to show emphatically that Lambe's message, as well as his prince, was bogus, to safeguard his own interests.

Nor was Snelgrave consistent though he was nearer the event and wrote at times as an eyewitness. Although he said that the negotiations between Huffon and Agaja for a free pass to the coast failed completely, yet almost in the same breath, he spoke of one Zunglar (Jongla) 'who was formerly the king's [i.e. Agaja's] agent for several years at Whydah, where I had seen him in my former voyages'.[3] If the negotiation had failed as completely as he implied, Jongla could not have remained Agaja's agent at Whydah for many years.

Moreover, Snelgrave spoke of one 'Buttanoe', Agaja's messenger, who 'spoke very good English', and also told the story of the Portuguese mulatto whom Agaja bought and brought to his court.[4] Jongla spoke at least two languages, English and French, and the implication is that Agaja kept all these linguists for trading direct with the different European nations on the coast. For if he was only allowed to trade with Whydah and Allada middlemen, linguists would not have been necessary, since the Dahomeans, the Allada and the Whydah spoke the same language. Indeed their presence among Agaja's officers was an eloquent witness to the ease with which the Dahomean citizens had access to the coast.

Norris's statement was made when the abolition issue was an important question in England. He was a slave trader of long standing and a complete anti-abolitionist.[5] He had once been thrown out of his slave-trading job by the American war of

[1] J. Atkins, *A Voyage to Guinea*, pp. 121–2.
[2] W. Snelgrave, *A New Account*, pp. 2–6.
[3] *Ibid.* pp. 56–61.　　　　　　　　　[4] *Ibid.*
[5] 'Report of the Lords of the Committee appointed for the consideration of all matters relating to Trade and Foreign Plantations' (1789).

74

independence, when he had to turn a smith 'for want of a better thing to do',[1] and he did not want to be deprived of it again by the humanitarians. He devoted the last section of his book to a detailed argument in defence of the continuation of the slave trade. It was part of his case to show that the Dahomeans loved slave trading.

What Norris heard in 1772, even if impartially reported, was not necessarily Agaja's intention in 1724 and 1727. Forty-five eventful years had passed since the invasion of Whydah and the changes in the national policy could easily have led to changes in the people's conception of the original intention. As will soon be plain, Agaja had been forced to become a supporter of the slave trade in 1730 and Tegbesu had put the slave trade before any other national activity since 1740.[2] No private citizen therefore could have told Norris that there were other reasons for invading Whydah when the official policy was 'trade before war'.

As for the oral traditions they must be regarded as propaganda spread by the *Agbadjigbeto* and probably generally widely believed. For in 1724 the Dahomeans were not completely prevented from trading directly with the Europeans on the coast. They had been trading directly with the Europeans through the Epe port as early as 1714, possibly earlier. It was partly because of this that the king of Allada had refused to close the port when the French director requested it in 1715.

The observation of Bulfinch Lambe who was in Agaja's court for about a year did not suggest that Agaja was greatly deprived of European goods, for he saw in the palace, three years before the conquest of Whydah

great quantities of plates, wrought gold and other rich things, also all sorts of fine gowns, cloaks, hats, caps etc., he also has all sorts of common goods beyond measure and gives away boogies like dirt and brandy like water.[3]

If Agaja was not shut off in 1724, still less was he in 1727. For after his conquest of Allada and the submission of Jakin, he had two ports at his own exclusive control. The first was Offra, which Soso had started to rebuild in 1717, and the second was Jakin.

[1] R. Norris to R. Miles, 29 June 1779 (T 70/1538); although Norris visited Dahomey in 1772, he did not write his account immediately.
[2] See chapter 4.
[3] W. Smith, *A New Voyage*, pp. 171–89.

The two ports were near each other and were about twenty-five miles east of Whydah. If all that Agaja wanted was to trade with the Europeans, he knew enough of the internal weakness of Whydah, controlled enough of the inland slave trade routes and was clever enough to realise that if he continued to develop the two ports and kept the inland routes closed to Whydah traders, the instability of Whydah and the abundance of the slaves that would come to his own ports would quickly induce the Europeans to abandon Whydah for his ports.

Despite this obvious fact that Agaja was hardly at any time completely shut off, he himself made diplomatic statements in 1727 and 1728 which might mislead the unwary as to his reasons for invading Whydah. In April 1727, a few weeks after the conquest of Whydah, he gave the Portuguese director, who had visited his court, the impression that he had invaded Whydah to be in direct contact with the European traders and professed that he was a friend of the Europeans, 'with whom he wanted all kind of commercial relations'.[1]

In the same month, when Snelgrave complained to him about the many indignities which the Europeans had suffered from Huffon and the Whydah people and how bad the trade had been because of the bad management of the Whydah authorities, Agaja said that 'his God had made him the instrument to punish the king of Whydah and his people for the many villanies they had been guilty of towards both blacks and whites'.[2] In September 1728 he told Delisle, an officer in the French fort, that he did not think it just that Africans should make profits out of the Europeans.[3]

These statements were made when Agaja was not yet in a position to dictate terms, and were probably intended to win the goodwill of the Europeans. Certainly they were all capable of more than one interpretation. 'All kinds of commercial relations' might mean 'not just the slave trade' which might mean in turn a diminution or even total abolition of that trade. The 'villanies' of which the Whydah were accused might be their excessive slave-trading activities. And Agaja's unwillingness to let the African profit out of the Europeans certainly meant that

---

[1] Viceroy of Brazil to King of Portugal, 18 June 1727, encl. a letter from the Portuguese director at Whydah dated 4 April 1727 (APB. OR. doc. 58).
[2] W. Snelgrave, *A New Account*, p. 64.
[3] 'Extrait du Registre', 13 Sept. 1728 (AN. C. 6/25).

he would not allow his subjects to trade freely in slaves, rather than that he would control the prices in favour of the Europeans.

Therefore neither the eighteenth-century slave captains, nor Agaja's diplomatic utterances, nor yet the popular 'textbook' oral traditions collected almost two centuries later can point to a correct assessment of Agaja's motives for invading the coastal Aja kingdoms.

The safest evidence to go on therefore would be Agaja's actions immediately after his victory. When these are considered, it immediately becomes clear that Agaja had very little sympathy for the slave trade when he invaded the Aja coast. His first motive appears to have been to sweep away the traditional political system, which had completely broken down and was no longer capable of providing basic security and justice. Such a policy was implied almost inevitably by Dahomey's rejection of the traditional system and its formation of an alternative.

The second motive would appear to have been to restrict and eventually stop the slave trade, which had been the cause of the breakdown of the traditional system in Aja, and to substitute other 'legitimate' items of trade between Europe and the new kingdom of Dahomey.

Indeed Dahomean opposition to the slave trade appears to go back beyond Agaja and may have been among the basic principles upon which the kingdom had been founded. As has been noticed, nascent Dahomey was twice recorded as preventing the Allada slave raiding in the last thirty years of the seventeenth-century.

The anonymous Aja, who, early in the eighteenth century, accused the Europeans of introducing 'the traffick in slaves' was a contemporary of Agaja. He was probably not the only Aja who felt that the form of contact which they had with the Europeans was not good for them and Agaja may have shared his views fully.

Agaja's own idea about the slave trade was probably fully discussed with Bulfinch Lambe, the first European of any standing he ever came into contact with. He seems to have impressed on Lambe that he wanted other kinds of Europeans than the slave traders. When Lambe had been in his court for eight months, during which time he must have had several discussions with Agaja, he recommended that:

if any tailor, carpenter, smith or any sort of white man that is free be willing to come here, he will find very good encouragement and be much caressed and get money if he can be contented with this life for a time.[1]

Agaja was supposed to have accepted the submission of Jakin after the conquest of Allada because of the experience of its traders and because of its commercial rivalry with Whydah.[2] In fact he made no attempt to persuade the European factors to settle in either Offra or Jakin, neither did the Europeans, who were always threatening to leave Whydah, approach him for permission to settle in any of his ports, despite the unsettled condition at Whydah.

Certainly the supply of slaves did not increase from Dahomean sources between 1724 and 1727. The Portuguese director wrote in July 1724 that as a result of Agaja's destruction of Allada, slaves had become abundant,[3] but such slaves could have been those sold by the slave-owning Allada people driven away from their homes and in extreme distress. They could equally have been Allada people who, in extreme distress, preferred slavery to a wretched death, as the Whydah were later reported to have done.[4] As soon as these sources dried up, the Europeans at Whydah felt the effect of Agaja's conquest. The slave routes were effectively shut and slaves became scarce and dear.[5] Offra port was laid waste and no attempt was made to reopen it for fifty years.[6]

Snelgrave's ship must have been the first slaving ship that reached Whydah after its conquest, when about eleven thousand captives were made. He personally demanded from Agaja enough slaves to fill his ship and Agaja promised to grant his wish. But it was only with very great difficulty that he got the six hundred slaves he wanted. At one point, when he needed only eighty more to complete his cargo, he sent a special messenger to the king to ask for his help in supplying them. Agaja replied that although he had many slaves who tilled his farm,

[1] W. Smith, *A New Voyage*, pp. 171–89.
[2] W. Snelgrave, *A New Account*, pp. 20–3; E. Dunglas in *E.D.* vol. XIX, p. 151.
[3] F. P. Mendes to V. F. Cezar de Meneses, 16 July 1724 (APB. OR. 19 doc. 36).     [4] W. Snelgrave, *A New Account*, p. 70.
[5] Tinker and Humphrey to R.A.C., 23 Feb. 1725 (T 70/7); 'Conseil de Marine', 13 Aug. 1728 (AN. C. 6/25).
[6] In 1776, under totally different circumstances, an unsuccessful attempt was made to reopen it. See below, chapter 5.

he had none for sale, and was in fact surprised that Snelgrave needed so many slaves. Many Portuguese slave ships which came after Snelgrave's stayed at Whydah for a long time hoping in vain that trade would revive.[1]

Before the conquest of Whydah, only Agaja sold slaves in his kingdom, and he sold mainly women. This practice he meant to continue after the conquest.[2] In April 1727 some Dahomeans who had believed that their conquest of the coast gave them the opportunity to trade as the former Allada and Whydah people had done, went to Jakin to sell their slaves to Snelgrave. As soon as Agaja heard it, he sent to arrest them all. Most of them fled, but some were caught. Their fate is not known, but the Dahomeans did not, after that, trade indiscriminately in slaves.[3]

Between 1 and 19 March 1727 Agaja's army laid siege to the European forts at Igelefe (written Grigwe or Gregoy by the Europeans). The European residents in all of them collected themselves in the French fort and put up a show of force, but it was only the large quantities of presents given to the Dahomean soldiers, to Jongla, Agaja's chief agent at Igelefe and to the Dahomean chiefs at Allada 'in order to influence them in our favour in this calamitous juncture' that induced the army to withdraw.[4] In November and December 1728 Agaja's army again attacked the English fort and again withdrew when they were given presents by the governor.[5]

In April 1727 Agaja ordered the remaining European factories still standing unburned at Sahe to be burned. This was accordingly done in the presence of their European owners who were just then being released from captivity. They were greatly surprised and complained bitterly to Agaja who denied giving any such orders.[6] As he neither punished those who had burned the factories nor ordered them to be rebuilt, it is difficult to believe that their destruction was contrary to his wish.

---

[1] W. Snelgrave, *A New Account*, pp. 70–107. Snelgrave spent 94 days at Jakin before he got his complete cargo of slaves. Before the conquest, the largest ships spent not more than 30 days.

[2] W. Smith, *A New Voyage*, pp. 171–89; W. Snelgrave, *A New Account*, p. 94.

[3] W. Smith, *A New Voyage*, pp. 171–89; W. Snelgrave, *A New Account*, p. 94.

[4] 'Accounts and Journals for Whydah', 21 March 1727 (T 70/598). Viceroy of Brazil to King of Portugal, Bahia, 18 June 1727 (APB. OR. 22 doc. 58).

[5] 'Accounts and Journals, C.C.C.', 31 Dec. 1728 (T 70/392).

[6] W. Smith, *A New Voyage*, p. 191; Viceroy of Brazil to King of Portugal, 1 June 1727 (APB. OR. 22 doc. 58).

The Europeans had not helped the Whydah against Dahomey and they had not in any way contested Agaja's authority in Whydah kingdom which, they admitted, 'had become his by right of conquest'. It would be difficult therefore to explain Agaja's hostility to them save on the assumption that he sought either to expel all the slave traders from his dominion or at least to impose upon them his own terms of trade.

That Agaja and the European directors were not thinking in the same terms when they talked of 'trade' is clear from their attitude to the conquered Whydah. The Europeans would have liked the old Whydah to become Agaja's subjects because they were experienced slave traders, and many Whydah would gladly have accepted such an offer. The Portuguese director went to Agaja early in April 1727 to plead their cause and to convince Agaja of the economic advantage of permitting their return.[1] Wilson, the English director, gave presents in February and May 1728 for the same purpose, but Agaja refused to allow the Whydah to return,[2] precisely for the reason adduced by the Europeans.

The European directors and traders realised from these actions that Agaja was opposed to their slave trading interests. They complained very bitterly and very loudly. D'Ayrie, the French factor at Jakin, advocated that it was time to find a route to the Mahi country, whence the slaves came, since the Dahomean soldiers had effectively prevented the traders from bringing the slaves down to the coast.[3] The viceroy of Brazil, judging from the reports he got from the Portuguese director and traders, said he considered the trade there was ruined and would remain ruined for a long time.[4] The English Company declared itself 'concerned that the trade of Whydah is in such precarious circumstances',[5] and the Dutch withdrew to Jakin and Epe and started intriguing against Agaja. All the Europeans who had hitherto regarded Agaja as their friend and deliverer from the tyrannical impositions of Huffon and the dwindling trade of

---

[1] 'Accounts and Journals for Whydah', 21 March 1727 (T 70/598); Viceroy of Brazil to King of Portugal, Bahia, 18 June 1727 (APB. OR. 22 doc. 58).
[2] 'Accounts and Journals C.C.C.', 13 June 1729 (T 70/392).
[3] 'Conseil de Marine', 13 Aug. 1728 (AN. C. 6/25).
[4] Viceroy of Brazil to King of Portugal, Bahia, 13 May 1729 (AHU. Codice 254 f. 61r. 62r.).
[5] Court of Assistants to J. Brathwaite, R. Cruikshank and B. Peak, 14 Aug. 1729 (T 70/54).

Whydah, immediately became his enemies and champions of the vanquished Whydah.

Even before his success at Whydah, Agaja had discovered that it was one thing to destroy the old political and economic systems in Aja but quite another to establish others in their places, for these systems had powerful defenders outside the old Aja states. These defenders of the *status quo* strenuously opposed Agaja between 1726 and 1730. The Little Popo and the Akwamu refused to recognise Agaja's right over the conquered territory[1] and the disillusioned European factors sought to bring back the old Whydah.

Of all the forces opposing Agaja's political designs during these years, Oyo was the most dangerous because it was the most powerful and because it felt its own political interests were directly involved. By the eighteenth century, the Yoruba kingdom of Oyo had grown into a large empire, controlling both Nupe (Tapa) and Borgu (Bariba)[2] in the north. To the south, Allada and therefore indirectly all the Aja country had been its tributary since the 1680s. It had a strong cavalry army which was the dread of all the surrounding states. It inflicted a sharp defeat on an Ashanti army in 1764 and remained throughout the eighteenth century the strongest imperial power in the whole of West Africa between the mouths of the Niger and the Volta and between latitude 10° north and the sea.

Yet in spite of its strength, the rulers of Oyo had never overthrown or rejected the *Ebi* social theory. The Alafin (kings of Oyo) continued to regard themselves as 'sons' of the Ooni (kings of Ife) and to go regularly to Ife for the final constitutional sanctions,[3] even though Oyo was much stronger militarily than Ife. To such rulers, Agaja's action in killing the 'father' of the Aja was the greatest sacrilege and if he was allowed to get away with it, there was no knowing where he would end or how many such law breakers would arise.

In the third decade of the eighteenth century, Oyo was ruled by capable men. Ojigi, the reigning Alafin, has been described as 'a powerful and warlike king'. He seems to have been the

[1] 'Conseil de Marine', 13 Aug. 1728 (AN. C. 6/25).
[2] S. Johnson, *History*, pp. 161–3; these traditions seem quite reliable and we shall see in chapters 5 and 6 that the Bariba and the Nupe achieved their independence in 1783 and 1791 respectively.
[3] Every Alafin up till today continues to go to Ife for the final authority before being crowned king.

choice of the Oyo army, and to have been installed for his known military ability. His Basorun, Yamba, was 'one of the most famous men in Yoruba history', and his Gbonka, Latoyo, was an army general of note.[1] Such men would not stand idly by while Agaja overthrew ancient customs and spread confusion.

The purport of diplomatic exchanges that took place between Oyo and Dahomey after Agaja's conquest of Allada in 1724 is not known. Whatever Agaja's terms may have been they did not satisfy Oyo. So on 14 April 1726 the Oyo army entered Dahomey.[2] Agaja's recent victory, his stock of firearms and some artillery, which he had captured during the sack of Allada, emboldened him to make a stand and hope for an even chance against the Oyo cavalry.

The battle that followed was short and terrible. The Oyo army killed a large number of the Dahomean soldiers and enslaved a still larger number. Abomey was burned and Agaja surrounded by his bodyguard and women escaped into the bush to save his life. The Oyo, having taught the upstart the lesson of his life, went back home.[3]

It was widely believed that Agaja was finished and that he would never again be able to threaten further the traditional order. Early in May 1726 'Hussar', the disappointed pretender to the Allada throne, who had originally invited Agaja for help, left his place of refuge and joined the 'Mina' (perhaps the Little Popo Accra), in order jointly to attack Jakin later that month and from there march steadily on to recover Allada. How the attempt fared is not known. Agaja was back at Abomey by 22 May, purposefully rebuilding his burned capital and his presence may have discouraged the invaders.

After this short and terrible experience Agaja had no cause to underrate the difficulties that would confront him in his

[1] S. Johnson, *History*, p. 74.
[2] Director of the Portuguese fort to Viceroy of Brazil, 22 May 1726 (APB. OR. 21 doc. 61); W. Snelgrave, *A New Account*, pp. 55–9. E. Dunglas in *E.D.* p. 147. Dunglas argues powerfully without any evidence but the words 'ancient treaty' that this invasion took place in 1712. The phrase may, however, refer to those that followed the Oyo invasions of Allada in the 1680s and in 1698. This firm date, given by a Portuguese eyewitness disposes of his doubts.
[3] Agaja's agents, obviously to boost up the morale of the Dahomeans, claimed a tactical victory over the Oyo at the end of this battle. The original version of their made-up story was repeated to Snelgrave in 1727 and later oral traditions have manufactured more stories.

attempt to take over the Aja country. Those difficulties, however, did not discourage him. Instead, he planned carefully to overcome them all. In the nine months between the withdrawal of the Oyo in May 1726 and Dahomey's invasion of Whydah in February 1727, Agaja, true to his nature, planned his tactics. He rightly calculated that he had enough military strength to deal with any opposition from the small neighbouring kingdoms. Only the Oyo presented a serious danger and those he hoped to buy off with presents. If they refused to be bought off, then he would defy and outwit them by burying his treasure, burning his farms and towns and fleeing to the European forts. These measures and the exigencies of the climate would, he thought, prevent them from occupying Dahomey for much longer than a month, and enable him to return to his capital after only a short inconvenience.

Accordingly, immediately after his conquest of Whydah in February 1727 Agaja sent presents to the Alafin of Oyo, whose messengers came to him at the Allada camp about the middle of April 1727.[1] He seems deliberately to have prolonged the negotiations in order that the onset of the rains might delay any Oyo invasion of Dahomey until the next dry season, and thus give him about a whole year during which he could prepare solidly for his flight.

The details of the negotiations are obscure, but, as Agaja had expected, they broke down. The Oyo probably felt that the Dahomean presents could not sufficiently atone for the break of established principles involved in Agaja's action. Besides all the princes of Allada, Weme and Whydah sent messengers to the Alafin, imploring him for help to regain their patrimony from the illegal grasp of Agaja.[2]

On 22 March 1728 the much dreaded Oyo army descended on Dahomey. According to his plan, Agaja buried his treasure, sent his subjects out of reach and completely burned all the

---

[1] J. Bazilio to Viceroy of Brazil, 17 July 1731 (APB. OR. 28 f. 129); W. Snelgrave, *A New Voyage*, p. 59.

[2] Viceroy of Brazil to King of Portugal, 5 April 1728 (APB. OR. 24 f. 40); Dupetitval to La Compagnie des Indes, 4 Oct. 1728 (AN. C. 6/25); W. Snelgrave, *A New Account*, pp. 121–2, 132; A. Dalzel, *History*, pp. 52–3; E. Dunglas in *E.D.* vol. XIX, pp. 158–9; S. Johnson, *History*, p. 174. Snelgrave, Dalzel and Dunglas are completely mixed up about the number of Oyo invasions and the events in each of them. Usually they record one or two; Oyo traditions say there were three, but the documents record four between 1726 and 1730.

provisions that might help the invading army. Not finding the Europeans friendly, he avoided taking refuge in any of their forts and ran into the bush instead. The Oyo army, deprived of both booty and provisions, found it impossible to remain long in Dahomey from which they had been forced to withdraw by the end of April 1728. There is no suggestion that Agaja offered them any presents to induce them to withdraw. He probably simply defied them.

Agaja's difficulties were not over, however, for another factor emerged with which he had not reckoned. During the Oyo invasion, the European directors and particularly Dupetitval, the French director, encouraged the old Whydah to re-establish in their kingdom and supplied them with everything they would need for such a settlement.[1] When Agaja later sought to drive the old Whydah away after the withdrawal of the Oyo, his army encountered a stiff resistance from the Europeans who collected themselves in the French fort. The Dahomeans attacked the fort on 1 May 1728, but after a whole day of fighting were forced to retire. They besieged the fort again on 14 May, forcing the European defenders to retire and to leave the old Whydah to defend themselves unaided. On 31 May the magazine in the fort caught fire and blew up, killing about three thousand of its Whydah defenders. The rest who had thus been deprived of an effective means of resistance were enslaved by the Dahomeans.[2]

By July 1728 Agaja had realised that he had to reckon not only with the Oyo but also with the Europeans. Their opposition had not been well concerted but might become so in future if adequate steps were not taken to deal with it. Agaja calculated that any future Oyo invasion could be rendered as ineffective as that of March 1728, provided the Europeans could be prevented from embarrassing him by encouraging the return of the old Whydah.

He therefore set about wooing the Europeans. In this task, Agaja came out at his diplomatic best. Because the French fort had served as the centre of opposition to his army in March 1727 and May 1728, Agaja secretly admired the valour of the French,

---

[1] 'Conseil de Marine', 11 Aug. 1728 (AN. C. 6/25); E. Dunglas in *E.D.* vol. XIX, p. 158; A. Dalzel, *History*, pp. 51–2; 'Accounts and Journals', C.C.C.', 31 Dec. 1728 (T 70/392). Both Dalzel and Dunglas mix up this episode with another which happened a year later.
[2] *Ibid.*

whom he regarded as the bravest Europeans whose friendship would be most valuable to him.

Dupetitval, the director of the French fort, was not unwilling to befriend Agaja. After his fort had been burned twice he had concluded that the interests of his country would be best served by being friendly with the winning side. In July 1728 he formally offered to help Agaja to oppose an Akwamu army which was then contemplating an invasion of Dahomey.[1]

The occasion gave Agaja the chance he had been looking for. He went about the task of winning over the French in a highly diplomatic way and frightened the French into professing their friendship for him. As if in a confidential talk with Antonio Pinto, a Portuguese factor at Jakin, he accused the French of plotting against Dahomey and promised to send his army against the French fort to ask for an explanation. Pinto repeated this to D'Ayrie, the French representative at Jakin, who promptly sent a messenger to warn Dupetitval of the impending danger. Dupetitval hurriedly summoned his council, where it was decided that a memorandum be sent immediately to Agaja protesting in the strongest terms that the French were his friends and wished to remain so.

This was immediately done and Delisle, the lieutenant of the fort, was despatched with the memorandum to Agaja on 24 August 1728. In it Dupetitval expressed surprise that the king of Dahomey could have believed the accusations that he had invited the Oyo to invade Dahomey, that he had given presents to the kings of Allada and Whydah, and that he had written unfavourable things about Dahomey to the king of France. He alleged that the accusations emanated from his enemies and that the Dahomean officers on the coast were surprised to hear them because they knew them to be untrue. He then recounted what he had done for Dahomey as evidence of his staunch friendship. He had, he said, not only given a friendly reception to Agaja's officers whenever sent to the fort, but had also made military preparations against the 'Mina' (i.e. the Akwamu) who intended to invade Dahomey; he had always regarded the Oyo, the Allada and Whydah peoples as enemies of trade and disturbers of the peace, with whom he could not therefore logically be in complicity against Dahomey. The fact that the king of France sent so many ships to Whydah, Dupetitval went on,

[1] 'Conseil de Marine', 11 Aug. 1728 (AN. C. 6/25).

was a positive proof that he was a friend and protector of Dahomey. This was precisely what Agaja wanted. He listened to the French protestations and declared himself persuaded at the last moment from taking a punitive expedition against them. He then gave Delisle such good treatment as to win his unqualified respect. Delisle stayed in Agaja's court until 4 October by which time he had committed the French to Agaja's cause as completely as Agaja himself desired.[1] It looked as though the latter would not only be able to flee to the French fort during the next Oyo invasion, but would also be able to rely on active help from the French against the Oyo. The powerful Oyo had, however, not been idle. Ojigi and his skilful advisers had decided upon drastic measures. They had determined to occupy Dahomey permanently, settle Oyo citizens there, and deprive Agaja of the whole of the kingdom. Their plan was to increase the severity of Oyo's action annually from 1729 onwards until Agaja was exhausted or caught. With this in mind, the Oyo army invaded Dahomey in 1729 and 1730.

During the 1729 invasion, the army and the colonists accompanying it set out about January and reached Dahomey around the middle of March.[2] Agaja repeated his earlier tactics and fled, but was hotly pursued by the Oyo army which advanced much farther south than it had ever done before, as far as Gome the northern province of the old Whydah kingdom, where the Aplogan and his people narrowly escaped with their lives.

Then instead of withdrawing as they usually did and as Agaja had expected, they settled down building a town, and occasionally attacking the Dahomeans in their forest hideouts. This went on until May, obviously much longer than Agaja had planned for or expected. Many Dahomeans died of hunger and a large number were killed.[3]

---

[1] 'Conseil de Marine', 18 and 24 Aug. 1728; 'Extrait du Registre des délibérations de la direction générale des Comptoire de Juda pour la Compagnie des Indes au fort St Louis Gregoy', 26 Aug.–4 Oct. 1728 (AN. C. 6/25).

[2] Viceroy of Brazil to King of Portugal, 28 July 1729 (APB. OR. 25 f. 158); 'Accounts and Journals, C.C.C.', 30 June 1729 (T 70/395); W. Snelgrave, *A New Account*, pp. 122–3; A. Dalzel, *History*, pp. 52–3.

[3] Viceroy of Brazil to King of Portugal, 28 July 1729 (APB. OR. 25 f. 158); 'Accounts and Journal, C.C.C.', 30 June 1729 (T 70/393). The name of the town they then founded is not recorded, but it probably was Cana (Calmina), which later became the Oyo headquarters in Dahomey.

To worsen the condition of the Dahomeans, the French did not carry out everything that Delisle had promised and the Europeans again embarrassed Agaja. When it looked as though the power of Agaja had been completely broken, the old Whydah approached all the European directors for co-operation in their effort to resettle in their ancient kingdom. The Portuguese seem to have refused all co-operation. Dupetitval prevaricated but he was finally persuaded by Gallot, his second in command, and offered to help. Testefolle the English director jumped eagerly at the opportunity and gave active encouragement.[1]

On 23 April 1729 Huffon and all his people solemnly came back to their ancient home. Testefolle announced enthusiastically that 'the king of Whidah and all his people returned and settled and trade began to flourish'. Gun salutes were fired for Huffon and his chiefs, all of whom were well entertained by the forts' officers, but the joy was shortlived.

It seems that the Oyo did not find things very easy, for Agaja had destroyed most of the crops. They were soon seriously short of supplies and had to withdraw about the end of May 1729. About the beginning of June, Agaja emerged from hiding and immediately started to reduce the forts to obedience once again. Huffon and his people immediately fled back to their Popo island.

Gallot had already arranged Dupetitval's punishment. Soon after April 1729 Gallot convinced the old Whydah that Dupetitval was in fact their enemy. The old Whydah therefore seized Dupetitval one morning, kept him in confinement and proclaimed Gallot director of the French fort. When they fled in June they took Dupetitval with them and soon announced his death.[2] Etienne Gallot, who had once served in Agaja's army and spoke some Fon, the language of Dahomey, was soon able to make his peace with Agaja.

The Dahomean army next encamped near the English fort, mainly to keep an eye on the old Whydah. Testefolle, already

---

[1] Charlot Testefolle to R.A.C., Whydah, 30 Oct. 1729 (T 70/7); 'Mémoire de la Compagnie des Indes', 8 Nov. 1730 (AN. C. 6/25); A. Dalzel, *History*, p. 54; E. Dunglas in *E.D.* vol. xix, p. 158.

[2] 'Mémoire de la Compagnie des Indes', 8 Nov. 1730 (AN. C. 6/25); A. Dalzel, *History*, p. 54; E. Dunglas in *E.D.* vol. xix, p. 158. D. Dalzel's and Dunglas's accounts of the death of Dupetitval and the circumstances surrounding it are substantially different from that given by Gallot, who was a principal character in the drama and who later confessed the villanous part he played in it. His account has been adopted here.

piqued by the failure of his attempt to resettle the Whydah, soon lost his nerve. He started to misuse all the Dahomeans in his fort and beat a Dahomean chief, with threats to deal in the same way with Agaja if he could secure him. For that treasonable statement the English fort was attacked on 4 November but was stoutly defended for six hours, when the Dahomeans retired. Testefolle was caught when he attempted to escape and was taken to Abomey where he was sentenced to death,[1] and executed.

Although Agaja was able to master the forts once again, these episodes suggested to him that he really could not count on European support against the Oyo who had shown themselves determined to wear out his resistance.

Before their next invasion in 1730 the Oyo tried to make their sources of provision much more secure. They made an alliance with the Mahi,[2] which would not only provide them with whatever they needed for maintenance, but would also deprive the Dahomeans of a refuge in that direction during the invasion. Oyo's plan and strategy seem to have been known to Huffon by December 1729 when he confidently told Edward Deane, the English director, that he and his people 'were resolved to return to their country in a short time and set trade on a flourishing foot again'.[3]

News of the Oyo advance reached the European forts at Igelefe on 3 January 1730, but the Oyo army did not reach Dahomey until about the end of February. Between 9 and 16 January, Agaja sent Dahomean citizens to Igelefe in such large numbers that all the old Whydah, who had been around, fled. He also sent one Budaka to keep the European directors calm and assure them that the Dahomeans at Igelefe would do no harm to the forts. Agaja himself fled to his usual forest retreat. On 21 February 1730 Huffon, who must have been watching the situation carefully told the European directors that, with the Oyo descending on Abomey, he was about to take

---

[1] 'Accounts and Journals, C.C.C.', 28 Feb. 1730 (T 70/395); Governor and Council, C.C.C., to R.A.C. 26 Dec. 1729 (T 70/7); Court of Assistance to John Brathwaite, 31 Dec. 1730 (T 70/54); A. Dalzel, *History*, pp. 57–8.

[2] Mallis de la Mine to Premenil, 8 Jan. 1732 (ADN. C. 739). For the history of the Mahi, see Cornevin, *Histoire du Dahomey*, pp. 140–2.

[3] 'Copybook and Diaries for Whydah', 30 Dec. 1729, 3, 9–17 Jan., 9 and 25 Feb. 1730 (T 70/1466).

possession again of his kingdom, and requested that they all send him the customary presents. All the directors thought Agaja was finished, took Huffon's success for granted and sent the required gifts.[1]

Agaja in his hideout found the prospect bleak. He offered the Oyo large quantities of presents rumoured to be goods worth six hundred slaves, in order to induce them to withdraw.[2] The Oyo knew Agaja too well by now to allow him to buy time, but they accepted his presents and feigned withdrawal. Agaja then summoned his scattered subjects to come out of their hiding and start the work of rebuilding, and those of them at Whydah set out for Abomey on 9 March.[2]

The Dahomeans soon realised that they were walking into an ambush. They were attacked by the Mahi as soon as they had emerged from their hideouts and when they attempted to defend themselves, the Oyo, who were thought to have gone, suddenly returned. Agaja managed to escape and his subjects who had left Igelefe on 9 March came back in a great panic on 20th.[3] Agaja realised beyond any doubt that the Oyo intended to settle near or at Abomey permanently, and therefore decided to evacuate it. On 7 April it was rumoured around the forts that Agaja was coming to settle at Allada permanently. On the 9th, the rumour was officially confirmed as the English director recorded cryptically: 'very few Dahomies to be seen. Messenger arrived from the king of Dahomey requiring that all chiefs (i.e. of the forts) go up to Dahomey to him to accompany him down to Arda'.[4]

The Europeans directors, unwilling to commit themselves except to the winning side, excused themselves. Agaja moved permanently to Allada soon after that date, and for the next thirteen years, Allada remained the capital of Dahomey.

The whole incident must have given Agaja pause for deep reflection. That Dahomey continued to exist at all in 1730 could be attributed partly to Agaja's farsighted plans, but more so to

---

[1] 'Copybook and Diaries for Whydah', 30 Dec. 1729, 3, 9–17 Jan., 9 and 25 Feb. 1730 (T 70/1466).

[2] Mallis de la Mine to Premenil, 8 Jan. 1732 (ADN. C. 739); 'Copybook and Diaries for Whydah', 9 and 20 March 1730 (T 70/1466).

[3] 'Copybook and Diaries for Whydah', 9, 20 March, 7 and 9 April 1730 (T 70/1466); Mallis de la Mine to Premenil, 8 Jan. 1732 (ADN. C. 739).

[4] Copybook and Diaries for Whydah', 9, 20 March, 7 and 9 April 1730 (T 70/1466); Mallis de la Mine to Premenil, 8 Jan. 1732 (ADN. C. 739).

the lack of effective co-operation between all the forces that had opposed him. The Akwamu and the Little Popo, who had refused to recognise his right, found themselves unable to co-operate and powerless to oppose him singly. Only the Akwamu once appeared on the Whydah beach with an army of about thirty thousand men, but they withdrew without striking a blow.[1] Although the old Whydah, helped by the European factors, had taken advantage of the Oyo invasions time and again to occupy Igelefe, they did not actively co-operate with the Oyo despite the fact that they stood to gain from such co-operation.

The circumstance most favourable to Dahomey was the complete lack of co-operation between the European directors and the Oyo, which may be accounted for by their mutual lack of enthusiasm for such an alliance. The Oyo had not yet forgotten that during the reign of Obalokun, certain Oyo messengers sent to a 'friendly' king in Europe did not return and they had since remained wary of befriending any Europeans established on the coast. The Europeans on their side had realised that they had burned their fingers by giving Agaja their passive encouragement to invade Whydah and were unwilling to have as their allies a still stronger power, occupying a much wider area, whose intentions were no more known than those of Agaja before the conquest of Whydah.

These factors might not continue to help Dahomey as they had done in the last four years. Indeed despite them, Abomey had been burned four times between 1726 and 1730, during which time the Dahomeans had spent as much time in hiding as in their own homes. Agaja had become greatly impoverished, and the documents no longer speak of his riches and generosity. Most of his gold plate and beautiful garments noticed by Lambe in 1724 had either been burned or looted by the Oyo invaders. Even the dried heads of his conquered enemies, which Agaja loved to exhibit to his subjects and show to his foreign visitors, had all been burned to ashes either by Agaja himself or by the Oyo. The expenses attendant on the rebuilding of his towns every time they were burned were a further drain on his diminished resources.

Agaja therefore decided that his revolutionary programme for a new political system in Aja and the substitution for the slave

[1] 'Conseil de Marine', 11 Aug. 1728; 'Extrait du Registre', 26 Aug. and 4 Oct 1728 (AN. C. 6/25).

trade of a new pattern of economic relations with Europe could not be achieved in the face of the determined opposition it had aroused. If he did not modify his policy, Dahomey might be completely destroyed.

He asked Bazilio, the Portuguese director, to help him to make a permanent peace with Ojigi,[1] to which request Bazilio agreed and for which he provided a large part of the preliminary presents that were sent to the Alafin and the Oyo chiefs. There then followed the first comprehensive settlement between Oyo and Dahomey and among the Aja, since Agaja overturned the traditional system. The details are not known, but its results were clear and far reaching.

Agaja was allowed to keep the whole of the Whydah kingdom and substantial part of Allada kingdom,[2] but was not allowed to return to Abomey. He therefore remained at Allada where he died in 1740.[3] The eastern boundary of the Dahomean kingdom was marked by Lake Nkoue, the So and the Weme rivers, and the whole of it became a tributary to Oyo. The Weme dynasty was reinstated.[4] The Allada dynasty and the remnant of the Allada people were settled in a new territory called Ajase Ipo, which became the kingdom of Porto Novo in the nineteenth century.[5] Both Weme and Ajase Ipo lay outside the eastern boundary and, like Dahomey, were tributaries to Oyo. Places

---

[1] Viceroy of Brazil to King of Portugal, 10 July 1730 (APB. OR. 27 f. 140); A. Dalzel, *History*, p. 59; A. F. C. Ryder, 'The Re-establishment of the Portuguese...' in *JHSN*, vol. 1 (1958), p. 161.

[2] Oyo never again invaded Dahomey on behalf of these kingdoms.

[3] Oral traditions in Dahomey relate that Agaja died at Allada but do not explain why. Tegbesu removed to Abomey in 1743. Levet to La Compagnie des Indes, 25 Feb. 1744 (AN. C. 6/25).

[4] In 1729 the prince of Weme was at Oyo asking for the help of the Alafin against Agaja. In 1732 Weme was sufficiently independent and safe from Dahomean wrath to harbour Agaja's son and his four thousand followers who had deserted from the Mahi campaign and for Hertog to be attempting to make an alliance between it and Jakin against Dahomey.

[5] De Chenevert and Abbé Bulet, 'Réflexions sur Juda', 1776 (AN. C. 6/27 *bis*). The relevant portion reads: 'Ardres à 7 lieues du N¼ N.Est, était la capitale de Ouedas: d'une division de ce peuple séparés en deux royaumes, celui d'Ardra et celui de Xavier. Le roy d'Ardres a conservé une partie de son royaume, c'est lui regne à Ardra et Porto Novo; celui de Xavier est au Grand Popo...'. Porto Novo was originally the name of the Port only; P. Labarthe, *Voyage à la côte de Guinée* (Paris, 1803), p. 115; C. W. Newbury, *The Western Slave Coast*, p. 30. The last two authorities suggest that the constitution of places like Badagry and Porto Novo as kingdoms was post 1724. Given the events of the time and the power of Agaja, they could only have been constituted and guaranteed by Oyo.

like Epe and Badagry, to which Allada and Whydah refugees had fled, secured immunity from Dahomean attack because they lay outside the eastern boundary of the Dahomean territory, but the ownership of the territory did not seem to have been clearly defined. Dahomey, Weme and Ajase Ipo were left to manage their internal administration and to borrow as much of Oyo practices as they wished.

As a guarantee that Agaja would observe these arrangements, one of his sons, who later became Tegbesu, king of Dahomey was given as a hostage to the Oyo. The treaty itself was sealed by an exchange of royal marriages, with Agaja sending his daughter to the Alafin Ojigi for a wife and Ojigi returning the compliment.[1]

In 1730 therefore, instead of Dahomey becoming the political master of the whole of Aja, it became one of the tributaries of Oyo, on the same level, as far as Oyo was concerned, as Badagry, Weme and Ajase Ipo. This settlement, restated eighteen years later, remained the basis of the political organisation among the Aja, and of their relationship with Oyo until the beginning of the third decade of the nineteenth century, when Dahomey recovered its independence and started on a fresh career of conquest.

The economic settlement was also in sight. On 12 May 1730, about the same time as the Dahomey–Oyo negotiations were going on, John Brathwaite, one of the three chief directors of Cape Coast Castle, arrived at Whydah specially to settle the quarrel between Agaja and Huffon in the interests of the slave trade.[2] He had acquired the reputation of a peacemaker between warring African kingdoms because, earlier on in 1730, he had helped to settle a quarrel between the Akwamu and the Accra to the satisfaction of both parties.[3]

He planned to persuade the Whydah to return to their ancient kingdom as subjects or tributaries of Agaja, and to persuade Agaja to accept them. The Royal African Company also wanted him to make a treaty with Huffon, should he be allowed back in his old kingdom, to allow the Company's ships to trade with the Portuguese for gold free of customs duties.[4] The

[1] A. Dalzel, *History*, p. 59; E. Dunglas in *E.D.* vol. xix, pp. 146–7. Dunglas's dating as already noted, is incorrect.
[2] J. Brathwaite to R.A.C., 1 June 1730 (T 70/7).
[3] Court of Assistant to J. Brathwaite, 31 Dec. 1730 (T 70/54).
[4] J. Brathwaite to R.A.C., 1 June 1730 (T 70/7); Court of Assistant to J. Brathwaite, 31 Dec. 1730/54).

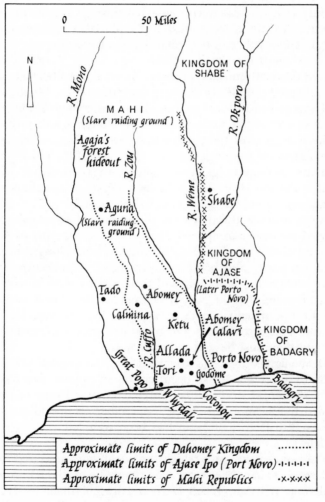

4. The kingdom of Dahomey and its neighbours
after the 1730 settlement.

The following labels appear within the map:

0   50 Miles

N

R. Mono

KINGDOM OF
SHABE

R. Okparo

MAHI
(Slave raiding ground)

Agaja's
forest
hideout

R. Zou

R. Weme

•Shabe

•Aguria
(Slave raiding
ground)

KINGDOM
OF
AJASE
(Later Porto
Novo)

Tado   •Abomey

Calmina   Ketu   •Abomey
Calavi

KINGDOM
OF
BADAGRY

R. Cuffo

•Allada   •Porto Novo

Great Poro

•Tori   •Godome

Whydah   Cotonou   Badagry

Approximate limits of Dahomey Kingdom ···········
Approximate limits of Ajase Ipo (Port Novo) ·I·I·I·I·I
Approximate limits of Mahi Republics ·X·X·X·X

Dahomean authorities were probably still too busy negotiating with the Oyo to give immediate attention to Brathwaite and the negotiations between him and Agaja did not start until the end of July 1730.[1] These were conducted through Deane, the substantive director of the English fort at Whydah, who set out for Allada on 29 July and remained there until 22 August.[1]

Once again the details of the negotiations have not been passed down. Brathwaite probably found the political situation in Dahomey completely different from that on the Gold Coast, and was forced to leave politics alone and confine his negotiations strictly to trade affairs. Although Huffon agreed to Brathwaite's suggestion that he should become Agaja's tributary, Agaja seems to have refused entirely to accept the old Whydah and he sent troops to Igelefe to frighten away those of them whom Brathwaite and Deane had been encouraging to come and settle in anticipation of the agreement to be reached.[2]

Agaja negotiated fully on the slave trade, however, which he offered no longer to oppose. Partly because the ruler of Jakin was not completely loyal, and to deprive him of any source of firearms, partly also because of the need to concentrate the slave trade in only one port and thus make it easy to control, Agaja insisted that the port of Jakin should be closed, and that the European activities be concentrated at Igelefe. He also insisted that certain classes of goods including all firearms and ammunition must be sold to him alone.

Deane agreed to Agaja's demand, and the English factory at Jakin to which goods had been sent on 16 August, began to be evacuated on 25 August 1730, three days after Deane had concluded the negotiations. By 17 September all unsold goods at the English factory at Jakin had been completely removed to Igelefe.[3]

This agreement, with which the negotiators appeared satisfied, seems to have been regarded as applying to all the European traders at Whydah. When Deane finally left Allada for Igelefe on 22 August he was accompanied by a detachment of the Dahomean army,[4] a sign of the new friendship between the

---

[1] 'Copybook and Diaries for Whydah', 29 July, 22 Aug. 1730 (T 70/1466); 'Accounts and Journals, C.C.C.', May–Dec. 1730 (T 70/396).
[2] J. Brathwaite to R.A.C., 16 Aug. 1730 (T 70/7).
[3] 'Copybook and diaries for Whydah', 25 Aug. and 17 Sept. 1730 (T 70/1466); J. Brathwaite to R.A.C., 16 Aug. 1730 (T 70/7).
[4] 'Copybook and Diaries for Whydah', 22 Aug. 1730 (T 70/1466).

Europeans and Agaja, and of the protection which the latter would henceforth give to the former.

All the other Europeans at Igelefe also showed their satisfaction at the conclusion of this treaty, though they did not seem to have closed their factories at Jakin as Agaja had demanded. The French and the Portuguese directors and their officers gathered at the English fort to celebrate the new accord. Sixty-three gun salutes were fired, twenty-one each in honour of the kings of England, France and Portugal. Healths were drunk on a lavish scale and altogether £18 was spent that afternoon by the English fort alone for the celebrations.[1]

For the Europeans, the occasion was worthy of this rejoicing, for at last Agaja had been converted to a slave trader. For Dahomey the agreement marked a fundamental change in policy and prepared the way for making the slave trade the basis of the Dahomean economy and for its transformation into the incorrigible slave-trading kingdom that it became in the nineteenth century. The conclusion of the two agreements, with Oyo and the European directors, also gave Dahomey a breathing space during which Agaja could gather up the remnants of his conquests and impose an administration and an economic system on such parts of them as were left to him by Oyo.

Not that Agaja had completely neglected any of these duties during the difficult years of the Oyo invasions. Whenever he found it convenient between his flights, he had sought to consolidate his hold over the conquered territories. In April 1728, soon after the Oyo's withdrawal, he sent his army to drive away the Whydah who had taken advantage of the Oyo invasion to resettle at Igelefe. In August he sent a Dahomean chief, called Lansu, to Jakin to overawe its ruler, a move that kept that ruler quiet for a time.[2] In September he reduced a province of Allada which lay south of Abomey but which had either revolted or had never before been effectively occupied.[3] While the Oyo invasions continued, however, none of these successes could be regarded as final.

With the security provided by the 1730 treaty, Agaja could assert his sole mastery over his kingdom. The reaction of Jakin

---

[1] 'Accounts and Journals, C.C.C.', May–Dec. 1730 (T 70/396).
[2] 'Conseil de Marine', 11 and 24 Aug. 1728 (AN. C. 6/25); 'Accounts and Journals, C.C.C.', 31 Dec. 1728 (T 70/392).
[3] 'Extrait du Registre', 23 Sept. and 4 Oct. 1728 (AN. C. 6/25).

and the Whydah to that agreement provided him with the opportunity.

The treaty between Dahomey and Oyo pleased neither the old Whydah nor the Jakin people, for neither secured their independence from Dahomey rule. Huffon, the king of Whydah, still in the Popo islands, at first decided to submit to Agaja and asked Bazilio to help him negotiate. Early in 1731 Bazilio submitted Huffon's proposal to Agaja who agreed to suspend hostilities while negotiations went on. Meanwhile, certain Dutch agents assured Huffon that they would give him arms and would enlist the support of the Fanti and the Oyo in his interest. Huffon therefore changed his mind about submitting to Agaja and the negotiations were called off.

In anticipation of the promised help by the Dutch, Huffon adopted a scorched earth policy against the Dahomean economy.[1] This is a strategy which the old Whydah repeatedly adopted from now on, whenever they found themselves too weak to fight Dahomey. In practice it meant making Igelefe port and beach unsafe for the European traders by plundering their goods, burning their tents and killing their agents, or blocking the lagoon passage between Great Popo and Igelefe. The old Whydah believed that Dahomey held on to Whydah kingdom because of its economic advantages, and would eventually withdraw if it was deprived of them.

In March 1731 they killed a Portuguese in the Popo river. On the night of 8 to 9 May, they made an attack on the French and the Portuguese tents on the beach at Igelefe during which the Portuguese fled but the French defended themselves.[2] On 13 April 1733 the Whydah prevented a French ship carrying provisions to the French fort from passing to Whydah, and on 18 May they arrested a Portuguese captain who had gone to trade among them, imprisoned him for eight days, plundered him of all his valuables and sent him back to Whydah.[2]

These activities inconvenienced the Europeans, but did not achieve their purpose. The blocking of the lagoon was neither sustained nor complete enough to force the Europeans away from Whydah, and the acting director of the French fort was, for

---

[1] J. Bazilio to Viceroy of Brazil, Ajuda, 17 July 1731 (APB. OR. 28, f. 129).
[2] Levet to La Compagnie des Indes, Juda, 26 Aug. 1733 (AN. C. 6/25); Mallis de la Mine to Premenil, 8 Jan. 1732 (ADN. C. 739); J. Bazilio to Viceroy of Brazil, Ajuda, 17 July 1731 (APB. OR. 28, f. 129).

instance, able to browbeat the old Whydah into allowing the French provision ship to pass. Their only effect was to drive the Europeans more and more on to the side of Agaja and to make them willing to co-operate with him against the old Whydah.

The Director of the English fort thought of building a fort on the seashore to be used against the incursions of the old Whydah. The Portuguese, the greatest sufferers from the Whydah activities, successfully urged Agaja to take military action. On 15 June 1733, between four and five hundred Dahomean soldiers came to Igelefe and seized about eighty old Whydah who were living in the English and the Portuguese forts without any murmur from the directors. On 9 August Agaja sent the rulers of Paom, Tori and the Aplogan of Gome, with their contingents, to reside permanently at Igelefe and make the incursions of the old Whydah impossible.[1]

It should be noticed that this was the first attempt made by Agaja to populate Igelefe with Dahomeans since its conquest in 1727. As can be inferred from the leaders sent, these 'Dahomeans' were simply those of the old Whydah and the Allada people who submitted to Agaja. Other attempts may have been made later, as has been suggested, to increase this nucleus.[2]

The Dutch, who had promised Huffon arms and aid for a military alliance, do not seem to have given much of either. From June 1733 to about the middle of 1734 a series of misfortunes befell the old Whydah which greatly weakened their fighting spirit for many years to come. On 15 June 1733 chief Assu, who had fled with Huffon from Whydah and had become the most influential leader of the resistance against Dahomey in the Popo islands, died after an illness of about twenty days. His eldest son 'Favory' (Fafore?) quickly succeeded to his title and his prestige. On 17 July 1733 Huffon himself died and a succession quarrel ensued. Fafore backed one contender, quickly gained the upper hand and brought his protégé to his own island, called the Assu island. Civil war ensued, and the other contender appealed to Agaja.[3]

Agaja promptly sent aid. The appellant and his supporters

---

[1] Levet to la Compagnie des Indes, 26 Aug. 1733 (AN. C. 6/25).
[2] C. W. Newbury, *The Western Slave Coast*, p. 25.
[3] Levet to la Compagnie des Indes, 26 Aug. 1733 (AN. C. 6/25). A. Dalzel, *History*, pp. 81–2. Dalzel is wrong on the date of the death of Huffon, which he puts at 1741; E. Dunglas in *E.D.* vol. XIX, p. 157.

were brought to Allada to submit to Agaja and unconfirmed rumours started to circulate that they would be allowed to resettle at Sahe. Meanwhile Agaja's army laid siege to the Assu island, the defenders of which were closely hemmed in and were dying off of hunger by November 1733. The Dahomeans dealt the final blow some time in 1734 when Delisle, an old friend of Agaja, who had become the director of the French fort, lent Agaja ships and cannons to finish the campaign.[1] If the economic policy of Agaja had not again forced discontented Dahomeans to flee to the old Whydah, the latter might never again have been able to oppose Dahomey.

Jakin's reaction to the 1730 settlement was different from Whydah's. Its ruler, like Huffon, had hoped that Oyo invasions would deliver Jakin from the Dahomean rule. When this hope was disappointed, he asked all the European directors to build forts in his territory, thinking that such forts might be an effective defence against Dahomean attack,[2] and increase his chances of securing firearms.

At first there was no response to these overtures, but in May 1731 events at Jakin took a new turn which caused Agaja some alarm. The Portuguese built a fortified mud fortress there and were planning a bigger one without consulting Agaja or in any way obtaining his permission.[3] The Dutch also started to make preparations to build strongholds at Jakin, and by August 1731, their agent, Mynheer Hertog, was actively negotiating an alliance which was expected to include Jakin, Oyo and Fanti.[4] Agaja's information services kept him well informed of all these developments.

The situation was particularly alarming because, by that time, Agaja was campaigning against the Mahi. He and his main army had left Allada on 20 May 1731 for Mahi,[5] probably in retaliation for the part which the Mahi had played in the Oyo invasion of Dahomey in 1730. They chose the rainy season partly to make sure that the Oyo would not be able to help the

[1] Levet to la Compagnie des Indes, 26 Aug. 1733 (AN. C. 6/25). A. Dalzel, *History*, pp. 81–2; Dunglas in *E.D.* vol. XIX, p. 157.
[2] Viceroy of Brazil to King of Portugal, Bahia, 29 April 1730 (APB. OR. 27).
[3] J. Bazilio to Viceroy of Brazil, Ajuda, 17 July 1731 (APB. OR. 28, f. 129).
[4] J. Bazilio to Viceroy of Brazil, Ajuda, 7 Sept. 1732. (AHU. S. Tome Caixa 4); W. Snelgrave, *A New Account*, pp. 150–1; A. Dalzel, *History*, pp. 60–1.
[5] Edward Deane to R.A.C., 26 June 1731 (T 70/7).

Mahi. The season was, however, not particularly favourable to the Dahomean infantry either.

On 26 June, after a month's siege, the Dahomean army suffered a very heavy defeat. A large section of the army was dispirited and asked that the siege be raised. Agaja became stubborn, executed the officers who advised retreat and maintained his ground. Discontent and desertion followed and one of Agaja's sons, perhaps the heir apparent, deserted to the king of Weme with about four thousand men under him.[1] These could make any hostile alliance which included Weme very dangerous to Dahomey. After a series of minor successes which in part offset the ignominious defeat of the previous June, Agaja returned in haste to his capital at Allada on 30 March 1732.

The situation demanded quick and decisive action which Agaja brilliantly took. On 1 April 1732 he caused it to be rumoured that his army had gone against Paom, 'a big city belonging to Ajuda', in order to hide his real objective and catch it unprepared. The following day, 2 April, his army suddenly attacked Jakin. By luck and presence of mind, the two most wanted men, Hertog and the ruler of Jakin escaped to Epe, but the whole town was burned, including all the factories except the Portuguese. Twenty Europeans and 4,538 Jakin, including the mother of the ruler, were taken captives. Goods to the value of eight hundred and fifty slaves were also seized. Altogether, it was a very rich booty.[2]

Jakin was effectively reduced. In September its ruler in exile at Epe asked Agaja for permission to come back on the conditions that he would be allowed to keep his garrison and would not be forced to go to Allada personally to make his submission. Agaja found the request so absurd that he thought it useless to waste any time in negotiation. He simply said he agreed. The ruler of Jakin found such an easy agreement coming from Agaja rather unconvincing and he remained in exile.[3] Dahomey did not appear completely satisfied that the

[1] W. Snelgrave, *A New Account*, p. 149; A. Dalzel, *History*, pp. 59–60.
[2] J. Bazilio to Viceroy of Brazil, Ajuda, 7 Sept. 1732 (AHU. S. Tome Caixa 4); W. Snelgrave, *A New Account*, pp. 150–1; A. Dalzel, *History*, pp. 61–3; E. Dunglas in *E.D.* vol. XIX, pp. 161–2; A. F. C. Ryder, 'The Re-establishment of the Portuguese...', in *JHSN* (1953), p. 166. Dalzel's dating is slightly inaccurate. It is possible that he has mixed up the date of the deaths of Huffon and of Agaja, for Agaja did not die soon after this event. Huffon died in 1733.
[3] See note 1 above.

spirit of resistance of the Jakin had been broken. On 24 November 1734 a Dahomean army again burned Jakin and remained encamped there for about a week. The reduction of Jakin and of Whydah between 1732 and 1734 left Agaja the sole master within the sphere conceded to him by the 1730 treaty.

It remained to give his whole territory an effective administration. The attempt had probably been going on since 1725, though the details are unknown and the Oyo invasions must necessarily have made such efforts at best disjointed. It is probable, however, that the traditional administrative boundaries remained largely unaltered, for there is no fundamental difference between the set-up described by Dapper and Du Marchais in the early seventeenth and early eighteenth centuries when a large part of the Aja had not yet come under Dahomey, and that described by Dawson in the late nineteenth century,[1] when Dahomey had been the sole kingdom for more than a century. Out of the administrative districts of the old kingdom of Whydah, Agaja seems to have kept Gome, Paom and Igelefe. He also seems to have kept Tori, Jakin and Allada divisions of the old Allada kingdom.[2] He probably did not tamper much with any of the other remaining districts, except as in the case of Sahe, where the wars may have wiped out the population.

The system of government and the terms under which the rulers of each administrative division held his office, however, changed. Dahomey being a centralised monarchy, no office under Agaja was inalienably hereditary. Every official was appointed for his ability and was liable to be transferred from one duty to another, to be promoted, demoted or dismissed by the king. He had his duties defined and limits set to his power. The practice under Agaja was probably not much different from that under Glele. Each officer

has to answer every question of that district [under him], to settle all petty disputes and to inform the king; but very serious cases he has to send to the capital to be settled by the chief minister or by the king himself.[3]

[1] J. Ogilby, *Africa*, p. 465; T. Astley, *Collections*, vol. III, pp. 8–9. Dawson to Fitzgerald, 17 Nov. 1862 (CA. 2/016).
[2] Levet to la Compagnie des Indes, Juda, 26 Aug. 1733 (AN. C. 6/26); W. Snelgrave, *A New Account*, pp. 9–10; A. Dalzel, *History*, pp. 17–18.
[3] J. Dawson to Fitzgerald, 17 Nov. 1862 (CA. 2/016).

Filling up the post of all the administrative districts of the old Allada kingdom probably presented no difficulties since the king of Allada had been killed. Agaja kept the ruler of Jakin as his officer until 1732, when he was driven to Epe, and he also kept the ruler of Tori. Up to 1730 he probably kept captains of the garrison stationed at Allada to take care of his new conquests. From 1730 to 1743 Allada was the capital of Dahomey kingdom, where the king himself resided.

Manning the administrative units of the old Whydah kingdom was slightly more difficult. First, Huffon was still alive. Theoretically, therefore, his traditional chiefs still held their rights. Secondly, the government of the coastal belt of Whydah involved a direct relationship with Europeans of which Agaja had had no previous experience, there never having been permanent European forts at Allada. However, Agaja retained the ruler of Gome, and probably the ruler of Paom, as his officers. The territory of Sahe had been burned and rendered uninhabited. For a whole year after the conquest of Whydah, Agaja could not decide how to govern Igelefe.[1] He simply continued to use his trade officers, Jongla, Buttenoe and others, to maintain contact with the Europeans, and his army to keep order.

Events moved a stage further after the withdrawal of the Oyo in 1728. Agaja probably then concluded that the old Whydah would never again be able to reoccupy their old kingdom. He certainly saw the need to have a regular basis of contact with the Europeans. On 7 September 1728 he appointed three officers, one for each of the European forts at Igelefe. He made Alege,[2] formerly the chief prison officer, the chief of the French, 'Ouroukaye',[2] probably the same as the official who appears as Budaka in the English records, the chief of the English, and 'Baagba'[2] the Portuguese chief. Surprisingly Jongla was dropped, probably because he was too keen on the slave trade before Agaja had made up his mind on it.

Delisle, the French officer who was present when the appointments were made, showed that he was pleased. Agaja, surprised but gratified, confessed that he had not chosen them

---

[1] W. Snelgrave, *A New Account*, pp. 9–10, 61–2; A. Dalzel, *History*, pp. 17–18; 'Extrait du Registre', 13 Sept. 1728 (ANC. 6/25); 'Accounts and Journals for Whydah', 21 March 1727 (T 70/598).
[2] These would appear to be personal names, not titles.

earlier because he did not know whether it was his right or
the privilege of the Europeans to choose their own Dahomean
chiefs.[1]

The duties of the three Dahomean officers were clearly defined. They were to take the customs duties on the ships of the
respective nations under them, to transmit the king's messages
to them and take theirs to the king, and to transact such trade as
the king decided on.[2]

How each of them fared between 1728 and 1733 is not completely known. Alege probably held his post right through,
though at one point he also acted as the English chief. Baagba
was soon dropped, and replaced by the veteran Jongla who
continued to be the Portuguese chief until 1733.[3] Budaka played
a very prominent part in keeping the English on the side of
Agaja during the critical months of 1730, but he too for some
unknown reason had been replaced by another officer called
Nançou (?Yansu) before 1733.[4] During the Oyo invasion of
1730, all the three officers were superseded by another Dahomean chief called 'Vodehay'[5] but they later resumed their normal duties after the settlement with Oyo.

The European directors, completely unused to Dahomean
etiquette and its strict 'civil service', were dissatisfied with this
arrangement. Their main grievance was that each of the Dahomean officers visited all the forts in turn, sometimes twice or
thrice daily, and put the directors to great entertainment expenses. But they did not confess this to Agaja. Instead they
complained of the behaviour of the Dahomean chiefs and falsely
accused Jongla of planning to take the French fort by force, an
accusation which Agaja did not believe.[6]

However, in January 1733, when all the directors went to
Allada for the *Anubomey* (annual customs), they jointly and
vigorously complained to Agaja that his officers were causing
injury to trade. Agaja realised that the directors were dissatisfied with the arrangement and recalled all three, Alege, Yansu,
and Jongla. He appointed in their place only one man, Tegan,

---

[1] 'Extrait du Registre', 13 and 23 Sept. 1729 (AN. C. 6/25); Copybook and
Diaries for Whydah, 7 Jan. 1730 (T 70/1466).
[2] *Ibid.*
[3] Levet to la Compagnie des Indes, 26 Aug. 1733 (AN. C. 6/25).
[4] *Ibid.*
[5] 'Accounts and journals, Cape Coast Castle', 28 Feb. 1730 (T 70/395).
[6] Levet to la Compagnie des Indes, 26 Aug. 1733 (AN. C. 6/25).

to whom he gave the title Yovogan, which meant White-man's chief.[1] Thus in January 1733 Tegan became the first man to occupy the unenviable post of the Yovogan of Whydah. With this, it may be said that the basic pattern of the administrative settlement of the new Dahomey kingdom was complete.

It remained for an economic pattern to emerge. It soon became clear that when Agaja finally subscribed to the slave trade in August 1730 he did no more than legalise his usual practice up to that time. After 1730 only Agaja, and nobody else in Dahomey, sold slaves to the Europeans and he conducted the trade through his officers. At Allada, the chief jailer took orders from him to sell a certain number of slaves of certain descriptions according to Agaja's need of European goods. Such slaves were then sent, as from 1733 onwards, to the Yovogan at Whydah, who sold them to the European forts and captains through his own 'trading boys', who were also king's officers. At Jakin, one Antonio Pinto a Portuguese factor, became Agaja's agent.

Certain classes of goods could only be sold to the king, others only to the chiefs, and some to everybody. As a rule, all guns and gun-powder, and every ounce of gold that entered Dahomey could only be sold to the king; similarly all white hats with gold or silver ribbons and corals of certain descriptions. The list could be amended by law from time to time. Goods once landed at Whydah could not be reshipped out of the country and no European once in Dahomey could leave without a royal permit. Lest there should be any doubt in the minds of the Europeans about this last provision, Agaja stationed a permanent military post on the beach.

The slave trade in Dahomey became in effect a royal monopoly. In 1733 when Guyonzuay, who had become the chief jailer after Alege, took advantage of his position to sell slaves without Agaja's authority, and did not give an account of his sales, he was promptly executed.[2] When one of the servants of the Yovogan sold slaves on his own account for gold, both the slaves and the gold were confiscated and the seller led in irons to Allada and presumably executed.[2] In the whole of Jakin, whenever Antonio Pinto was away, not one slave could be obtained by the Europeans.

To the Europeans, Agaja's monopoly and strict control was

---

[1] Dubelay to la Compagnie des Indes, 26 Aug. 1733 (AN. C. 6/25).
[2] Levet to la Compagnie des Indes, Juda, 26 Aug. 1733 (AN. C. 6/25).

distasteful. It increased the prices of slaves because Agaja demanded just what goods he needed and gave the number of slaves he thought reasonable. For instance, in November 1733 Dubelay reckoned that Agaja demanded three thousand and thirty guns of all kinds and descriptions, ten thousand pounds of gun-powder, six cases of organs 'with 12 or 14 airs' and one hundred and fifty pounds of large corals, for three or four hundred slaves. Alternatively, he would take eighty thousand pounds of cowries, one thousand two hundred anchors of brandy, two thousand five hundred pieces of platilles and eight hundred pieces of salempory.[1] None of these goods were the cheap and gaudy kind that Europeans had been pleased to exchange for slaves in the past.

Agaja demanded any amount of goods he needed on credit and could only be refused at the owners' risk. In February 1733 when Levet, the acting French director, refused to sell his entire stock of gunpowder to Agaja on credit, he was ordered out of the country. Dubelay, who was present at the council meeting that decided Levet's expulsion, remarked that the rulers of Dahomey would not be trifled with.[2]

Finally trade became slow and the European ships could no longer count on quick round voyages. The Portuguese complained that in 1730 each round trip took fifteen or sixteen months instead of the six or seven months it used to take before the Dahomean conquest of Whydah.[3] Snelgrave accurately reflected the frustration of the European traders when he wrote of Whydah in 1734: 'there is no prospect of trade there again for many years, or at least as long as the conqueror lives. What little there is is carried on chiefly at Appah' (Epe).[4]

The Europeans therefore tried the traditional solution by planning to abandon Dahomey. The English built a factory at Epe and one of their chief agents at the Cape Coast Castle who visited Whydah in 1735 recommended that the English fort should be removed from Whydah and built at Keta.[5] But nothing

[1] Dubelay to la Compagnie des Indes, 21 Nov. 1733 (AN. C. 6/25). Platilles and salempory were kinds of cloth.
[2] Levet to la Compagnie des Indes, Juda, 26 Aug. 1733. (AN. C. 6/25). Dubelay to la Compagnie des Indes, 21 Nov. 1733 (AN. C. 6/25).
[3] Viceroy of Brazil to King of Portugal, 29 April 1730 (APB. OR. 27).
[4] W. Snelgrave, *A New Account*, p. 156.
[5] Court of Assistants to E. Stephens, G. Wheeler and W. Rogers, 10 July 1735 (T 70/54).

came out of the suggestion. The French traders started to extend their trading activities from Cape Mesurado to Badagry and Epe[1] and to avoid trading at Whydah.

The reaction of the Dahomean citizens to Agaja's measures cannot be exactly described for internal events in Dahomey between 1733 and 1740 are confused and obscure. It seems probable, however, that the measures, and particularly the economic ones, were greatly resented by some of the most important chiefs in Dahomey. Most of them probably believed that they had possessed the coastal kingdoms to enjoy the slave trade with the Europeans and felt bitterly disappointed at being deprived of the fruits of their success. Some of them therefore staged a series of revolts which Agaja mercilessly put down between 1733 and 1736, to ensure his own unimpaired control of the slave trade in Dahomey.

In 1733 the Possu, lieutenant-general of the Dahomean forces, was accused of planning to desert the kingdom to join the ruler of Savalu in Mahi and was executed on 9 June.[2] In December Gome, the Aplogan's territory, was burned and the Aplogan himself narrowly escaped.[3] On 24 November 1734 Agaja again attacked Jakin where he heavily punished the European traders[4] who seem to have continued to trade there despite Agaja's known opposition to such activities. The following year the Mehu, the second highest officer in the kingdom, led a revolt which was mercilessly put down,[5] and Ashampo, one of the ablest generals of Agaja, successfully escaped to Little Popo after he had received warnings that Agaja was about to seize him. At Little Popo he was welcomed and seems to have been made the general of their army.[5] There may have been many more desertions of less known public figures.

Although Agaja was enabled by these strong measures to remain master in Dahomey without sacrificing any of his principles, he had created new problems for himself. The series of revolts and the desertions greatly weakened Dahomey internally. The fact that the European traders were trading in large numbers in the neighbouring ports raised the possibility that

---

[1] 'Enregistrement des rapports de capitaines au long course', 13, 28 Feb. 1737, 13 Jan., 28 June 1738, 3 July 1739, 20 June 1740 (ADN. B. 4587).
[2] Levet to la Compagnie des Indes, 26 Aug. 1733 (AN. C. 6/25).
[3] J. Dubelay to la Compagnie des Indes, 7 Jan. 1734 (AN. C. 6/25).
[4] 'Enregistrement des raports...', 26 Nov. 1736 (ADN. 4587).
[5] A. Dalzel, *History*, pp. 68–71, 97–8.

the states behind those ports could obtain arms and threaten the security of Dahomey from without. The danger would be more serious if the Dahomean deserters joined the external aggressors. This fear of external aggression which from now on continued to haunt the Dahomean rulers was not entirely unfounded. It was partly through the importation of large quantities of arms that Agaja was able to conquer the coastal states. The presence of the Dutch at Little Popo, whither Ashampo had fled, and at Badagry where Hertog continued his hostile activities, further justified Agaja's fear of external aggression, for the Dutch were notorious for inciting one kingdom against another.[1] Their promise to Huffon in 1731 to help him make an alliance against Agaja, their help for the ruler of Jakin against Agaja and the activities of Hertog at Badagry whither he had withdrawn in 1734, were such as to justify this reputation.

Agaja's operations in the last years of his life therefore had two aims. The first was to prevent external invasions, and the second was to root out Dutch influence from the immediate vicinity of Dahomey.

In 1736 and again in 1738, certain unidentified enemies attacked Jakin.[2] The aggressors may have been the Badagry people acting under the instigation of Hertog. Agaja sent his army to aid Jakin and attack Badagry and it was during these Dahomean attacks that Hertog died fighting in June 1737.[3] In the following month, a Dahomean force destroyed the Dutch factory at Keta and captured the factor. The Dutch were, however, too well practised in local political intrigues to be attacked with impunity. As a result of their obscure manoeuvres, Ashampo was soon in the field at the head of a combined army of Krepi and Little Popo Accra. The Dahomeans were intercepted and completely wiped out and Ashampo followed up his victory with a raid on Igelefe.[4]

This crushing reverse still further weakened a Dahomey already upset by internal dissension. Agaja was by now loosing his grip on the internal administration of Dahomey and the very survival of his dynasty appeared doubtful. In 1737 an English

[1] P. Labarthe, *Voyage à la Côte de Guinée*, pp. 110–11.
[2] A. F. C. Ryder, 'The Re-establishment of the Portuguese...', in *JHSN*, pp. 169–70.
[3] 'Enregistrement des rapports...', 3 Feb. 1738 (ADN. B. 4587).
[4] Steimark's declaration, 4 Dec. 1737 (WIC). I owe this information and reference to Mr Ivor Wilks of the University of Ghana.

visitor to Whydah observed that 'the power of the king of Dahomey...is at present at so low an ebb that it has been lately employed, and often without success, upon his own tributary subjects'.[1]

Agaja was no longer able to enforce his royal monopoly on the slave trade in which complete freedom again became the rule. He blamed his misfortune on Bazilio whom he arrested and imprisoned for six months.

Worse was, however, to befall Agaja. The attack on Badagry in June 1737 contravened the 1730 settlement made with Oyo which, by implication, forbade Agaja from extending his military operations east of Lake Nokue and the Weme river. Moreover, it is probable that the series of internal revolts and falling trade since 1733 had greatly impoverishd Agaja and made him unable to pay the annual tributes regularly to Oyo.

The Oyo army therefore came down against Dahomey about the beginning of 1739.[2] The attack appears to have been unexpected by Agaja who precipitately ran into hiding while the Oyo again wasted the country.

Agaja was now a tired old man. The chaotic situation inside Dahomey and the renewed external attacks, particularly by the Oyo must have greatly disheartened him. He died soon after he re-emerged from his forest hideout about May 1740.[3]

With his death passed one of the greatest kings of Dahomey and one of the great military leaders and state builders of history. Dalzel's homage to him is likely to remain the aptest epitaph ever:

Trudo, considered as a conqueror, seems little inferior to any other of that class which has swoln the page of history. Like them he waded to glory through an ocean of innocent blood; and like them experienced the vicissitudes of fortune. Yet he never lost his magnanimity

---

[1] King of Portugal to Viceroy of Brazil, 22 July 1740, enclosing a letter from a Treasury officer dated 18 Sept. 1739 (APB. OR. 53 doc. 41); 'A description of the castles and forts belonging to the Royal African Company, 1737' (T 70/1470).

[2] A. Dalzel, *History*, pp. 71–4; Dalzel's dating is not quite accurate. Isaac Gregory, the English director, did not reach Whydah until March or April 1739.

[3] The various dates, 1727, 1728, 1732, etc., usually given as the date of Agaja's death, can be taken as incorrect. See Viceroy of Brazil to King of Portugal, 18 May 1741 (APB. OR. 38); Conseil de direction to la Compagnie des Indes, 18 Nov. 1753 (AN. C. 6/25).

nor wept like Alexander when his general refused to follow him; he knew how to enforce obedience and drove when he could not lead them to conquest.[1]

No one could go through the documents of this period tattered, scattered and incomplete as they are, without being enormously impressed by the personality of Agaja. A middle sized, stout, athletic figure with spare shoulders, Agaja had a majestic bearing and an attractive countenance that never failed to impress his visitors.[2] Dubelay, a French director, saw nothing incongruous in seeing a physical similarity between him and the celebrated French writer Molière, though he thought his request for a suit of armour was 'Don Quixotic'.[3] Bulfinch Lambe and Delisle remained in his court for fairly long periods and saw enough of him to know the quality of his mind and to study his temperament.

From their accounts Agaja emerges as a far-sighted man who knew his own mind, and was not easily deflected from his purpose except by sound reason. He had a quick mind and knew how to wriggle out of unfavourable positions.

He was open to constructive ideas and was eager to learn any new methods that might be useful. He learnt the art of making leather cartouch boxes for his powder from the Mali,[4] the art of firing the great guns from Lambe,[4] of building fortresses from Delisle, and of forming a guard of honour from Gallot. He was greatly interested in reading and writing which he affected to practise with the aid of both his Portuguese mulatto slave and Lambe.

He could be unpredictably generous, magnanimous in victory and endowed with that sense of humour which men of great hearts possess. He knew too how to create fear in his enemies and respect in his friends, as well as to support the morale of his people in very adverse circumstances.

It was he, in his thirty-two years reign, who finally attempted to complete the task that the Wegbaja dynasty had set itself— to sweep away the old political system in Aja and to stop the

[1] A. Dalzel, *History*, pp. 63–4.
[2] W. Snelgrave, *A New Account*, p. 80.
[3] J. Dubelay to la Compagnie des Indes..., 21 Nov. 1733 (AN. C. 6/25).
[4] W. Snelgrave, *A New Voyage*, pp. 171–89. Not much is known of the role of the Mali in the growth of Dahomey. Twenty-four of them were said to have been in Agaja's camp in 1724. They were said to have come from the ancient state of Mali and were Muslims.

slave trade. Although he succeeded in ending the old political organisation in Aja, he brought on Dahomey a series of Oyo invasions and a stubborn resistance from the European slave traders. In the end he submitted to the Oyo, the defenders of the traditional order, and was forced to make the slave trade into a state enterprise in Dahomey. His vigorous attempt to enforce the royal monopoly over the slave trade brought internal revolts and desertions and led to renewed external aggression. By 1740, when Agaja died, these had greatly disorganised the internal administration of Dahomey, weakened the power of the monarchy and threatened the very existence of the kingdom.

In spite of these difficulties, Agaja laid down a firm basis of administration throughout his territories which he had greatly enlarged. And in his failure he left one intangible but important legacy. To the very last he maintained the principle of absolute authority of the king within Dahomey unimpaired. It was through the application of this principle that Tegbesu, who succeeded Agaja, was able to re-establish the kingdom of Dahomey.

# 4

## Reconstruction continued, 1740-67

In 1740 Dahomey had to be rebuilt almost from nothing. Although Agaja had created a tradition of how the enlarged kingdom should be governed, and had left unimpaired the principle of absolute monarchical control of its internal affairs, at his death the authority of the monarchy had fallen into disrespect. The trade of the kingdom had diminished to vanishing point and its very existence was threatened by renewed Oyo invasions and the raids of the Little Popo and the old Whydah.

Agaja had died without an obvious successor. So-Amamu or Zingah, his eldest son had weakened his own chances when he deserted the Dahomean army during the Mahi campaign of 1731. He put forward his claim nevertheless, but was challenged by Avissu, the youngest of the four eligible princes. Manoeuvres followed during which each candidate gave presents to those who were likely to influence the election. Finally Avissu was elected and he chose Tegbesu as his title.[1]

Probably the kingmakers took largely into consideration the relationship and attitude of each contestant to Oyo. Agaja died just as a new series of Oyo invasions was beginning. Therefore, whoever was to rule Dahomey after him would have to be capable of making peace with Oyo without betraying Dahomean interests. So-Amamu, because of his desertion in 1731, did not seem to possess the qualities needed.

Avissu, on the other hand, possessed them. He had served Dahomey by being a hostage at Oyo and through that stay had become familiar with the Oyo nobles and their manners. It would be very much easier for him than for anyone else to treat with the Oyo authorities. His election might to some extent

---

[1] E. Dunglas in *E.D.* vol. XIX, pp. 165–7; Le Herisse: *L'Ancien Royaume*, pp. 161, 299–300. These authors record different oral traditions which agree in essentials; R. Norris, *Memoirs*, pp. 7–8 and A. Dalzel, *History*, confirm that Agaja's successor was not his eldest son.

satisfy the pride of the Oyo and incline them to offer lenient terms of submission. Whether Oyo actually supported his election is not however known.

That the desire to placate Oyo formed a large element in Tegbesu's election is further suggested by political developments in Dahomey from 1789 onwards. When antagonism to Oyo grew, opposition to the Tegbesu line also developed. As will be seen, Kpengla, Tegbesu's son and successor, adopted the policy of independence from Oyo rule. From then on Tegbesu's line was increasingly challenged. Kpengla's son and successor, Agonglo, was murdered in a palace revolt and Agonglo's son and successor, Adandozan, was deposed in 1818 when Gezo vigorously carried out the anti-Oyo, pro-independence policy of Dahomey.

The greatest immediate danger confronting Dahomey at the accession of Tegbesu was then the renewed Oyo invasions which had started in 1739. Just how many times the Oyo came down between 1740 and 1748, when Tegbesu again made his submission, is uncertain. Dalzel says that they came every year until 1747,[1] but perhaps he exaggerates. Certainly they came in 1742 or 1743[2] and threatened to come in 1748.[3] The causes of these invasions are obscure, but the 1748 threat followed immediately after Tegbesu's attack on Epe in 1747[4] and suggests that the overlordship of Epe and perhaps of some other small territories between Jakin and Badagry was still being disputed by Dahomey.

Whenever the Oyo army came down or threatened to come, the Dahomeans simply followed the tradition laid down by Agaja. The king and his court ran into some remote forest and the citizens were distributed in small parties to safe places. One director of the English fort, Isaac Gregory, who was at Allada during one of these invasions, was taken away to the king's secret hideout.[5] These invasions, apart from being the greatest threat, were also the root cause of most of the other difficulties confronting Dahomey at Tegbesu's succession.

They encouraged the Little Popo and the old Whydah to re-

---

[1] R. Norris, *Memoirs*, pp. 15–16; A Dalzel, *History*, p. 74.
[2] Levet to la Compagnie des Indes, 20 Aug. 1743 (AN. C. 6/25).
[3] 'Accounts and Journals, C.C.C.', 1 Jan.–30 June 1748 (T 70/424).
[4] 'Accounts and Journals, C.C.C.', Nov. and Dec. 1747 (T 70/423).
[5] A. Dalzel, *History*, p. 74; R. Norris, *Memoirs*, p. 15; E. Dunglas in *E.D.* vol. XIX, p. 170.

sume their raids on Igelefe and the Whydah beach.[1] Again we
do not know exactly how many times they came. They probably
came whenever the Oyo invaded Dahomey and sent Tegbesu
into hiding. They certainly attacked the forts during the Oyo
invasion of 1743 and in 1747. On the first of these occasions
there was a pitched battle between them and the Dahomeans
during which Bazilio helped the old Whydah.

In the second raid, they suddenly appeared on the beach in
the morning of 8 August 1747 and overpowered the Dahomean
garrison stationed there, but ran away before the Dahomean
troops at Igelefe could reach the scene of action. Rumours then
started that Ashampo of Little Popo had gathered an army to
invade Dahomey kingdom from the beach, and fears of this
impending invasion, which never took place, persisted until
December.[2]

The Dahomean administration was at best fitful and always
weak while the invasions lasted. For example, the law which had
restricted the slave trade to the king alone was openly dis-
regarded and ordinary Dahomeans continued to trade in slaves,
even though the trade was small.[3]

The European directors started to disobey the law which forbade the re-export of goods once landed in Dahomey, and to
behave in other ways which were harmful to Dahomean interests
but which were friendly to the winning side. Levens, the French
director, refused to admit the Dahomeans who had been sent to
his fort for safety during the Oyo invasion.[4] Bazilio, the Portuguese director, maintained a very close liaison with the old
Whydah by a nightly exchange of messengers, and openly supported them in war against Dahomey, nominating a new general

---

[1] Levet to la Compagnie des Indes, 20 Aug. 1743 (AN. C. 6/25); Conselho
Ultramarino to King of Portugal, Lisbon, 29 Oct. 1744 (AHU. S. Tome
Caixa 5); A. F. C. Ryder, 'The Re-establishment of the Portuguese', in
*JHSN*, p. 171. Contrary to Ryder's opinion, the Dahomean charges
against Bazilio were well attested by other Europeans at Whydah. Levet
wrote of those charges: 'Quoyqu avant que de me rendre à Ardre, je
fusse informé de touttes ces vérités, je fis cependant mois possible auprès
du Roy, qui étoit fort en colère, pour rebattre les coups...'.

[2] 'Accounts and Journals, C.C.C.', Nov. and Dec. 1747, Sept.–Dec. 1747
(T 70/423).

[3] Levet to la Compagnie des Indes, Juda, 2 Jan. 1746 (AN. C. 6/25).

[4] Levet to la Compagnie des Indes, 20 Aug. 1743 (AN. C. 6/25); Conselho
Ultramarino to King of Portugal, Lisbon, 29 Oct. 1744 (AHU. S. Tome
Caixa 5); A. F. C. Ryder, 'The Re-establishment of the Portuguese...',
in *JHSN*, p. 171.

for them when one had fallen in battle. Moreover, he harboured many hundreds of them in his fort, and was supplying the Epe and the Badagry with firearms. At Igelefe, he had himself assumed the right to make laws by forbidding all the Portuguese captains to sell their gold to anyone else but himself.

The chaos and the insecurity consequent upon these developments greatly impoverished the monarchy and the Dahomeans in general. Tegbesu inherited practically no money from Agaja's treasury and one of his very first acts on accession was to borrow or buy goods on credit from the Europeans.[1] The slave trade almost completely disappeared from Whydah in the early years of his reign.

In 1740 the English fort was doing practically no trade. From about 1742 to December 1745 no goods or provisions were sent to it and at the end of December 1745 the total value of the goods there was only £247. 10s. 8d.[2] A mutiny encouraged by Tegbesu in order that he might seize the gunpowder in the fort must have further discouraged the English trade, which was not increased by the decision to place the fort once more under the authority of Cape Coast Castle in 1746. After a long neglect, goods worth £21. 5s. were consigned to Whydah in September and October 1746.

By that time the fort was occupied by only two officers, who did nothing but watch it going progressively to ruin. Towards the end of that year, one of the two occupants, the director, died. The other, considering himself unfit to be director, appealed for reinforcement to the captain of a naval vessel which chanced to be in Whydah harbour at the time and William Devaynes was sent by the captain. On reaching the fort, Devaynes found very little Company property there.[3]

The disturbance caused by the enemy invasion of Dahomey was only one of the reasons for the decay of the English trade at Whydah. Another, and perhaps much more important, reason was that the Royal African Company was heavily in debt. Although

---

[1] 'Journal and Ledgers, C.C.C.', 1 May–31 Oct. 1746 (T 70/204); 'Accounts and Journals, C.C.C.', 1 Sept.–31 Dec. 1746 (T 70/422); Conseil de direction to la Compagnie des Indes, 18 Feb. 1753 (AN. C. 6/25).

[2] 'Accounts and Journals, C.C.C.', July 1740–June 1745. (T 70/413–21); 'Journal and Ledgers, C.C.C.', Nov. and Dec. 1745 (T 70/702), Sept. and Oct. 1746 (T 70/704); 'Minutes of the Court of Assistants', 29 Sept. 1744 (T 70/95); Levet to la Compagnie des Indes, 13 Oct. 1746 (AN. C. 6/25).

[3] Viceroy of Brazil to King of Portugal, Bahia, 8 March 1748 (AHU. S. Tome Caixa 6); W. Devaynes to Melvil, 23 Sept. 1753 (T 70/1520).

Parliament gave it a grant of £20,000 in 1744, it could not repay the debts it had contracted before December 1743.[1] In such circumstances, the Company doubtless confined its activities to places in West Africa where conditions were calm enough to ensure a profitable return, and the port of Dahomey was not one of those in the early 1740s.

The French trade at Whydah was no more flourishing than the English. When Levet reached Whydah in June 1743, he found the French fort in its worst condition ever. The roofs were gone, all the walls were almost fallen, hardly any provisions were left, and those were rotten. In 1744, despairing of peaceful conditions ever returning to Dahomey, he proposed that the French activities at Whydah be carried on from two big ships to be stationed permanently in the harbour, from which officers should go ashore only when necessary. This should protect the French from the old Whydah raids and from the Oyo invasions.[2] The Anglo-French war which broke out in 1744, however, prevented his plan from being adopted.[3]

Meanwhile the French trade at Whydah almost completely vanished. One French Company's ship that came there soon after Levet's proposal, departed without a single slave bought. Probably because of this, not a single ship belonging to the French Company came to Whydah to trade between 5 December 1744 and 1 February 1746.[4] Levet thought that the French Company's trade at Whydah was at an end, and he never had the satisfaction of seeing it re-established, as he was expelled from Whydah on 16 September 1747.[5]

The Portuguese trade did not seem to suffer as much as the English and the French. Although the Portuguese fort was blown up by the Dahomeans in 1743, gold and tobacco, their two main articles of trade, secured for them the best offers. The Portuguese themselves considered Whydah the only place in West Africa capable of supplying them with the bulk of the six thousand healthy slaves which they required annually for import into Brazil.[6] Their activities, however, did not greatly

---

[1] 'Minutes of the Court of Assistants', 29 Sept. 1744 (T 70/95).
[2] Levet to la Compagnie des Indes, Juda, 14 March 1743, 31 Jan. 1744 (AN. C. 6/25).
[3] Gaston Martin, *L'Ere des Negriers 1714–1774* (Paris, 1931), p. 215.
[4] Levet to la Compagnie des Indes, Juda, 1 Feb. 1746, 1 Oct. 1747 (AN. C. 6/25); A. F. C. Ryder, 'The Re-establishment of the Portuguese...', in *JHSN*, p. 180.      [5] *Ibid.*      [6] *Ibid.*

enrich the Dahomean monarchy because the Portuguese director did not allow gold to be sold to the king. Moreover, with the
trade in everybody's hands, and Bazilio siding with the old
Whydah against Agaja, it is unlikely that duty was regularly
paid to the king on all sales.

Not only was Tegbesu thus impoverished by being deprived
of the duties that should have accrued through trade, but also
the European captains, particularly the French from Nantes,
continued to trade at Little Popo, Great Popo, Epe and Badagry
where they not only enriched the inhabitants, but also supplied
them with firearms which threatened the security of Dahomey.

The case of *L'Achille* which traded between Cape Mesurado
and Epe, avoiding Whydah, between March and September,
1741[1] and that of *Le Triton* which brought Levet to Whydah in
June 1743 and then went on to trade at Epe,[2] were two of hundreds of similar cases. It was not uncommon for captains of
ships to be instructed, as the Captain of *La Reine des Angers*
was, positively to avoid Whydah, unless they were absolutely
sure beforehand that the conditions there were calm.[3]

By 1744 the ports of Little Popo, Epe and Badagry not only
rivalled, but individually had more trade than Whydah. The
European traders showed that they preferred those neighbouring
ports where, they said, slaves were abundant, and the European
goods, no matter how poor in quality, fetched high prices.[4]

Tegbesu's duties were therefore to re-establish the authority
of the monarchy, bring about the cessation of the Oyo invasions
and the Little Popo and the old Whydah raids, and make the
Whydah port once more the centre of slave export in the Yoruba-
Aja country. These duties required ruthlessness, diplomacy,
administrative capacity and business acumen, qualities which
are not necessarily complementary, but which Tegbesu possessed in a very high degree.

As soon as Tegbesu ascended the throne, he set about making
his title secure, in order to re-establish the absolute authority of
the crown. First, he ordered his elder brother who had contested
the throne with him to be sewn up in a hammock and drowned
in the sea, since royal blood must not be shed. He also ordered

[1] 'Enregistrement des rapports...', 7 June 1742 (ADN. B. 4588).
[2] Levet to la Compagnie des Indes, 14 June 1743 (AN. C. 6/25).
[3] 'Journal de Trait du Navire Negrier "La Reine des Angers" ' (ADN. 16/J/9).
[4] Levet to la Compagnie des Indes, 31 Jan. 1744 (AN. C. 6/25).

all his accomplices to be executed or sold into slavery. He deprived the sons of another brother of all chances of succession by putting a curse upon them.[1]

Tradition explains that Tegbesu took these steps because his eldest brother and his supporters were unwilling to acquiesce in their defeat and were preparing to seize the throne by force, and because the cursed brother had reproached him for high-handedness. Perhaps there was some truth in these explanations, but behind Tegbesu's actions lay the desire to eliminate all those who could question his or his descendants' title.

He seems to have sold into slavery many Dahomean princes who might contest the throne with his own descendants. Don Jeromino or Jeronimo, called Fruku by the Dahomeans, was one of such princes. He was a playmate of the future Kpengla, but was sold into slavery probably to give Kpengla a chance to ascend the throne. He was, however, brought back from slavery in Brazil by Kpengla, after he had spent twenty-four years there and he made a bid for the throne after Kpengla's death.[2] We shall never know how many such princes were sold, but Fruku could not have been the only one.

Tegbesu was also known to have executed many Dahomean citizens whom he considered too rich and any army captain who had lived too long or was too popular for his own convenience. He adopted the convenient Oyo practice of executing every army officer who lost a war.[3]

He restated the law governing the succession, probably with his own amendment. The crown was hereditary in the male line, but it was left to the king to designate which of his sons should succeed him. Irrespective of the number of children that the king might have by his several wives, a successor could only be chosen from among the children born by the six wives designated as being legally capable of supplying a successor.[4]

All these measures left him the undisputed master in Dahomey.

---

[1] E. Dunglas in *E.D.* vol. xix, pp. 165–7; Le Herisse, *L'Ancien Royaume*, pp. 299–300.

[2] Abson to Miles, 14 Dec. 1782 (T 70/1485); A. Dalzel, *History*, p. 223.

[3] Guestard, 'Mémoire...', 1750; Levet to la Compagnie des Indes, 13 Oct. 1746 (AN. C. 6/25); R. Norris, *Memoirs*, pp. 49–53; A. Dalzel, *History*, p. 69. Generally Norris and Dalzel mix up the events of the last years of Agaja's reign and those of the early years of Tegbesu's because of the wrong date which they ascribe to Agaja's death.

[4] De Chenevert and Abbé Bullet: 'Réflexions sur Juda', 1776 (AN. C. 6/27 *bis*).

Contemporary European observers who did not understand his motives completely misinterpreted his actions. Levet, the director of the French fort from 1743 to 1747, thought he was devoid of natural reason and justice. Norris and Dalzel thought him an unmitigated tyrant.

By 1751 Tegbesu's policy of liquidating all rivals had been immensely successful. In that year he designated his eldest son, who was about sixteen years old, as his successor. His intention was widely proclaimed and generally accepted. He then asked Guestard, the French director, to send the prince to France for education. For three years Guestard evaded this request because his instructions forbade him from encouraging Africans to come and study in France, and he could not tell Tegbesu this in so many words.[1]

When Tegbesu saw that foreign education would be unattainable for his son, he decided to find out whether new rivals would challenge his son's right to the throne. On 20 June 1754 it was announced that the king was dead and had been succeeded by his son. For about the next six months Tegbesu kept away from public engagements during which his son probably acted. The Dahomean chiefs at Igelefe declared that they were going to Cana to meet the new king and carried presents along with them. Everybody not privy to the scheme sincerely believed that Tegbesu was dead. As no one challenged his son's right to the throne, his ruse and policy were both proved successful.

Six months afterwards, when Guestard went to Abomey expecting to see the young king, he was shocked to find Tegbesu alive and well. Tegbesu enjoyed Guestard's astonishment and explained things away by saying that he had merely wanted to entice his enemies who might wish to take advantage of his death to bring war on Dahomey.[2]

The authority of the king could not be complete without an obedient and efficient administration. To this task Tegbesu must have addressed himself. Though we do not know the details, he probably set up new chiefs in command of those administrative districts which had lacked them during the uncertain days of the Oyo invasions. What is known is that he applied himself early to the task of re-establishing the Daho-

---

[1] Conseil de direction to la Compagnie des Indes, 10 July 1754; Guestard to la Compagnie des Indes, 10 July 1754 (AN. C. 6/25).
[2] *Ibid.*

mean capital at Abomey. For without a secure centre, control would be difficult.

In 1743, after one of the Oyo invasions, he succeeded in persuading the Oyo, with the aid of lavish presents, to allow him to return to Abomey. About August of that year, he removed the court thither from Allada. In a rather quiet way of announcing this great success, he sent for the European directors to come and see him in his new capital to discuss trade.[1] Levet, who went, found Abomey 'the most unhealthy place in all the Guinea Coast'. Thirteen years of evacuation had certainly made a great difference to the city, but Tegbesu set about purposefully rebuilding it and making it the centre of the Dahomean administration.

We do not know much about the organisation of Tegbesu's court at Abomey. His stay in Oyo had certainly familiarised him with Oyo court institutions, some of which he introduced into his own court. The most notable of these introductions was the *Ilari* system.

The *Ilari* were the people whom the Europeans called 'half heads' from the way their hair was cut. They were, throughout the Yoruba country, messengers-cum-civil-servants used by certain classes of Oba (Kings). The advantage of this class of people for Tegbesu was that they were mobile, could be sent to any part of the kingdom and thus used to check any remote officer or coordinate any national plans. From 1745 onwards, the *Ilari* were frequently sent down to the Europeans' forts.[2]

Tegbesu must also have created chiefs to fill up any vacant posts or new vacancies which he may have created for the overall national administration. Only a few of the national officers were well known during his reign. The Temigan (later Migan) was the equivalent of a modern prime minister for he was the general overseer of 'all sorts of affairs'. The Mehu, next in rank to him, was in charge of finance and commerce. The Agau was the General of the army. The Ajau was the 'first Counsellor', and the Diau was the chief eunuch and guardian of the king's harem. There were also many other lesser ministers and officials stationed in the capital, each with his own specialised functions.

[1] Levet to la Compagnie des Indes, 25 Feb. 1744 (AN. C. 6/25).

[2] 'Journals and Ledgers C.C.C.', 1 Jan. to 30 April 1746 (T 70/704). 'Half heads' were first mentioned as messengers of the king of Dahomey in January 1746. Henceforth they became recognised as the normal royal messengers.

All the most important chiefs had lieutenants. The Aplogan[1] was the Migan's assistant; the Yovogan, governor of Whydah, was the Mehu's assistant and the Sogan, master of the horses, was the Agau's assistant. The Posu and the Fusupo were probably commanders of the right and the left wings of the army.[2]

The position of the administrative division of Whydah was of vital importance to Dahomey, especially as Tegbesu believed 'that it was better to trade than to make war'. It was essential that the officers there should be absolutely under the authority of the king, reliable, able to bring as much wealth to the king as possible without ruining the trade, and entirely free from the temptation to amass wealth for themselves, at the expense of the royal interest.

These conditions were difficult to satisfy. An excessive zeal to serve the king might lead to extortion, which would either scare away the ships and thus diminish trade, or make the directors complain to the king. Either of these developments might cost the responsible minister his head. On the other hand, failure to satisfy the king might give rise to the suspicion that the officer was either incompetent or amassing wealth for himself, both of which faults might also incur the death penalty. The result was that execution became the normal occupational hazard of the civil administrators of Whydah.

The multiplication of officials increased rather than diminished this risk. Up to 1746 the Yovogan, based at Igelefe, was the sole administrator of the Whydah division. In that year, an officer called the 'Coki' was appointed.[3] The following year another officer called the 'Bunio' was also appointed.[4] In theory these two officers were to assist the Yovogan as members of his council. In fact they were spies on him and on each other. As all the posts were completely at the disposal of the king, an under-officer who was a good spy or tell-tale could expect to occupy the highest post.

Tegan, who had been appointed the Yovogan by Agaja in

---

[1] Aplogan means owner or chief of the Aplo (or lance).
[2] De Chenevert and Abbé Bullet: 'Réflexions sur Juda', 1776 (AN. C. 6/27 *bis*). The title of the Sogan was probably a new one created during the reign of the Tegbesu, for at the end of his reign there were only sixteen horses in Dahomey and not a single cavalry man.
[3] 'Journals and Ledgers, C.C.C.', Nov. and Dec. 1746 (T 70/704).
[4] 'Accounts and Journal, C.C.C.', Sept.–Dec. 1747 (T 70/423).

January 1733, occupied the post until 1743. In that year he lost his head because Levet, the French director, had been displeased with his zeal in the service of Dahomey. Levet alleged that 'it was he who by his dark practices planned and carried out the deportation of Levens, and has for some time been sending messengers to propose to several officers of this fort that he would make them directors.'[1] In addition, he said that he had given 'insults and continuous vexations' to the French and the Portuguese.

On 20 July 1743 he represented Tegan to Tegbesu in such a thoroughly unfavourable way that on the 27th Tegan was seized when he visited Allada to rejoice with the king on the successful blowing up of the Portuguese fort. Within fourteen hours he was beheaded and all his property was confiscated by the king.[1]

Tegan's fate was not unique. Of the nine more Yovogan appointed between 1743 and 1763, five were beheaded, three of them between April and November 1755, and one, in 1760, after occupying the post for only twenty days. Three were recalled in disgrace and presumably executed and the ninth, still alive in 1763, had been severely wounded by the old Whydah and narrowly escaped death. Most of the executions had been decided on the basis of unproved allegation.[2] Nor did the under-officers escape. Of the five Coki sent to Whydah between August 1754 and October 1759, only one died a natural death.[3]

Although these executions, like the liquidation of all his rivals, revealed Tegbesu's ruthlessness, they nevertheless strengthened the king's hold on Whydah administration, and may be typical of the way in which Tegbesu kept on their toes all the officers whom he sent to all the administration divisions of his kingdom.

Because of the continuous threat posed by Ashampo of Little Popo and the old Whydah against the port and the forts at

[1] Levet to la Compagnie des Indes, 20 Aug. 1743 (AN. C. 6/25). This would seem to be the real end of Tegan whom Norris and Dalzel call Tauga. Norris and Dalzel were probably mixed up about this first Yovogan and the man who headed the revolt, instigated by Tegbesu, against the English fort in 1745. In either case, the fascinating story about the fidelity of Tegan's wives is difficult to fit in. See R. Norris, *Memoirs*, pp. 40–8; A. Dalzel, *History*, pp. 91–6.

[2] 'Accounts and Journals, C.C.C.', 1 Jan.–30 June 1748 (T 70/424); 'Accounts and Daybooks for Whydah', 30 April, 30 June, Dec. 1755, 30 June 1756 (T 70/1158); 18 and 28 April 1760, 4 Oct. 1761 (T 70/1159). C. W. Newbury, *The Western Slave Coast*, p. 25.

[3] 'Accounts and Daybooks for Whydah', 31 Aug. 1754, 30 April 1755, Sept. and Oct. 1756, 19 Aug. 1757, Sept. and Oct. 1759 (T 70/1158).

Igelefe, it was essential, in settling the Whydah administration, that the coastal garrison should be strengthened. The military post under the command of the Cockeracoe, established by Agaja, had grown into a small town called 'Cockeracoe Croom'. In the early 1740s, this garrison was not strong enough to withstand the incursions from the west. In 1747 it was badly defeated. Between August and December 1747, therefore, Tegbesu strengthened the garrison village. Not only did he replace the Cockeracoe who had been killed by the Little Popo, but he also sent down one more officer, the Cockavo and his contingent to live there permanently.[1] He made it a regular habit to send down two officers and their contingents as an extra precaution whenever an invasion was expected from Ashampo and the old Whydah.[1] For every major threat, he sent down the Agau and all the generals under him.

No administrative settlement of Whydah could be complete without bringing the directors of the forts fully into the system. Tegbesu realised that their position was of very great importance indeed in his scheme. Dahomeans called them 'guardians' of the country[2] because they could attract ships to Whydah harbour by giving a favourable report of the harbour, and could drive ships away by giving an unfavourable one. Tegbesu therefore made it a policy never to allow in Dahomey any director whose friendliness to the Dahomean authorities was not beyond doubt. He also associated the directors with all his efforts to revive the Dahomean trade in slaves.

One of the first things he did on his accession was to deport Levens, the French director,[3] and Bazilio, the Portuguese director for the unfriendly parts they had both played during the Oyo and Little Popo invasions of 1739-43. Between 1742 and 1766, three more Portuguese directors and two more French were deported from Dahomey.[4] Whenever Tegbesu was asked

---

[1] 'Accounts and Journals, C.C.C.', Sept.–Dec. 1747 (T 70/423).
[2] Levet to la Compagnie des Indes, 31 Jan. 1744 (AN. C. 6/25). S. Berbain, *Le Comptoir Français de Juda au XVIII<sup>e</sup> Siècle* (Paris, 1942), p. 97, gives the procedure as described by a French trader, which confirms the Dahomean view of the role of the directors.
[3] Levet to la Compagnie des Indes, 20 Aug. 1743 (AN. C. 6/25); 'Extrait d'une lettre particulière écritte de Juda', 16 Aug. 1743 (AN. C. 6/25); Conselho Ultramarino to King of Portugal, Lisbon, 29 Oct. 1744 (AHU. S. Tome Caixa 5); A. F. C. Ryder, 'The Re-establishment of the Portuguese...', in *JHSN*, p. 171; A. Dalzel, *History*, pp. 83–5. Dalzel's dating is inaccurate.　　　　[4] See Appendix 2.

why he had taken such actions, he replied that those officers were not friends of the country and were attempting to spoil the slave trade.

It was, however, not only by deportation that he kept the European directors loyal to the Dahomean interest. He also tried hard to bring them into the administrative system of Dahomey. He made it a practice to get personally acquainted with every new director, both formally and informally. In 1743 he invited Levet to visit him at Allada immediately after his arrival,[1] and in 1746 he invited Turner, the English director, to come and spend some time with him at Dido,[2] somewhere north of Abomey. During these visits, the directors were made to feel free to discuss their complaints with the king or give suggestions on Whydah trade. On other occasions they were also encouraged to take their complaints to the king. If Tegbesu had anything he wanted to discuss with them he said it then or he invited all the directors at some other time to tell them.

In this way the directors came to know and accept their rights, duties and places within the administrative system of Dahomey. Generally they were regarded as being just like any other Dahomean chiefs even though their special position as foreigners was recognised. They too accepted the position by giving presents whenever they visited the king just as any Dahomean chief did.[3] They also had gifts bestowed on them in return just as on any Dahomean chief. They acquired the right to complain to the king whenever they felt they had been wronged by any of the king's officers. By this right they came to have a large say on the conduct of any Yovogan and, as Tegan's case shows, their opinion of any Yovogan could make or unmake that officer. This regularised position greatly attached most of the European directors during Tegbesu's reign to the Dahomean interest and brought them out in defence of Dahomey when the Little Popo and the old Whydah renewed their raids on Dahomey after 1752.

[1] Levet to la Compagnie des Indes, Juda, 14 June 1743 (AN. C. 6/25).
[2] Levet to la Compagnie des Indes, Juda, 25 Feb. 1744 (AN. C. 6/25); 'Journals and Ledgers, C.C.C.', Jan. and Feb. 1746 (T 70/703); Nov. and Dec. 1746 (T 70/704); 'Accounts and Journals, C.C.C.', Nov. and Dec. 1747 (T 70/423); to cite only a few examples of when Tegbesu invited directors for personal acquaintance.
[3] By 1751 this had become the normal practice. 'Accounts and Journals, C.C.C.', 20 Jan.–30 June 1751 (T 70/425); Conseil de direction to la Compagnie des Indes, 18 Feb. 1753 (AN. C. 6/25).

Stability could not exist in Dahomey while the Oyo persisted in their invasions. The only way to get them to stop was to offer them terms that they would be ready to accept, and to observe such conditions as they might impose. Tegbesu's long residence in Oyo must have given him a fairly accurate idea of the power of Oyo and of the men who ran its affairs. It must also have made him wary of offending Oyo. Indeed, it seems that throughout his reign he studiously avoided any action that might cause an Oyo invasion of Dahomey. However, it was not until after a few Oyo invasions, and threats of invasion that he reached a definitive settlement with them.

He gave the Oyo a very lavish present in 1743 after one of their invasions. In the middle of 1746 he also asked the forts to defray some of the customary presents demanded by Oyo.[1] It was not, however, until 1748 that a settlement was reached.

In March of that year, news reached the forts at Igelefe that the Oyo were up in arms against Dahomey, that Tegbesu 'had quitted his habitation and carried all his valuable movables into the bush, and that he was making large dashes to avoid the impending blow'. In a hurry the Yovogan and the most important officers at Igelefe were summoned to the king's secret hideout for urgent advice and necessary contributions.[2]

The preliminary presents were very effective, for the Oyo did not invade Dahomey. Negotiations then followed on a definitive peace treaty, which was happily concluded, probably around April, definitely before 30 June 1748.[2]

The terms were probably largely a confirmation of those reached in 1730. In addition Tegbesu must have been told to leave the ports east of Jakin in peace for, until towards the end of the century when Oyo's power started to decline, Dahomey never again attacked any place east of Jakin, though it would have liked to attack Epe particularly to destroy the port.

Probably during these negotiations also, the annual tributes to be paid perpetually to Oyo were settled. Traditions both at Abomey and Oyo are remarkably agreed on these annual tributes. They consisted of forty-one men, forty-one young women, forty-one guns, four hundred bags of cowries and four hundred corals.[3]

---

[1] 'Journals and Ledgers, C.C.C.', Nov. and Dec. 1746 (T 70/704).
[2] 'Accounts and Journals, C.C.C.', 1 Jan.–30 June 1748 (T 70/424).
[3] Le Herisse, *L'Ancien Royaume*, p. 319; E. Dunglas in *E.D.* vol. xix, pp. 146, 171.

*Dahomey and its Neighbours*

This was a very heavy tribute. A bag (*oke*) of cowries consisted of twenty thousand pieces. Four hundred bags would therefore consist of eight million pieces. In the mid-eighteenth century, when twenty thousand pieces were worth four pounds,[1] eight million pieces would be worth £1,600. When the value of all the other articles of the tribute are added, the extent of Oyo's power and the burden which Dahomey had to bear annually through this submission can be estimated. This tribute was paid annually in November, and carried from Cana, where the Oyo officers checked it, to Oyo by a Dahomean chief specially created for the purpose. It was paid for the next seventy years until shortly after 1818 when Gezo successfully declared his independence.

There was more to the 1748 treaty than the mere annual payment of tribute by Dahomey. The payments indicated that ultimate sovereignty in Dahomey remained with the Alafin of Oyo. This gave Oyo enormous responsibilities as well as rights in Dahomey. For instance, Oyo undertook the defence of Dahomey against external aggression and stationed its forces for this purpose in the Atakpame area. In 1764, when one Odanquah of Ashanti trespassed with his soldiers into the area, the Oyo forces wiped out his whole twenty thousand soldiers.[2]

Oyo also made laws for Dahomey, though we shall never know how many. The one law which the Dahomean kings long remembered with wounded pride was that which prohibited any Dahomean, be he king or commoner, from wearing silk damask in Cana.[3] Cana itself appears to have been the Oyo headquarters, where the kings of Dahomey had a palace but no authority at all and where any Dahomean was free to live. Generally no Dahomean law bound any Oyo citizen in Dahomey.

Oyo could ask Dahomey to send contingents to any military

---

[1] I have arrived at this and subsequent amounts in this work, by a series of calculations and equations as follows: 40 cowries = 1 tockey, 5 tockies (200 cowries) = 1 gallina; 20 gallinas = 1 cabess; 5 cabesses (20,000 cowries) = 1 ounce. Every Yoruba also knows that 20,000 cowries = 1 oke (bag). In 1750, 8 ounces = 1 mark of gold, i.e. about £32; 1 ounce (bag) would therefore be about £4. See Guestard, 'Memoir...', 1750; A. Dalzel, *History*, pp. 133–5, notes, where the value of cowries would seem to have been less towards 1790.

[2] William Mutter to African Committee, 27 May 1764 (T 70/31). This is probably the engagement recorded by Dupuis as having taken place between Dahomey and Ashanti during the reign of Osei Akwasi, king of Ashanti, see Dupuis, *Journal of a Residence in Ashantee* (1824), pp. 238–9.

[3] Dawson to Fitzgerald, 17 Nov. 1862 (C. A. 2/016).

124

expeditions that it might wish to make, or could commission Dahomey to fight such wars under, or without, Oyo officers. It could also prevent Dahomey from undertaking any war. Between 1783 and 1789 Abiodun, the Alafin, exercised all these rights successfully to the great annoyance of the Dahomean authorities.[1]

The kings of Oyo became the heirs of all the most important chiefs in Dahomey, from the king downwards. In accordance with this right, when the Mehu died in 1779, Abiodun demanded all his movable property, including his wives.[2] It is probable, too, that every Dahomean king on accession was required to send presents to Oyo, though we have no definite example of this usage. Certainly, whenever an Alafin ascended the throne or did something noteworthy, the king of Dahomey sent presents to Oyo. In 1774, when Abiodun overcame Gaha in a civil war in Oyo, Kpengla sent presents.[3]

These rights are enormous and there may be many more than are known. They certainly show that the overlordship of Oyo over Dahomey was not as nebulous and as remote as the oral traditions would lead us to suppose, and will explain the hearty dislike with which the Dahomeans regarded the rule of Oyo. Only the purely internal administration was left to Dahomey.

In some respects, even this settlement would appear to have been very generous and its term much lighter than those which Oyo made with some other tributary states. For there is no tradition which suggests that the Oyo placed any *Ajele* (resident superintendents) in any of the Dahomey towns, as they were, for example, in the Egba towns. Moreover, Dahomey was allowed to retain its own army and seems to have been allowed military initiative northwards and westwards of Abomey, wherever Oyo interests were not likely to be harmed. These concessions allowed Dahomey to revive and grow in future.[4]

The conclusion of the peace treaty in 1748 was an occasion of the greatest joy to the Dahomeans as it must have been pleasing to the Oyo. All round Dahomey it was celebrated with dances and feasts. At Igelefe, the Yovogan, the war generals and captains, councillors, chiefs, traders and all the inhabitants of the town

---

[1] Numerous examples of this occur between 1774 and 1789 as will be seen in the next chapter.

[2] A. Dalzel, *History*, pp. 173–7. Dalzel's dating of the Mehu's death is inaccurate.     [3] A. Dalzel, *History*, p. 158.

[4] 'Accounts and Journals, C.C.C.', 1 Jan.–30 June 1748 (T 70/424).

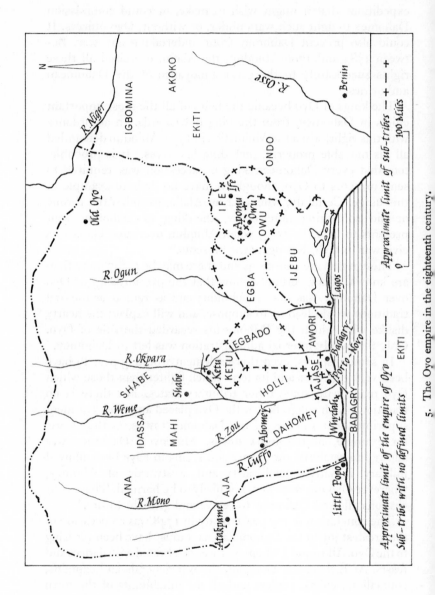

5. The Oyo empire in the eighteenth century.

danced round the forts. The European communities were called upon to provide presents. The English fort alone expended liquors worth £13 on the one day of celebration.[1]

With his own constitutional position secure, the administration put in order and the danger of Oyo invasion removed, Tegbesu could concentrate wholeheartedly on the promotion of the slave trade, which he had regarded since his accession as one of his primary objectives. Indeed, most of the administrative measures which he took at Whydah and his settlement with the Oyo were designedly encouraging to the export trade of slaves in Dahomey.

It was certainly the keystone of Tegbesu's policy that the energies of the country were to be devoted to the slave trade rather than to military adventure. This was probably partly because the militarism of Agaja, though successful in its earlier years, had nearly ended in the complete destruction of Dahomey. It may also have been that Tegbesu saw the slave trade as the best way to refill the empty coffers which he had inherited.

His policy was stated in 1754 when he heard of the impending Anglo-French war and tried to offer his good offices to bring peace. Devaynes the English director reported that

the king of Dahomey sent down two of his half heads as messengers accompanied by the Viceroy and other caboceers to desire I would write home to the king and company to desire in a friendly way that they would be at peace as he heard there was a report of an approaching war in Europe and that it was better to trade than to make war.[2]

He tried first to secure a complete monopoly of the trade in Dahomey for the crown, then to make Igelefe the only slaving port in Yoruba-Aja and finally to create an atmosphere in which the trade would flourish. At the end of 1744 or early 1745 he rounded up and executed all the Dahomean private slave exporters at Igelefe. He then invited the Migan and the Mehu to recommend two or three officers each, who were sent to Igelefe as 'king's traders' and in whose hands the whole export trade in slaves in Dahomey was concentrated.[3]

This action at once restored the king's monopoly and avoided

---

[1] 'Accounts and Journals, C.C.C.', 1 Jan.–30 June 1748 (T 70/424).
[2] Thomas Melvil to African Committee, 30 Nov. 1754 (T 70/1523).
[3] Levet to la Compagnie des Indes, 1 Feb. 1746 (AN. C. 6/25).

the kind of dissatisfaction which Agaja's single-handed mono-poly had caused. He reimposed Agaja's law which stipulated that goods once landed in Dahomey could not be re-exported and he maintained that it was his right, and not the directors', to decide who should trade at Whydah port and in what com-modities. So he expelled Bazilio, partly for forbidding the Portuguese traders to trade freely in gold, and Levet, partly for preventing the French officers in the fort from trading.

Early in 1746, in May 1747 and again in May 1748, he pro-claimed a law designed to make Whydah the entrepôt of the Yoruba-Aja country. He ruled that the paths were free and open for anybody to go to and come from Epe, Weme and Ajara to bring the slaves from those places to Igelefe for export. At the same time he ruled that European captains must not go to any of those places to trade, and he made it clear that if any of them were caught trading there, they would be ill-treated.[1]

This dislike of Europeans trading in the neighbouring ports is a recurring theme in Dahomey's relations with all its neigh-bours. The attempt to centralise the trade at Whydah recalls Allada's policy between 1640 and 1670. The refusal of the Europeans to obey this law after its first promulgation led to Tegbesu's raid on Epe in 1747, where he seized all the European traders.

Tegbesu saw to it that the European forts in his territory were kept in a fit condition to carry on the trade. He showed a particular concern whenever any of them was in difficulty, either for lack of a director or of means of sustenance.

Although he had blown up the Portuguese fort in 1743 in an attempt to reassert his authority over Igelefe, and over the Europeans, he had offered to rebuild it free of charge as soon as Bazilio, the director he hated, was safely out of the country, and he had appointed another director to take care of the fort until the Portuguese authorities appointed one. When his nominee died in 1746, he showed the same concern that the fort should not be without a head, though Nunes, the Portuguese whom he appointed, was a rogue whom he had to drive out of the country as soon as he discovered his true character.[2]

---

[1] 'Journals and Ledgers, C.C.C.', Nov. and Dec. 1746 (T 70/704); 'Ac-counts and Journals, C.C.C.', Nov. and Dec. 1747 (T 70/423), 1 Jan.–30 June 1748 (T 70/424).

[2] Conselho Ultramarino to King of Portugal, Lisbon, 29 Oct. 1744 (AHU. S. Tome Caixa 5); Levet to La Compagnie, 20 Aug. 1743 (AN. C. 6/25);

In the same way, he appointed Druno de la Court to succeed Levet, the French director whom he had expelled in 1747, and also lent the French fort 4,000 'livres' of cowries free of interest to tide over the difficulties of its lack of provision.[1] When the English fort had no substantive director between the departure of Gregory, late in 1745, and the arrival of Turner on 1 January 1746, Tegbesu sent two *Ilari* to wait constantly at the English fort and to see that it came to no harm. When Turner came, he was welcomed like a royal visitor.[2]

One factor outside the control of Tegbesu helped to increase the number of ships that came to Whydah port from 1749 onwards. In that year, the British decided to enforce the exclusion of the French from any trade on the Gold Coast. They laid claim to the whole of Anomabu where the French used to trade and, in spite of French protests, maintained the ban by force in 1750 and 1751. When the British fort at Anomabu was built, their control of the trade of the area was complete and a great number of French ships which would have traded at Amissa and Koromantine, increasingly came to Whydah from 1750 onwards.[3]

To make sure that the monarchy derived as much financial advantage as possible from these exertions, Tegbesu created, or resuscitated, a very efficient system of collecting taxes from all parts of the kingdom. The inhabitants nearest the capital were asked to pay in kind by working for the king for a specific number of days in the year. Those farther away paid in cash (cowries) or with the products of their farms. Collectors were posted everywhere, on the high roads, in the market places, at the entrance to the forts and on the beach.[4]

In the first half of 1751 Tegbesu took one more step in the interest of making Whydah the greatest centre for slave export

'Journal and Ledgers, C.C.C.', 1 Jan.–30 April 1746 (T 70/804); A. F. C. Ryder, 'The Re-establishment of the Portuguese...', in *JHSN*, pp. 172–8.

[1] 'Accounts and Journals, C.C.C.', 1 Sept.–31 Dec. 1747 (T 70/423); 20 Jan.–30 June 1751 (T 70/425); Conseil de direction to la Compagnie des Indes, 18 Feb. and 1 April 1753 (AN. C. 6/25).

[2] 'Accounts and Journals, C.C.C.', Nov. and Dec. 1746 (T 70/704).

[3] J. R. and W. H. to the French Captain at Cormantine and Amissa, 22 Feb. 1749; Le Chevalier de Glanderes to John Roberts and Council, 12 Feb. 1750; J. R. and W. H. to R.A.C., 24 March 1750 (T 70/68); Thomas Melville to African Committee, 11 June 1752 (T 70/518).

[4] De Chenevert and Abbé Bullet, 'Réflexions sur Juda', 1776 (AN. C. 6/27 *bis*).

in Yoruba-Aja. On the advice of the director of the Portuguese fort, he sent a two-man economic mission to the Viceroy of Brazil to ask for an increase in the Brazilian trade to Whydah and to give Tegbesu's friendly greeting to the Viceroy.[1] Tegbesu chose Brazil rather than any European country, probably for continuity of foreign policy, for it was the Portuguese who had first befriended his father Agaja. It was also probably their trade which remained the most constant during the depression of the last years of Agaja and of the early years of Tegbesu.

The mission, however, was accorded a very discourteous reception by the Viceroy of Brazil who lodged the ambassadors in a Jesuit convent, and refused to recognise them as ministers of the king of Dahomey. His excuse was that Tegbesu had blown up the Portuguese fort in 1743 and had not rebuilt it. In exchange for four women, three men, six specially manufactured *ofi* garments and a sheep which Tegbesu sent to the king of Portugal through the Viceroy, the Viceroy gave the ambassadors some dresses and a high-toned message. He stipulated that if Tegbesu wanted any trade with the Portuguese, he must repair the Portuguese fort, and restore all the Portuguese property that had been taken away by the Dahomean authorities.

The mission was therefore a failure. It had not been necessary. Portuguese needs, and not Dahomean invitation, forced them to stay in Whydah. Portuguese trade did not diminish because their fortress was blown up in 1743 nor could the mission have increased it appreciably unless there had been an increased demand for slaves in the Brazilian market.

This really was one of the main weaknesses of the methods which Tegbesu was employing to raise the fortunes of Dahomey. The revival which he sought was based on two external factors. The first was the transatlantic slave trade, which depended on European politics, needs and moods. The second was Oyo, the action of which was again conditioned by all kinds of local political and economic developments. Both these two factors were completely outside the control of the Dahomean authorities. To that extent therefore, Dahomean wealth could only last so long as these external conditions were concurrently favourable to it.

[1] Censelho Ultramarino to King of Portugal, Lisbon, 5 May 1752 (A. H. U. Codice 254 F. 245 V.).

That they might not always be continuously favourable was shown by the outbreak of the Seven Years War and the passing of a Portuguese law regulating their captains' trade in West Africa. Tegbesu's message to the king of England in 1754 about the impending Anglo-French war was sent partly because he realized that any such war was bound to affect his own economy. When the message failed to have any effect he re-enacted the law which made Whydah a neutral port.[1] In spite of his efforts, the outbreak of the war meant a great decrease in the number of ships calling at Whydah simply because fewer ships came out from Europe.

Equally disadvantageous to the Dahomean economy was the unexpected change in Portuguese trading habits. Late in 1756 or early 1757, the Brazilian authorities ruled that Portuguese ships going to 'Costa da Mina' must trade there in turns, one at a time. Tegbesu thought that the law encroached on his own prerogative and protested very strongly. In spite of his protests, however, the Portuguese directors from 1757 onwards enforced the law very rigorously on the Portuguese captains, and were not deterred by Tegbesu's deportation of the first director who attempted to do so.[2] Whydah port was at a disadvantage because it was there only that the Portuguese authority had a representative who could enforce the law. Impatient or even lawless captains therefore went to the other ports near Whydah, causing a loss to the Dahomean economy.

The second major weakness of Tegbesu's methods was perhaps a much more dangerous one than the first. His policy of putting trade before war meant that the Dahomean army was badly neglected. Observers who saw the soldiers trained under Tegbesu remarked that they had no discipline and knew no tactics.[3] That was a great deterioration from the days of Agaja. It may have been that the terrible Oyo invasions, and Tegbesu's first-hand acquaintance with the might of Oyo had convinced him that it was a waste of time and national resources to encourage militarism in Dahomey.

---

[1] 'Accounts and Daybooks for Whydah', 31 Dec. 1755 (T 70/1158).
[2] Theodozio Rodrigues da Costa to Viceroy of Brazil, Ajuda, 10 Dec. 1757 (APB. OR. 61, f. 153); 'Accounts and Daybooks for Whydah', May and June 1759 (T 70/1159); Felix Jose da Govea to Viceroy of Brazil, Ajuda, 29 Jan. 1761 (APB. OR. 69, f. 97).
[3] De Chenevert and Abbé Bullet, 'Réflexions sur Juda', 1776 (AN. C. 6/27 bis).

It is certainly no accident that the Dahomean oral traditions recall only two major wars fought during the long reign of Tegbesu, one against the Mahi and the other against Za. All the other campaigns were minor ones, probably the mere despatch of raiding parties rather than wars.[1]

Of the two major wars, only the one against the Gbowele province of Mahi undertaken in 1753 could strictly speaking be regarded as being a war, for the one against Za was more like the quelling of a civil rebellion. Dahomey traditions say that the cause of the war against the Mahi was that a Dahomean criminal had fled to Gbowele and had not been returned despite Tegbesu's insistent demands. Contemporaries said that the war was provoked purely and simply by Tegbesu, who insisted that the Mahi must have a king instead of being a republic. There followed a brief campaign. On 10 March 1753 the Dahomeans announced that they had been victorious.[2] It is, however, doubtful whether their victory was anything final or spectacular.

The neglect of the army meant that often the raiding parties were unsuccessful and Dahomey was unable to procure for itself the slaves needed for export. Therefore it gradually came to depend on those sold to it by the Oyo traders. Since those traders sold to many ports, the Dahomean supply became insecure.

Tegbesu's exertions also produced unfavourable reactions which increased the insecurity of his achievements. His repressive measures drove away many people from Dahomey. These exiles were able to live in other territories under the general peace imposed by Oyo. This meant that Dahomey no longer had any special advantages to offer anyone seeking security or adventure as it had during Agaja's reign. It was therefore no longer attractive to new immigrants who might have made good the losses through emigration. By 1750 the population of Dahomey was noticeably diminished, a further contributory cause of military weakness. At the same time the neighbouring territories, to which the Dahomean exiles had fled,

---

[1] Le Herrise, *L'Ancien Royaume*, p. 301; R. Norris, *Memoirs*, pp. 21–4; A. Dalzel, *History*, pp. 75–7; Norris, followed by Dalzel, implies that the campaign against Mahi continued for many years, but his account is confused.

[2] 'Accounts and Daybooks for Whydah', 10 March 1753 (T 70/1158); Conseil de direction to la Compagnie des Indes, 18 Feb. 1753 (AN. C. 6/25); A. Dalzel, *History*, pp. 75–7. Dalzel's dating is inaccurate.

disliked Dahomey intensely,[1] whether as a result of the activities
of the Dahomean exiles is uncertain.

Moreover there were internal revolts in Dahomey itself. Two
of these have been recorded, one in 1754 and the other in 1758.
Both are obscure, but they appear to have been serious. In the
former, the rulers of Tori and Ajara revolted simultaneously,
but they were taken alive after a brief campaign and the movement collapsed. The second was hatched in Abomey itself and
headed by a man who appears to have been very important,
though his identity is not disclosed. He was, however, caught and
beheaded in September 1758. His head was publicly exhibited,
not only at Abomey, but also at Igelefe.[2]

The state monopoly of the slave trade in Dahomey was not
advantageous to the European slave traders, and indeed displeased them. It meant that the king could charge whatever
price he wished for his slaves, demand the European goods he
needed and pay whatever price he thought reasonable for such
goods. Levet, the director of the French fort, put the frustration
of the resident European traders as follows: 'if anyone has
some merchandise to sell, he must sell it to them at the price
they want or he may keep his ware since he can only sell to the
[king's] merchants who find too dear everything that is not
given to them free'.[3]

Levet also pointed out that the slave trade in Dahomey was
not regarded as a free economic activity, but as part of the
national or even international politics, to be rigidly controlled
by the king.

Indeed the Dahomean authorities made it plain that they expected the directors of the forts to encourage ships from their
several countries to come to trade only at Whydah and to prevent
them from going to any of the other neighbouring ports. Whenever a ship went past the Whydah harbour or simply sent its
boats there from Little or Great Popo, the representative of the
nation, whose ship it was, was subjected to official inquisition.
If any director remained long in Dahomey without his nation
sending large numbers of ships, he was regarded as an enemy of
the king, treated with disdain and sometimes ejected from the

---

[1] Guestard, 'Mémoire...', 1750 (AN. C. 6/25).
[2] 'Accounts and Daybooks for Whydah', 31 Oct. 1754, Sept.–Oct. 1758
(T 70/1158).
[3] Levet to la Compagnie des Indes, 1 Feb. 1746 (AN. C. 6/25).

country.[1] These attitudes made the resident directors fear to offend Tegbesu but drove away the European slave captains.

The weaknesses of, and the reactions to, Tegbesu's policies and methods did not yet constitute a serious threat to the ends which he sought. In general, Tegbesu was immensely successful up to 1767. By 1747 he had put the finances of the monarchy in order. By 1750 'the commerce of Whydah was easily very large',[2] and in the early 1750s the export trade of Whydah, which was almost nil in 1740, exceeded those of Badagry and Epe. The measure of his success can be appreciated by a look at the volume and organisation of the trade at Whydah in 1750.

It was then estimated that about nine thousand slaves were exported annually from Whydah by the French and the Portuguese alone. The English trade there was still much less important but they too must have been taking a few hundred out. These slaves were made up from the Fon, the Whydah, the Allada (all Aja) and the Anago (Yoruba). The Portuguese bought the Aja but not the Yoruba, and exported about four thousand of the total. The French bought the rest.[3]

Each slave cost between 6 and 8 'ounces' or between £24 and £32 in eighteenth-century money. On this reckoning Tegbesu's income in 1750 from the slaves exported by the French and Portuguese amounted to something between £216,000 and £288,000. If to this we add the customs duties that the ships paid before they were allowed to trade,[4] the annual presents and other presents to Tegbesu, and the unknown value of the English trade, it will be agreed that Tegbesu's income from the slave export in the mid-eighteenth century was very substantial.

The Dahomean citizens who were lucky enough not to have been sold into slavery, also profited from the sale of their less fortunate kinsfolk. The slave trade as revived by Tegbesu was a

---

[1] Levet to la Compagnie des Indes, 31 Jan. 1744, 20 Aug. 1743 (AN. C. 6/25).
[2] Guestard, 'Mémoire pour servir à l'intelligence du Commerce de Juda...', 1750 (AN. C. 6/25).
[3] *Ibid.*
[4] The customs duties varied from time to time according to the law imposed by the king of Dahomey. In the 1790s every three-masted ship paid the value of twelve slaves in goods. In 1803 the value of seven slaves was paid for every mast. C. W. Newbury, *The Western Slave Coast*, p. 27; John Macleod, *A Voyage to Africa*, etc. (London, 1820), p. 11.

highly organised, if inhuman, business. From the moment of his arrival at Whydah harbour to that of his departure with a full cargo, each slaving captain had temporary establishments to facilitate his trade. At the beach he erected a tent, which served him as a clearing house, in which goods from his ship could be kept, en route for the forts. Here also the slaves he purchased could be kept, on their way to the ship's hold. At Igelefe, he also had another establishment, usually beneath the walls of the fort which belonged to his nation.

For his use in these two establishments, he employed, for the whole of his stay, Dahomean citizens who served him as porters, canoemen, messengers, storekeepers, labourers, washerwomen, water carriers, rollers of water, slave prison keepers and night-watchmen. He also had the services of the beach garrison.

All these workers had their daily pay standardised. A porter earned three tockies (120 cowries) for each load from the beach to the forts. If the parcel was heavier than normal, he took more in proportion to the weight. Each canoeman was paid a hat and a covercloth before the captain descended on land, the chief canoeman being paid more. After landing, each was given one anchor of brandy (8 gallons) for successfully crossing the terrible bar. Every Sunday, each crew was paid one cabess of cowries (20,000 cowries) and a flagon of brandy. At the end of the trade, they all had another cabess of cowries and an anchor of brandy.

On landing, each slave captain paid the chief of the beach garrison an anchor of brandy and a hat. On departure, he paid a covercloth, a barrel of flour and a quart of salt meat. The erection of a hut at the beach cost the captain four cabesses of cowries (80,000) and an anchor of brandy.

Messengers were paid two tockies (80 cowries) daily, and a flagon of brandy every Sunday. At the end of the trade, each messenger was paid an anchor of brandy and a piece of cloth. Each of the store labourers got two tockies daily and half a piece of cloth at the end of the trade.

The woman water carrier, the washerwoman, the day watch and the rollers of water casks, took two tockies each per day with further payments in cloth or brandy. The public crier who announced the permission for a captain to open his trade was paid ten gallinas (2,000 cowries) and a flagon of brandy. The messenger who went to inform the king of the arrival of a captain, was paid five gallinas (1,000 cowries). If he was a 'king's boy', he had double payment.[1]

These wages were fairly high in relation to the cost of living. It was possible to feed well for a whole day on something between three and five cowries, so that a man who earned 80 cowries a day was doing well indeed. The more ships that called at Whydah port, the more workers would benefit from high wages, the steadier would the wages be, and the more prosperous would the Dahomeans appear.

It is no wonder then that in the last years of Tegbesu's reign and even in the early years of his successor, Dahomey wore a prosperous look, to a degree which astounded Norris. The kingdom was packed with towns and villages whose population, reduced though they must have been if compared with what they had been fifty years earlier, were still contented and well fed. The king himself, far from being a wanted fugitive, hiding in remote forests, had seven palaces. Tegbesu lived in very great affluence as Norris's visit to his court in 1772 showed, and as the eyewitness report of the *Ato Anubomey* (Annual Customs) of the same year would suggest.

During this ceremony, it was the practice to mount a daily exhibition of the king's belongings. Each day's exhibition must be different from the next one and no one single item was exhibited twice for the whole three months of the *Ato* ceremony.

Norris commented on some of the daily exhibitions which he saw while he was present. Of that mounted on 12 February 1772, when the daily exhibition had been going on for about two months, he said,

the variety and abundance of rich silks, silver bracelets and other ornaments, coral and a profusion of other valuable beads exceeded my expectation, besides there was another display of forty women with silver helmets.[2]

On the final day of the *Ato*

a large stage is erected near one of the palace gates adorned with flags and umbrellas and surrounded with a fence of thorns to keep off the rabble. On it are piled heaps of silesias, checks and callicoes, a great many fine cloths that are manufactured in Eyeo country, and a prodigious quantity of cowries.[2]

[1] Guestard, 'Mémoire...', 1750 (AN. C. 6/25).
[2] R. Norris, *Memoirs*, pp. viii–ix, 84–112.

It was not only Norris who witnessed to the affluent state of Dahomey. Mills, a former governor of the Cape Coast Castle, who visited Igelefe for the first time in February 1777 on his way back to England, preferred the place to the Gold Coast. He wrote:

> The natives both males and females are most civil, good kind people I ever saw, full of compliments and as quick and tame as you possibly can imagine...The country appears amazingly populous, and they appear happy, contented and cheerful...The people here are exceeding fond of wearing many clothes about them both men and women, they are also fond of their own manufactured cloths and wear grass ones...[1]

In fact Mills admired what he saw so much that he said he would have settled in Dahomey had it not been for the consideration he had for his friends and family.[1]

Though Mills might not know it, there were sumptuary laws. Only the king wore sandals and he alone could be carried in a hammock. All other Dahomeans walked barefoot. The court dress, which was the same as the military dress, and in which all who attended the court were obliged to appear, was a short sleeveless upper garment over whatever kind of drawers one chose. Only a war captain had an umbrella, and every chief had a mule presented to him on appointment by the king, as a sign of his dignity.[2] As we have already noticed, no Dahomean was permitted to wear silk damask in Cana.

These few details show that the kingdom of Dahomey under Tegbesu was well organised, and the society a well-ordered one in which each individual knew his rights as well as his duties.

Meanwhile the growing wealth of Whydah port under the secure hold of Tegbesu made the old Whydah uneasy and aroused the envy of Ashampo of Little Popo, Agaja's old enemy. From 1752 onwards they renewed, with increasing vigour, not only the scorched earth tactics adopted by Huffon in 1731, but also their determination to deprive Tegbesu of Whydah.

Between 1752 and 1763 they came against Dahomey six

---

[1] David Mills to R. Miles, 5 Feb. 1777 (T 70/1534).
[2] De Chenevert and Abbé Bullet, 'Réflexions sur Juda', 1776 (AN. C. 6/27 *bis*).

times.[1] They defeated the Dahomean army three times, and on two occasions out of those three, they remained masters of the beach and the forts unchallenged for days.[1] The allegiance of the forts to Tegbesu, and the active support which the English fort gave to Dahomey during the 1755 and 1756 invasions, largely prevented the old Whydah from becoming the complete masters of Igelefe.[2]

The most serious of the Whydah invasions occurred in 1763.[3] At 8 a.m. on 12 July of that year, a Whydah force of some eight thousand well-drilled men appeared at Igelefe, led by Ofori, son of Ashampo. They easily overcame the Dahomean army on the beach, and marched towards the forts. Honu, the Yovogan, who opposed them with about a thousand men was soon wounded and carried off the field. The Coki then took command, but he too was easily made to beat a retreat.

The old Whydah and the Little Popo then started to burn Igelefe and to pursue the disorderly Dahomean army. At this point the English and the French forts unexpectedly opened fire on the invaders. Goodson, the director of the English fort, took command of the Dahomean forces, distributing powder and rum freely for the Dahomean soldiers and his own garrison, and ordering the wounded to be dressed with silesia supplied by his fort. By 2 p.m., in the face of this combined attack, the invaders' ranks had been broken. Ofori, their commander, escaped, but shot himself for grief and only a skeleton army survived to tell the tale of their disaster.

Although the old Whydah and the Little Popo were so dismally defeated, their invasions had demonstrated the weakness into which the Dahomean army had fallen and were not without adverse effects on the trade of Dahomey. From about 1752 onwards, ships increasingly avoided Whydah where they stood a real chance of being pillaged and suffering losses from Tegbesu's

---

[1] 'Accounts and Daybooks for Whydah', 1 May 1752, 4 Jan. 1753, May–Oct. 1753, 31 Dec. 1753, 28 Feb. 1754, 31 Aug. 1755, 31 Oct. 1755 (T 70/1158); Conseil de direction to la Compagnie des Indes, 25 Nov. 1755 (AN. C. 6/25); 'Accounts and Daybooks for Whydah', Sept. and Oct. 1756 (T 70/1158); A. Dalzel, *History*, pp. 100–2; E. Dunglas in *E.D.* vol. XIX, pp. 177–82. Dalzel's accounts of these events are incomplete.

[2] 'Accounts and Daybooks for Whydah', 31 Oct. 1755, Sept. and Oct. 1756 (T 70/1158).

[3] A. Dalzel, *History*, pp. 102–4; 'Accounts and Daybooks for Whydah', 12 July 1763 (T 70/1159) 'Mémoire sur le Fort Juda', post 1763; 'Le Royaume de Juda', n.d. (AN. C. 6/25).

policies.[1] In 1754 more ships went to Badagry, Epe, and Little Popo than went to Whydah. In 1755 very few ships indeed went to Whydah and the drift was not stopped by all the protests which Tegbesu delivered to the directors of the fort.[2] By 1763 Porto Novo, the new port of the kingdom of Ajase Ipo was being used both by the English and the French.[3]

Dahomey's problem was increased by the Portuguese law, already referred to, and the Seven Years War. The drift of the ships not only caused the usual security problem for Dahomey but also a serious problem of unemployment, since Tegbesu's earlier successes had raised a large labour force whose livelihood depended on casual work with the slave ships. Stealing and burglary became common, a real threat at Igelefe and an added reason for ships to avoid the Whydah port.[4]

On 5 December 1763 Tegbesu sent a public crier to Igelefe, 'to proclaim through the whole place two days together that whoever stole the value of even a single cowrie the king was determined to punish with death'.[4] However, the end of the Seven Years War, and the complete overthrow of the old Whydah and Little Popo invaders, both in 1763, brought ships flocking to Whydah in 1764[5] and restored normal conditions at Igelefe. All the forts sank back into routine administration, and the stealing and the burglary stopped. At the end of 1764 the French director was able to say that the Whydah trade 'has always been the best and certainly preferable to the trade in other ports lower down the coast', and to express the fear that too many ships and an unnecessary competition among the captains might spoil the trade.

Yet the position could no longer be the same as before the old Whydah invasions started. In 1765 the total export of the slaves from Whydah port was about five thousand.[6] This com-

---

[1] 'Enregistrement des rapports...', 16 June, 19 June, 3 July, 10 Aug., 26 Sept., 15 Oct., 13, 19 Nov. 1753 (ADN. B. 4592); Conseil de direction to la Compagnie des Indes, 18 Dec. 1752, 25 Nov. 1757 (AN. C. 6/25).

[2] 'Accounts and Daybooks for Whydah', Feb. 1758 (T 70/1158); May and June 1759 to 20 July 1761 (T 70/1159).

[3] 'Accounts and Daybooks for Whydah', 3 Aug. 1763 (T 70/1159); 'Côte d'Afrique, Mémoire sur le fort Juda', post 1763 (AN. C. 6/26).

[4] Captain Jenkinson to African Committee, 28 July 1762 (T 70/31). 'Accounts and Daybooks for Whydah', 17, 21 and 28 March 1763 (T 70/1159).

[5] Conseil de direction to la Compagnie des Indes, 29 Nov. 1764 (AN. C. 6/26).

[6] 'Côte d'Afrique', 1765 (AN. C. 6/26).

pared very unfavourably with the nine thousand in 1750. The combined total of the slaves exported from Little Popo, Great Popo, Epe, Porto Novo, Badagry and Lagos was also about five thousand.[1] No doubt Whydah trade was predominant but as it depended largely on Oyo suppliers, its continued lead depended on Oyo preferences. The phenomenal growth of Porto Novo which in 1765 was exporting one thousand two hundred slaves,[2] more than the combined total of the long-established ports of Epe and Badagry, suggests that the days of Whydah as the leading port in the Yoruba-Aja country were numbered.

However, in 1767 Dahomey was enjoying a standard of affluence and orderliness which it was not to surpass for the rest of the century and which indeed its rulers would have to struggle from then on to maintain. The credit for this phenomenal progress from the gloomy days of 1740 goes entirely to Tegbesu.

Between 1740 and 1766 he had reconstructed Dahomey from the tattered ruins left by Agaja. He had made his own constitutional position and that of his descendants secure, he had rebuilt Abomey, re-established the internal administration, and reintegrated the Europeans into the system. He had bought peace from Oyo by submission and had concentrated the whole national energy on the slave trade which he revived and made a complete royal monopoly. Although his methods had caused a dwindling in the population of Dahomey, and had produced revolts and dissatisfaction among the Europeans, yet he had greatly enriched both the monarchy and the general populace and had produced such an orderly and contented community as was not surpassed again for the rest of the century.

His policies had, however, placed Dahomey at the mercy of external factors that might not always be favourable and he had neglected the army. The years which followed were to see the grave consequences of these mistakes.

---

[1] 'Côte d'Afrique', 1765 (AN. C. 6/26).       [2] *Ibid.*

# 5

## Weaknesses in the new system, 1767-89

From 1767 onwards the long-term implications of Tegbesu's economic settlement became the dominant issues in the national life of Dahomey. By making the slave trade the basis of the economy of Dahomey, Tegbesu had placed the kingdom at the mercy of external factors which the Dahomeans could neither control nor even influence. This became increasingly clear as international conditions became less favourable to the unfettered movement of European shipping. The experience of the next two decades would show that the Dahomeans no longer controlled an important factor governing the stability of their kingdom and that the slave trade was, after all, not a secure basis for the national economy.

Between 1767 and 1789 both the Dahomean authorities and the European director constantly complained of the 'badness of the trade' in Dahomey. The number of slaves available started to decrease, slowly at first, from about 1765. In 1774 the decrease was reaching an alarming stage, but the European directors still thought that it was either a passing trouble or simply a question of imperfect distribution. Guestard, the director of the French fort, said he hoped that Kpengla would easily re-establish the declining trade of Dahomey and put the other faults right.[1]

Soon, however, all the European directors realised that the problem was more deep-rooted and that the supply of the slaves had declined generally in Dahomey. Between June and October 1774 they all, individually and collectively, complained to Kpengla that slaves were too few in Dahomey and asked him to do something about it,[2] though they did not specify what.

[1] Guestard to Ministre de Colonies, 7 June 1774 (AN. C. 6/25).
[2] De Warell to Messrs de la Chambre du Commerce de La Rochelle, 15 Nov. 1774 (CCR. Cartoon XIX); 'An Account of the forts belonging to the British and foreign nations in these parts of Africa called Guinea', 1774 (T 70/1532); 'Accounts and Daybooks for Whydah', 14 Oct. 1774 (T 70/1161).

Olivier Montaguere, who succeeded Guestard, said there was hardly any trade at Igelefe in 1776,[1] and the attempt by Norris, made towards the end of 1777, to collect some long-standing debts, shows that the trade had not yet revived by then.[2] Norris arrived at Igelefe about the middle of September 1777, the first English trader to be seen in Whydah port since the beginning of that year. By the end of December he had been able to collect only seventy slaves out of the one hundred due to him. At the same time he had managed to buy four hundred and forty slaves from various other ports near Whydah.

That Norris's experience at Igelefe was neither peculiar nor caused by the unwillingness of the Dahomeans to repay their debts is shown by the account of a young French slave trader, Proa, who was on board a slaving ship that reached Whydah at the end of July 1777. On their plans and prospects he wrote: 'We had hoped to make a quick trade and to complete our cargo in a couple of months, but the slaves were not very abundant at Whydah market'.[3]

In 1783 and 1784 both Abson, the English director, and Montaguere warned their nationals that if too many of their ships came to Whydah, they would make ruinous voyages.[4] The Portuguese director, confirming the same impression, said that the slaves in Dahomey were too few even for the Portuguese ships alone.[5] In 1788 Paget Bayley, an English naval officer who visited the Whydah port, reported that 'the trade is by no means abundant'.[6]

While the Europeans were thus complaining of the paucity of the slaves in Dahomey, the Dahomean authorities were also

[1] O. Montaguere to Ministre de Colonies, 6 Oct. 1777 (AN. C. 6/26).
[2] R. Norris to Richard Miles, 4, 10, 17, 18 Sept. and 29 Dec. 1777 (T 70/1534).
[3] 'Mémoire de Proa, le Navigateur', 1777 (unpublished). I am grateful to M. Jean Marchand for kindly allowing me to consult this account when I was in Paris. M. Marchand is a descendant of Proa and is preparing for publication this very interesting account of a young French sailor in the slave trade in the eighteenth century. Proa was about 18 years old when he wrote the Journal.
[4] O. Montaguere, 'Extraits...', 2 March 1783 (AN. C. 6/26); L. Abson to R. Miles, 1 Oct. 1783, 30 Dec. 1783 (T 70/1545); L. Abson to J. Fayrer, 30 Sept. 1784; L. Abson to R. Savage, 30 Sept. 1784 (T 70/1551).
[5] F. Antonio da Fonseca e Aragão, director of the Portuguese fort, to King of Portugal, 25 June 1784 (AHU. S. Tome Caixa x).
[6] Paget Bayley and L. Abson, 'Observation on the state and conditions of [William's] fort and the trade thereof', 27 March 1788 (Adm. I/1506, part II).

justifiably complaining that the Europeans did not send their ships to Whydah. There are, of course, no complete figures showing the number of the ships that called at Whydah port during this period, nor have we any means of comparing the annual fluctuations. Such figures as are available and the complaints of the Dahomean authorities show, however, that many fewer ships came to trade in Whydah port between 1767 and 1781 than, say, in 1750.

No English ship came to trade in Whydah between 1764 and 1767,[1] and only one came between 1767 and 1770.[2] No French ones were seen in Cape Coast harbour to pick up boats and canoemen for the Whydah trade between June 1778 and October 1779.[3] Gaston Martin's figures tend to show that the Nantes trade to Whydah between 1767 and 1775 was relatively on the decline.[4]

In May 1768, April 1777, November 1778, October 1785 and July 1786,[5] Tegbesu and Kpengla sent messengers to the European directors to find out why the European ships no longer came to trade in the Whydah port as they used to do. These messages signify that the lack of European ships was beyond argument. They were not formal exchanges of politeness, but expressions of serious concern on the part of the Dahomean authorities. The fewer the ships, the more pressing the demand and the higher the status of the messenger sent. In November 1778 the Mehu himself came down and stayed at Igelefe for six days,[6] although he was at that time a very old man and as the holder of the second highest office in the kingdom would not normally have absented himself from Abomey except on the most urgent business. In October 1785 Kpengla was prepared to make the lack of ships in Whydah an international issue. He threatened to report Abson to the king of England for preventing English ships from coming to trade in Whydah.[6]

[1] A. Dalzel to African Committee, 27 Sept. 1768 (T 70/31).
[2] A. Dalzel to Andrew Dalzel, 13 April 1771 (E.U.L. DK. 7/52).
[3] R. Miles to African Committee, 21 Oct. 1779 (T 70/1537).
[4] Gaston-Martin, *L'Ere des Negriers*, p. 289; S. Berbain, *Le Comptoir Français*, pp. 42–6, is not very clear on this as she does not break down her figures.
[5] 'Accounts and Daybooks for Whydah', 18 May 1768 (T 70/1160); 30 April 1777, 1 and 12 Nov. 1778 (T 70/1161); 2 Oct. 1785, 20 July 1786 (T 70/1162).
[6] 'Accounts and Daybooks for Whydah', 1, 6 and 12 Nov. 1778 (T 70/1161), 20 July 1786 (T 70/1162).

The fact that both the Europeans and the Dahomeans complained means that often between 1767 and 1783 there were
neither ships nor slaves in Dahomey, and that at times when the
one was available the other was not. Tegbesu had unreservedly
tied the fortune of Dahomey to the slave-trade economy and
had struggled with a measure of success, from 1740, to have a
constant supply of slaves and ships. How then did this situation
arise?

When the European directors and traders had to account
officially for this decline in the slave trade of Dahomey, they
often gave uncomplimentary stock reasons to prove that the
fault lay with the Dahomeans. In the late 1760s and the 1770s
their general excuse was 'the villainy' of the Yovogan and the
'thievish inclinations' of the Dahomeans.[1] In the 1780s it was
that the Dahomean authorities were either unwilling or too
slow to pay their debts to certain European captains.[2]

Although these excuses were not entirely unfounded, none
of them was ever a strong cause for the European desertion of
the Whydah port. Villainy and thievish inclinations were common features with both the African and the European slave
traders. Guestard, twice director of the French fort at Whydah
and altogether thirty-four years in the African slave trade, said
that often what the Europeans called stealing on the part of the
Africans was the dishonesty which they had learnt from the
Europeans themselves. He affirmed that the European traders
diluted their brandy with large quantities of water, sometimes
as much as half. They would cut away large slices inside a
piece of cloth, tuck in a piece of wood or other material and
wrap the rest well round to conceal the trick.[3]

Indeed, the kings of Dahomey maintained that their subjects learnt dishonesty from the Europeans. Tegbesu kept a huge
pot of watery brandy, which he had bought from the Europeans,
constantly by himself. Whenever a director complained to him
that his subjects stole, he gave that director a glassful of the

---

[1] A. Dalzel to African Committee, 27 Sept. 1768 (T 70/31).

[2] 'Accounts and Daybooks for Whydah', 2 Oct. 1785 (T 70/1162).

[3] Guestard to Ministre de Colonies, 16 June 1770 (AN. C. 6/25). Writing of
the character of the French captains who came to trade at Whydah, Guestard
said, 'Où ils excellent la pluspart, c'est en mauvaise foi. Ils mettent beau-
coup d'eau dans leur eau de vie, ils ont de marchandise dont ils coupent de
morceau et les reploient de façon que ne paroisse pas...par ces ruses
grossières, ils perdent entièrement la confiance de commerce.'

liquor and assured him that if he could stop his fellow Europeans indulging in such bad practices, stealing would stop entirely at Igelefe.[1]

Generally, where theft occurred, it appears to have been resorted to by the Dahomeans as an extra-legal means of redress against offending Europeans. An example of this was the case of two English captains, Copeland and Jenkinson, who came to trade at Igelefe in 1762. Jenkinson related the half amusing, half pathetic story:

> When I came on shore, I found Captain Copeland was gone up to the king of Dahomey to seek redress for some goods which the blacks have stole [*sic*] from him... Since his return, I have lost no goods, but him they keep taking from more or less everyday; poor man, I am really sorry for him.[2]

Usually, stealing was a capital crime in Dahomey and its penalty was death. Jenkinson, however, did not say whether anyone was punished for this crime against Copeland.

Equally weak was the excuse that the Dahomeans did not willingly repay their debts. Both the Dahomean and the European traders freely gave one another credit and some Europeans were as remiss in paying back as some Dahomeans. In October 1785 Kpengla explained at length to Abson that he had sold slaves on credit to certain English captains and that one captain Fayrer was still owing him.[3]

There were however, other, more probable reasons, which arose out of Tegbesu's policy and from the international conditions which governed the slave trade.

Tegbesu following his policy of 'peaceful slave trade' had relied largely on the slaves brought in from outside Dahomey and particularly on those supplied by the Oyo traders. That the Oyo supply would not always be available to the Igelefe market was shown by the change in Oyo policy from about 1774 onwards.

In May of that year, Abiodun overthrew his Basorun, Gaha,[4] who had been the *de facto* ruler of the Oyo Empire

---

[1] See note 3, p. 144.

[2] Captain Jenkins to African Committee, 28 July 1762 (T 70/31).

[3] 'Accounts and Daybooks for Whydah', 2 Oct. 1786 (T 70/1162).

[4] S. Johnson, *History*, pp. 182–6; A. Dalzel, *History*, p. 157. Dalzel's story of a king of Oyo fighting against his 'Ochenoo' (Osorun, another name for Basorun) makes it plain that the incident was the same one as Abiodun fighting against Gaha. This has made it possible to date this incident at May 1774.

since 1754.[1] Abiodun was a trader by profession before he became the Alafin,[2] and as soon as he was secure on the throne he threw all his energy into encouraging the slave trade. By 1776 his exertion had led to the foundation or extension of a flourishing slave market at Abomey-Calavi, which was wholly stocked and controlled by the Oyo. At that date, the slaves were supplied from that market to Igelefe, Epe, Porto Novo and Badagry.[3]

Soon Abiodun decided to make Porto Novo, the port of Ajase Ipo, the main Oyo port. He called it his own 'callabash' out of which no one but himself would be permitted to eat.[4] Abiodun's choice of port may partly have been dictated, and was certainly helped, by the traditional trade regulations at Porto Novo, which were more generous than those obtaining at Whydah.

Any Oyo trader at Igelefe would have to sell his slaves to the king's traders, who alone could resell to the European exporters. At Igelefe also, certain imported articles like firearms, iron and corals were allowed to be bought only by the king of Dahomey. At Porto Novo, on the other hand, an Oyo trader could sell direct to the Europeans and thus earn a greater profit, and he could buy any kind of European manufactures he wanted.[5]

The adoption of Porto Novo as the main Oyo port meant that Dahomey was deprived of the most important source of its slave supply. It is significant that the European complaints became loud just when the change in Oyo policy was taking place. The only way by which Dahomey could make up the shortage was to get its own slaves by its own raiding, but that proved impossible, again as a result of Tegbesu's policy.

---

[1] The date of Basorun's seizure of power has also been fixed by a comparison of Johnson's tradition and documentary evidence. Johnson (*History*, p. 178) relates that two Alafin were executed in quick succession when Gaha rose to power. In a letter dated 22 October 1754, written at Igelefe in Dahomey to Thomas Melvil, Governor of Cape Coast Castle, Devaynes said: 'the king of Io [i.e. Oyo] is dead and they are fighting who shall have the stool. Two that have been seated on it within these two months are both killed.' T. Melvil to African Committee, 30 Nov. 1754 (T 70/1523).

[2] S. Johnson, *History*, p. 187, 'Long before his accession, he was a trader in potash'.

[3] Chenevert and Abbé Bullet, 'Réflexions...', 1776 (AN. C. 6/27 *bis*). Abomey-Calavi is still existing, north of Godomey.

[4] A. Dalzel, *History*, pp. 195–6.

[5] Market regulations were part of the internal affairs of each kingdom. They varied from place to place, and each trader, even if he was from the imperial capital, was requested to abide by the local market laws.

Another implication of the policy of 'trade before war' was that the army had been neglected and therefore weakened. When Tegbesu died in 1774 the whole of the Dahomean infantry numbered three thousand, out of which an inadequate three hundred were posted to Igelefe to guard the beach and protect the forts. There were, in addition, sixteen horses but not a single cavalryman. The infantry was badly trained and the only tactics it knew was to go in great secrecy and surprise unsuspecting villages.[1] The army had, both in number and training, greatly deteriorated from the great days of Agaja.

The Dahomean army, even at its most efficient, depended on the arms supplied by the Europeans, who entirely controlled the quantity and the quality. From about 1764 onwards these European suppliers brought only firearms of very poor quality.

In March 1765 Tegbesu complained that a parcel of guns which he had bought from the English burst whenever fired and hurt several of his soldiers,[2] instead of killing the enemy. Between 1764 and 1770, when the English captains avoided trading at Whydah, the French traders, 'finding they have no competitors', gradually introduced 'worse manufactures'.[3] In August and again in November 1773 Tegbesu complained about the French arms. Guestard admitted that the guns were badly welded together and wrote to the French traders at Nantes to send better ones.[4]

When the Nantes Chamber of Commerce replied in June 1775, they showed no intention of trying to remedy the fault. They irrelevantly maintained that their guns ought to be more acceptable to the Dahomeans than the English guns, and implausibly suggested incompetent handling as the reason for frequent accidents.[5] There was therefore no immediate probability that the badly trained and shrunken Dahomean army would get good weapons, even if they were driven to fight.

---

[1] Chenevert and Abbé Bullet, 'Réflexions sur Juda' 1776 (AN. C. 6/27 *bis*); O. Montaguere to Ministre de Colonies, 6 Oct. 1777 (AN. C. 6/26). The garrison at Igelefe alone around 1750 was estimated at about eight thousand men. The number of horses was an improvement. In 1727 there were only two.

[2] 'Accounts and Daybooks for Whydah', 10 March 1765 (T 70/1160).

[3] A. Dalzel to African Committee, 27 Sept. 1768 (T 70/31).

[4] 'Accounts and Daybooks for Whydah', 10 Aug. 1773 (T 70/1163); Guestard to MM. le Chambre du Commerce à Nantes, 16 Nov. 1773 (ADN. C. 727).

[5] MM. de la Chambre du Commerce à Nantes to M. de Warel, 3 June 1775 (ADN. C. 604).

The first result was that Dahomey could not increase its own supply of slaves. Tegbesu, pursuing his peaceful trade policy to the end, sent out no raiding parties in the last five years of his reign. The first three expeditions which Kpengla sent out at the beginning of his reign in 1775 and 1776[1] were heavily defeated. The others sent out between 1776 and 1781 did not succeed in bringing many captives back. More often than not they were defeated.[2]

Another consequence of the weakness of the army was much more serious. It made it impossible for Dahomey to guard the Whydah beach effectively, thus rendering Dahomey a prey to enemy invasions and preventing the Dahomeans from effectively protecting the lives and property of the Europeans who resorted thither. This problem became acute from 1767 onwards when the old Whydah resumed their predatory raids on Igelefe and the Whydah beach.

Between April 1767 and August 1781 the raiders came at least eleven times. Of these, seven were between April 1767 and October 1770, one each in March 1772, June 1775, June 1780 and from June to August 1781.[3] Their disastrous defeat of July 1763 had taught them to limit their aims and change their tactics. Instead of seeking to occupy Whydah by defeating Dahomey in war as they had attempted before 1763, they now adopted the policy of rendering the Whydah port and the beach unsafe for European goods and captains. In that way they expected to injure the economy of Dahomey and perhaps force the Dahomeans to abandon Whydah when they no longer

---

[1] Chenevert and Abbé Bullet, 'Réflexions...', 1776 (AN. C. 6/27 *bis*); O. Montaguere to Ministre de Colonies, 6 Oct. 1777 (AN. C. 6/26); A. Dalzel, *History*, pp. 163–4.

[2] L. Abson to R. Norris, 21 June 1778 (T 70/1551); A. Dalzel, *History*, pp. 165–6; 'Accounts and Daybooks for Whydah', 2 January 1779 (T 70/1162). These expeditions will be dealt with more fully later. Their general purpose was to increase the Dahomean stock of slaves. They were indeed raids rather than wars and were certainly not motivated by the 'insatiable thirst after blood, the barbarous vanity of being considered the scourge of mankind and the savage pomp of dwelling in a house garnished with skulls...' as Dalzel so damagingly affirms.

[3] Dalzel to African Committee, 1767, March 1768 (T 70/31); 'Accounts and Daybooks for Whydah', 29 Feb. 1768 (T 70/1160); L. Abson to African Committee, 24 Oct. 1770 (T 70/31); 'Accounts and Daybooks for Whydah', Aug.–Oct. 1770 (T 70/1160); Guestard to Ministre de Colonies, 15 Oct. 1770 (AN. C. 6/26); 'Accounts and Daybooks for Whydah', 10 March 1772, June 1775 (T 70/1161); 17 June 1780, 6, 20, 27 June, 7 July and 29 Aug. 1871 (T 70/1162).

gained anything from its occupation. This was the same kind of scorched earth policy which Huffon had adopted in 1731.

For this kind of operation, they needed not a large army, which since 1763 they probably had not got, but small bands of men who could rob, kill and flee in their boats before the Dahomeans or anyone else could catch them. The pattern of the new attacks was set in April 1767. On the very day that Archibald Dalzel arrived to take over the directorship of the English fort, a party of the raiders visited the beach, beyond which 'they advanced no further but contented themselves with the plunder they found at the waterside consisting of brandy just landed from a French vessel and a box of silk belonging to a Portuguese captain'.[1]

It was these same tactics that they adopted during the four raids which they made between August and October 1770. In the first, they carried away goods belonging to a French captain. During the second, they took away a few slaves belonging to a Portuguese captain and either burned, broke or carried away every boat they found on the landing. On the third occasion, they roamed the beach, completely unopposed, from 16 to 20 September and killed two Dahomeans in a skirmish, but they got no European plunder. On the fourth occasion, they carried away three European tent-keepers, whom they presumably killed later.[2]

The complete inability of the Dahomeans to check this danger sometimes forced the Europeans to take their own measures. Once in 1780 the Europeans hired 'free people for bringing the canoes on this side of the river, in consequence of a report that the Popoes intend coming to the beach with a hostile intention'.[2]

In 1781 the Dahomeans tried unsuccessfully to check the invaders. The Agau set out against them about 27 June, but within two weeks, he was back without having accomplished anything. A week later, the old Whydah and their allies again invaded the Whydah beach and put the Agau on the defensive.

[1] A. Dalzel to African Committee, 1767 (T 70/31).
[2] L. Abson to African Committee, 24 Oct. 1770 (T 70/31); 'Accounts and Daybooks for Whydah', Aug.–Oct. 1770 (T 70/1160); Guestard to Ministre de Colonies, 15 Oct. 1770 (AN. C. 6/26). Guestard said that the raiders came five times in the series, but Abson gave the details of only four raids; 'Accounts and Daybooks for Whydah', 17 June 1780, 6, 20, 27 and 29 Aug. 1781 (T 70/1162).

They maintained their pressure until August.[1] Kpengla borrowed iron bars from the directors to be made into shot and used against the invaders, but he was unable to deal effectively with them.

Even if the slaves had been abundant in Dahomey and the port had been safe, it is still almost certain that the number of ships that came to Whydah during these years would still have diminished greatly, since European conditions too were adverse.

The English deserted Whydah after 1764 for two main reasons. The first was that generally they did not like Whydah port 'as it is equally open to us the French and the Portuguese'.[2] They preferred places like some of their forts on the Gold Coast where they had absolute monopoly. Moreover, in the competition which resulted from 'open port' conditions, 'the French have the knack of pleasing the negroes better and underselling the English',[2] and the tobacco which the Portuguese imported from Brazil had secured the monopoly of African favour which neither the French nor the English could break.

The second and immediate reason for the English desertion was that in 1764, certain Liverpool merchants sent a few ships to Whydah. Those ships found others in the harbour and keen competition drove up the price of the slaves. Consequently the Liverpool ships made ruinous voyages, the report of which effectively discouraged any English captain until 1770 from coming to trade at Whydah.[2]

A much more protracted reason for the paucity of all European shipping at Whydah was the American war of Independence. As early as 1776, one James Charles was already complaining that the unhappy dispute had entirely spoilt the African trade. 'All our African ships are laid up as fast as they get home, they that's so lucky to "scape the American privateers". We have Guinea captains, mates and doctors strolling the streets eighteen to the dozen.'[3]

As the war progressed, its direct and indirect effects discouraged more and more ships from going out to trade. By September 1777 West Indian credit was running low, and the planters were asking for up to four years before paying for a

---

[1] See note 2, p. 149.
[2] Archibald Dalzel to Andrew Dalzel, 1 April 1769, 13 April 1771 (EUL. DK. 7/52).
[3] James Charles to R. Miles, 14 Nov. 1776 (T 70/1534).

cargo of slaves.[1] By the middle of 1779 the insurance rates had become almost prohibitively high, the cost of fitting out slave ships had risen sharply and at the same time the prices of slaves in the West Indies had fallen,[2] a trend that continued into 1780.[3]

These disadvantages were strong enough to discourage even the veteran English slave traders and to convince them that other jobs would be more profitable while the war lasted. Archibald Dalzel, the erstwhile director of the English fort at Whydah, who had set up his own slave-trading business, left London, the centre of his activities, for his native Scotland and was preparing to go to Mississippi whether as a permanent or temporary immigrant is uncertain. Norris started a tools factory[4] and the other traders continued to be discouraged from going to sea up to the beginning of 1782,[5] though some ventured out in 1781.

The American war must have had a similar effect on the French slave-trading activities.[6]

Two conclusions can therefore be drawn from the decline of the trade of Dahomey and the causes leading to it. The first is that 'peaceful slave trade' was impossible. Only wars could provide an ample supply of slaves. The second is that the slave trade itself was not a reliable basis for the economy because the factors governing it were beyond the control of any one power.

The rulers of Dahomey did not reach this radical conclusion. Either willingly or by force of circumstances, they held to the slave-trade economy and did all they could to revive and make it prosper once again at Igelefe.

Tegbesu believed, in part correctly, that the cure for the trouble lay in bringing more European ships to Whydah port and he thought that that could be achieved simply by making the port safe for them. Following his peaceful policy to the end, he

[1] R. Norris to R. Miles, 4 Sept. 1777 (T 70/1534).
[2] R. Norris to R. Miles, 29 June 1779 (T 70/1538).
[3] John Coghlan to J. Roberts, 18 Nov. 1780 (T 70/1542 (I)).
[4] R. Norris to R. Miles, 29 June 1779 (T 70/1538).
[5] J. T. Hodgson to R. Miles, 19 Jan. 1782 (T 70/1545).
[6] S. Berbain, *Le Comptoir Français*, pp. 42–6. Though Berbain did not break down her figures, a close examination would suggest a decline in the French slave-trading activities between 1777 and 1782; Gaston Martin, *L'Ere des Negriers*, p. 15.

sought to put an end to the Whydah and Popo raids by methods of diplomacy.

About 10 August 1769 he created a king for the old Whydah and gave him the title 'Agbangla'[1] after one of the greatest of the kings of ancient Whydah, who reigned from about 1670 to 1703. He then sent him to the European forts where many of the old Whydah could see him and where the European directors gave him presents.[1] This move was meant to appease the old Whydah and show them that any of them who wanted to return to their ancient homes, as Dahomean citizens under their own king, were free to do so.

Tegbesu then tried to conclude a peace treaty with the Popo. As it would have been impolitic to declare his intentions he worked through Dalzel, then the English director at Whydah, who between 15 and 23 July 1769 agreed to help in the task.[2] On 24 July 1769 Dalzel sent a messenger to Popo to ask the king 'to open a communication with the Gold Coast'. Negotiations then followed and on 17 August the king of Popo sent a messenger to the forts agreeing to open communication between Igelefe and Popo 'for the conveniency of sending letters to the Gold Coast by land'.[2]

A week later, Tegbesu publicly announced his 'intention to open all the paths and for the future live in amity with all his neighbours'.[3] The king of Popo did not reject these feelers, and throughout September and October 1769, messengers went backwards and forwards between Abomey and Little Popo. On 23 November 1769 Tegbesu announced that he was at peace with the Popo. Three weeks later, for the benefit of those who may not have heard it the first time, or to confirm what he had said earlier, he again announced that the peace treaty with the Popo had been concluded.[4]

The terms of this treaty are not known, but the peace itself was shortlived. The old Whydah and the Popo were up in arms again in August 1770 and they continued their depredations intermittently until the beginning of 1772, as has already been noticed.

In October 1770, soon after the raids were renewed, two French captains went to Tegbesu at Abomey and offered to land the artillery of their ships on the beach to be used against

---

[1] 'Accounts and Daybooks for Whydah', Aug.–Dec. 1769 (T 70/1161).
[2] *Ibid.*      [3] *Ibid.*      [4] *Ibid.*

the invaders. Tegbesu gladly accepted their offer, but Guestard, the director of the French fort, prevented the step being taken. He warned the captains that he believed that after the guns had been used successfully against the old Whydah, they would be turned against the European forts.[1]

Tegbesu therefore decided on another peace treaty with the raiders. This time he did not try to divide their forces. On 29 April 1772 he bluntly asked Lionel Abson, who had become the director of the English fort in 1770, to help him to make peace with the Popo.

Abson tried to adopt the 1769 plan, and, as if on his own initiative, asked the king of Popo to open the road between Igelefe and his teritory. The trick was, however, quickly discovered and his messenger returned with those of the king of Popo and together they all went to Tegbesu at Abomey to negotiate. No fast conclusions were reached at the first meeting. On 13 July 1772 the Mehu was sent down to Igelefe, accompanied by the Agau and invested with full powers 'to settle all differences with the Popo'.[2] At Igelefe, the two state officers from Abomey were joined by the Yovogan and all his under officers. Soon after that date a peace treaty was again concluded.

Again the terms of this treaty are unknown. Considering Tegbesu's purpose, it is probable that he asked, and the old Whydah and the Popo agreed, that the raids on Whydah beach and on the shipping be stopped. In return he may have granted permission to any Whydah who wanted to resettle at Igelefe, and freedom of the Igelefe market to any Popo traders who wanted to come and trade. Between 1772 and 1775 the raids on the Whydah beach completely stopped, though they were resumed actively from 1777 onwards.

The peace was therefore still being observed when Kpengla ascended the throne of Dahomey in May 1774. Kpengla was not a younger brother of Tegbesu, as the Dahomean oral traditions would have it.[3] He was in fact the son of Tegbesu, and the same

---

[1] Guestard to Ministre de Colonies, 15 Oct. 1770 (AN. C. 6/26).
[2] 'Accounts and Daybooks for Whydah', 29 April–13 July 1772 (T 70/1161); R. Norris, *Memoirs*, p. 60; A. Dalzel, *History*, pp. 104–5.
[3] Guestard to Ministre de Colonies, 7 June 1774 (AN. C. 6/26); Le Herisse, *L'Ancien Royaume*, p. 17; E. Dunglas in *E.D.* vol. xx, pp. 3–5. Guestard's evidence seems conclusive that Kpengla was the son and not the brother of Tegbesu. Guestard had known the prince since 1751 when he was first

prince who had been designated his successor since 1751 and he was about thirty-nine years old at his accession. He seems to have ascended under the name of Adamusu[1] and was very popular with all the sections of the community, both African and European. Guestard, who had known him for about twenty-five years, thought that he had an engaging character and real ability.[1] Everyone expected that with his youthful vigour Kpengla would be able to arrest the decline in the fortune of Dahomey.

His first actions did not disappoint his admirers. Immediately on accession, he asked all sections to forget all past differences and close ranks.[2] At the final act of his coronation ceremony, which occurred in June 1775, when he ceremonially took the throne of Allada, he made a very stirring policy speech. The text has not survived, but two points remained vivid in the minds of his hearers. First, he promised that he would revive the declining slave trade and see to it that the slaves exported through the Whydah port were provided entirely from the captives made by the Dahomean soldiers, whose expedition would therefore be made more effective. No slaves would be bought from the inland countries. Secondly, he promised that he would shake off the Oyo yoke and secure independence for Dahomey.[3]

Kpengla's militant speech was in complete contrast to Tegbesu's peaceful policy. It shows that Kpengla had grasped another aspect of the problem confronting Dahomey. It was

designated successor, and had once been falsely told that the young man had succeeded his father. If the prince had lost his title Guestard would surely have commented on it. The story related at length by Dunglas that Tegbesu did not have a legitimate heir and that Gnansoumou (Yansumu?) his brother succeeded him, seems designed to show that cases of brother succession in Dahomey was common and so legitimise Gezo's otherwise unconstitutional seizure of power in 1818. Kpengla's first assumed name was probably Adamusu. The English called it 'Adahoonzou', the French called it 'Adamouzou'. The name is still remembered in his praise names but only by a few Dahomeans.

[1] *Ibid.*

[2] 'Accounts and Daybooks for Whydah', 19 Aug. and 18 Sept. 1774 (T 70/1161).

[3] Chenevert and Abbé Bullet, 'Réflexions...', 1776 (AN. C. 6/27 *bis*); 'Accounts and Daybooks for Whydah', June 1775 (T 70/1161). The Dahomean traditions recorded by Dunglas in *E.D.* vol. xx, pp. 31–4, attribute the adoption of independence policy to Agonglo but, in view of this documentary evidence firmly attributing it to Kpengla, the traditional story must have got confused.

necessary to fight to secure captives and provide one of the conditions that would encourage the ships to come to Whydah. Kpengla also realised that so long as Dahomey was under Oyo, it would be impossible to deal effectively with Porto Novo, which was rapidly becoming the greatest rival of Whydah port.

Keen European observers, however, thought that these two political objectives were impracticable for many years to come. The Dahomean army was still too weak to enforce the first and it was so much hot air at that time for Dahomey to talk of declaring independence of Oyo. Indeed, for the rest of Kpengla's reign, nothing more was publicly heard of this policy, and no move, as far as is known, was taken to realise it.

However, Kpengla vigorously pursued his declared policy of increasing the supply of slaves from Dahomean raids. Soon after his accession he declared the paths between Porto Novo and Igelefe closed and sent raiders to make them unsafe. His excuse was that he had a misunderstanding with certain chiefs between Igelefe and Porto Novo,[1] but in fact the measure appears designed to force the Dahomeans to make their own captives. However, in March 1777, when he found that this measure did not produce as many slaves as he had expected, he reopened the roads.[1]

Between 1775 and 1781 he regularly sent out raiding parties which, as has been noticed, were almost regularly defeated, sometimes disastrously. Early in 1775 he sent a raiding party to the country of the Seretchi,[2] but his army was defeated.[3] Between 1775 and 1776 he sent two more expeditions out to some undisclosed destination both of which ended in utter defeat.[4] In the second of these, the Dahomean party of about eight hundred was completely wiped out. The raiding party sent out at the end of July 1777 only avoided being taken captives themselves.[5] An expedition against the Mahi between March and June 1778 brought back a few slaves,[6] but that against Aguna

---

[1] O. Montaguere to Ministre de Colonies, 6 Oct. 1777 (AN. C. 6/26).
[2] The Seretchi lived between Great Popo and Lake Aheme.
[3] A. Dalzel, *History*, pp. 163–4; Le Herisse, *L'Ancien Royaume*, p. 306.
[4] Chenevert and Abbé Bullet, 'Réflexions...', 1776 (AN. C. 6/27 *bis*).
[5] 'Accounts and Daybooks for Whydah', 2 Aug. 1777 (T 70/1161); A. Dalzel, *History*, pp. 165–6; Dalzel mixes up the Dahomean raids at this point. The Mahi campaign took place in 1778 and was not successful as he would seem to imply. The expeditions were slave raids, not wars with any political motives.
[6] L. Abson to R. Norris, 21 June 1778 (T 70/1551).

towards the end of 1778 came back defeated early in January 1779. Kpengla then begged for arms from the Europeans and was later able to announce a 'complete' victory. The raid sent out at the end of 1779 ended disastrously on 3 January 1780.[1]

Some of these raids failed mainly because the soldiers did not have sufficient powder and bullets, which could only be obtained from the European traders. Kpengla was therefore forced back to Tegbesu's earlier conclusion that the first prerequisite for an economic revival was a constant supply of European ships.

He accepted a proposition suggested to him early in his reign by Sessu, an exiled Badagrian chief then in Abomey, that one way of procuring the European ships and therefore arms, was to establish another Dahomean port at Jakin, east of Whydah, nearer the area which had become the favourite of the European captains. Sessu promised that he would personally see to it that the new port had a sufficient supply of slaves. In that way some of the ships that went to Porto Novo and Badagry might be drawn away.[2]

Sessu's suggestion, though useful to Kpengla, was not altruistic. Before 1776 he had been a contender for the throne of the Akran of Badagry against another prince 'Guinguin' (Gangan), had lost and had then withdrawn to Porto Novo. Between June and October 1776 he had attacked Badagry in a bid to gain the throne, but had been defeated again and forced to withdraw to Abomey.[3] His suggestion that Kpengla should consider establishing a new port at Jakin was made in the hope that such a port would somehow decrease the trade of Badagry to the advantage of himself who would become Kpengla's representative in the new port. Kpengla, however, saw it as a way of attracting the ships and the arms he so much needed.

On 30 October he sought the opinion of the European directors on whether the venture would be advantageous to trade and asked for their co-operation. Although the directors realised that the port was too near Whydah, had no independent source of slaves and would generally be disadvantageous to their own

---

[1] 'Accounts and Daybooks for Whydah', 2 and 24 Jan. 1779, 3 Jan. 1780 (T 70/1162).

[2] De Warel to Ministre de Colonies, 1 Nov. 1776 (AN. C. 6/26).

[3] 'Report of the Captain of "Duc de Bougonne" of Nantes', 24 Sept. 1775 (ADN. B. 4595); Chenevert and Abbé Bullet, 'Réflexions...', 1776 (AN. C. 6/27 *bis*).

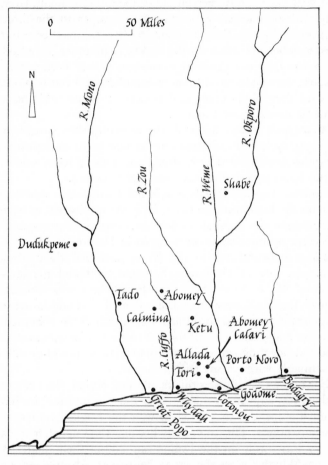

6. The kingdom of Dahomey and its neighbours towards the
end of the eighteenth century.

interests, so great was their suspicion of each other's intentions that they all replied in the affirmative and offered to co-operate.[1] A year passed, however, and no ships called at Jakin. In April, July and September, Kpengla sent messages to the directors urging them to use their influence to direct ships there,[2] but his messages bore no fruit. At the end of September, he asked the European forts to contribute to the cost of maintaining the port because they had agreed to its re-establishment but had refused to send their ships there, and because he alone could not continue to shoulder the expense.[3]

As a result of this demand, the directors were forced to tell Kpengla their real objections to his new port, undoubtedly to his great disappointment.[4] After that, nothing more was heard of the Jakin port and it was presumably closed.

Nothing remained to Kpengla but to maintain moral pressure on the European directors. The Mehu himself, as we have seen, spent six days at Igelefe in November 1778 and his successor in office came down again in December 1780.[5]

To give confidence to the Europeans that their property would be safe in Dahomey, Kpengla tightened the laws on stealing. On 8 November 1777 he made a proclamation at Igelefe that 'whoever stole the value of a single cowrie, the king was determined to punish with death'.[6] On 8 September 1781 he made the law still more stringent. If any persons were detected 'stealing whitemen's property, they should be killed',[6] presumably without any trial.

For many years during this depressing period, the Dahomean authorities appear to have been most interested in having English ships and they tried to woo the English traders more than any others. This was surely because the English had played a very active role on the Dahomean side in their quarrel with the old Whydah since the 1750s. Moreover, Abson's reputation was very high in the 1770s as a result of his part in the peace of 1772.

[1] 'Accounts and Daybooks for Whydah', 30 Oct. 1776 (T 70/1161); De Warel to Ministre de Colonies, 1 Nov. 1776 (AN. C. 6/26).
[2] 'Accounts and Daybooks for Whydah', 30 April, 10 July and 1 Oct. 1777 (T 70/1161).
[3] *Ibid.*
[4] O. Montaguere to Ministre de Colonies, 6 Oct. 1777 (AN. C. 6/26).
[5] 'Accounts and Daybooks for Whydah', Dec. 1780 (T 70/1162).
[6] 'Accounts and Daybooks for Whydah', 18 Nov. 1777 (T 70/1161); 8 Sept. 1781 (T 70/1162).

In September 1779 the king called Majerican, the Dahomean interpreter of the English fort,[1] to Abomey for consultation on the best means to attract English ships. At his own suggestion Majerican was despatched on an embassy to Cape Coast Castle 'to lay the state of [Kpengla's] wants before the governor', but the visit had no practical result.

In 1781, when it had become quite apparent that the English were not greatly interested in his port, Kpengla asked the French and the Portuguese directors to write to their countries and their governments and to ask them to send more ships to his port.[2]

When none of these measures brought more European ships and the coffers of the monarchy continued to run low, Kpengla decided to seek greater advantages from the internal slave trade. First, he ordered out of Igelefe all the non-Dahomean traders, except the Oyo, whom he could not properly regard as foreigners, on the pretext that they had disclosed his secret war preparations to his enemies. He then fixed the price of slaves for Dahomean traders at thirty-two cabesses (64,000 cowries) for a male and twenty-six (52,000 cowries) for a female slave, and set his agents to buy at those prices to be resold to the European exporters at higher prices.[3]

Not satisfied that his subjects were disposing of their slaves fast enough at those prices, he made another law that anyone who had two slaves must sell one to the king. If anyone had three, he must sell two to the king.

It was bad enough for prices to be fixed when the demand was much greater than the supply and a higher one could easily be obtained, it was worse to be forced to part with one's property at such an unsatisfactory price. So the Dahomean traders were discouraged from venturing out to buy slaves. Since Kpengla had earlier driven out the non-Dahomean traders, the result of his measures was to cause an even greater decrease in the number of slaves available in Dahomey.

The Dahomean traders, who were all king's officers, appreciated this situation and complained in a body to the king. They were, however, accused of conspiracy and had to purge themselves with heavy fines, after protracted litigation, on 1 May

---

[1] 'Accounts and Daybooks for Whydah', 11, 15, 16, 20, 31 (*sic!*) Sept., and 9 Dec. 1779 (T 70/1162).
[2] 'Accounts and Daybooks for Whydah', 8 Sept. 1781 (T 70/1162).
[3] A. Dalzel, *History*, pp. 213–15.

1779. After that all the chiefs at Igelefe gathered at the house of the Yovogan and swore fealty to the king.[1]

Having now tried almost every method to attract the European ships and failed, Kpengla, completely at the end of his wits, accused the directors in his kingdom of having declared a war on him and by implication asked them to show why he should not regard them as his enemies from then on.[2] But even this threat did not produce an improvement.

The result of Kpengla's failure was a deep depression which continued from 1767 to 1782 and caused widespread hardship. From 1776 onwards, by far the greatest number of the European and the Brazilian ships which resorted to the 'slave coast' went to trade at Porto Novo.[3] Figures are not available to show this, particularly because no European forts were ever built there, but the documents give an unmistakable impression of a thriving commerce at Porto Novo. Dalzel records that in 1786 there were at one time eleven French ships in Porto Novo while there was only one brig in Whydah port.[4] John Adams, who made ten voyages to the area between 1786 and 1800, also conveys the impression that Porto Novo was, for a long time during this period, the leading port in the Yoruba-Aja country.[5]

The fact that Porto Novo, formerly a weaker neighbour of Dahomey, continued to flourish under the protection and encouragement of Oyo, while Dahomey was so depressed, was both humiliating and dangerous.

Because the national energy had been directed towards the promotion of the slave trade, industry and agriculture were sadly neglected. Abson, sending a locally manufactured cloth to Miles at Cape Coast Castle in 1783, was apologetic for the decline in quality.

I send you a good Whydah cloth which I hope you will find to your liking; they are both scarce and inferior to what they used to be. The

---

[1] A. Dalzel, *History*, pp. 213–15; 'Accounts and Daybooks for Whydah', 1 May 1779 (T 70/1162).

[2] 'Accounts and Daybooks for Whydah', 14 April 1780 (T 70/1162).

[3] R. Miles to R. Norris, 15 Jan. 1778 (T 70/1483). Miles wrote, 'The Portuguese begin to find their way to the coast again now as much as ever.' These ships could only trade at Porto Novo since at this time there was no trade in Whydah port and Lagos port was considered too small.

[4] A. Dalzel, *History*, p. 194.

[5] Captain John Adams, *Sketches taken during ten voyages to Africa between 1786 and 1800* (London, 1821), pp. 17–18.

king when we goe [*sic*] to visit him always apologises when he is about giving us our cloths, knowing they are not so good as formerly.[1]

Much more serious, however, was the neglect of agriculture. In 1780, for the first recorded time in the eighteenth century, a serious famine broke out in Dahomey and the Dahomeans took to eating unfamiliar wild fruits. As a result, an epidemic of an unknown disease broke out in the following year and killed a great many Dahomeans.[2]

By 1777 burglary had again become a serious problem at Igelefe,[3] a sign that the casual labourers employed by the ship's captains no longer had enough work. In January 1779 Kpengla himself asked the directors to supply him with guns and gun-powder either free of charge or on credit.[4] The *Anubomey*, politically the most important annual ceremony in Dahomey, was twice fixed and twice postponed in 1780,[5] obviously be-cause Kpengla had no money to finance the heavy expenses involved.

The clearest indication of the impoverishment of the Daho-means is shown by the affairs of Lionel Abson, the English director since 1770, whose fortune was completely ruined by the help he had given, over a period of years, to needy Daho-means. At the end of 1782 several chiefs from the Migan downwards, and several Dahomean traders, owed Abson alone one hundred and twenty slaves, three hundred and fifteen 'ounces' of choice goods, five hundred and thirty-nine 'ounces' and six 'ackies' of cowries, three ounces of gold and two hundred and twenty-eight pounds of ivory. That excluded the debt owed by the king who 'commands from you what he knows you have by you with that impudence not to be borne'.[6] It is impossible to calculate accurately how much the known debts owed to Abson would be worth in eighteenth-century money, but it could hardly be much less than £16,000.

Abson was not the richest European director then at Igelefe. Olivier Montaguere appears to have been much richer and he

---

[1] L. Abson to R. Miles, 30 Dec. 1783 (T 70/1545).
[2] A. Dalzel, *History*, p. 178; 'Accounts and Daybooks for Whydah', 12 Sept. 1780 (T 70/1162). Dalzel's dating of this famine is inaccurate.
[3] 'Accounts and Daybooks for Whydah', 18 Nov. 1777 (T 70/1161).
[4] 'Accounts and Daybooks for Whydah', 2 Jan. 1779 (T 70/1162).
[5] 'Accounts and Daybooks for Whydah', 7, 14, 19, 20, 21 and 26 Jan., 6 and 28 Feb. 1780 (T 70/1162).
[6] L. Abson to R. Miles, 14 Dec. 1782 (T 70/1545).

could hardly have given less than Abson did to the Dahomeans of all classes. He probably gave more as he was seriously competing with Abson to gain the favour of the Dahomean authorities.[1] In November 1781 he himself declared that for some time past, the king and all the chiefs of Dahomey had been well disposed towards him because he had continuously and increasingly given them presents and goods on credit, 'which is the only way to maintain their friendship at a time when they are always in urgent need'.[2]

A large amount must also have been borrowed from the Portuguese director and traders in Dahomey, but the details are not known.

This decline in fortune came at a very awkward time for Dahomey. For just then political changes in Oyo increased the burden of the tribute paid by Dahomey to Oyo. Abiodun, who ascended the Oyo throne in 1774, saw clearly the economic advantages which Oyo could derive from its tributaries and he decided to extract those advantages much more fully than any of his predecessors are known to have done. There were therefore many occasions during this period when the impoverished Kpengla was forced to satisfy the Oyo demands under threats of invasion. Two examples, which are probably typical of many more, have been recorded.

When the death of the Mehu of Dahomey was announced on 27 January 1779[3] Abiodun's representative at Abomey demanded his movable property and one hundred of his wives. Though the Mehu had lived to a ripe old age, he, like most Dahomeans at this time, probably left a heavy debt rather than wealth behind, and it fell to Kpengla to find the means of satisfying the Oyo. Kpengla therefore sent a few items. About the following April, Abiodun sent to demand the rest of the Mehu's property, with a threat that if they were not sent promptly, he would send his Basorun to fetch them. So well did the Dahomeans remember and dread the power of Gaha, that five years after his death, anyone holding his office still made them tremble. Kpengla not only sent what he called the rest of the

---

[1] L. Abson to R. Miles, 31 Dec. 1783 (T 70/1545).

[2] O. Montaguere to Ministre de Colonies, 24 Nov. 1781 (AN. C. 6/26).

[3] 'Accounts and Daybooks for Whydah', 27 Jan. 1779 (T 70/1162); A. Dalzel, *History*, pp. 173–4; E. Dunglas in *E.D.* vol. xx. Dalzel is in error about the date of the death of the Mehu. Dunglas worsens the error by rationalising without any further evidence whatsoever.

Mehu's property, but also some of the captives brought back from the Aguna campaign, undertaken just before the death of the Mehu.[1]

The second occasion arose out of the non-payment of corals which were normally payable to Oyo. During these years of depression (it is not known exactly when) Kpengla withheld this payment with the excuse that coral was no longer available.[2] Abiodun, discovering that the Oyo merchants were in fact still able to purchase corals from Igelefe, was greatly incensed at Kpengla's deception and sent immediately to remind Kpengla that he 'held his dominions no longer than whilst he regularly paid his tributes, and when he neglected it Dahomey belonged to Eyeo'.[3] Kpengla was forced to pacify the Alafin with heavy presents.

In the last nine years of Kpengla's reign, several of the factors that had caused the trade depression in Dahomey disappeared, making conditions appear favourable to the revival of the slave trade in Dahomey. In October 1781 British ships, emboldened by the growing preponderance of the British Navy in the Atlantic, started to come to Whydah.[4] The flow was increased by the end of the American war in 1783. In fact the peace seems to have produced a new enthusiasm throughout Europe for the pursuit of the slave trade. From then on until 1789 ships came in large numbers to all parts of West Africa.

Once again, there are no complete figures, though the few available illustrate the trend well enough. Between January and August 1783 Liverpool alone sent fifty-nine ships to all parts of West Africa and was fitting out twenty-five more.[5] In Septem-

---

[1] 'Accounts and Daybooks for Whydah', 2 and 24 Jan. 1779 (T 70/1162); A. Dalzel, *History*, pp. 174–7. Dalzel was completely mixed up about the sequence of the events here. Kpengla sent a raiding expedition against Aguna towards the end of 1778. By 2 Jan. 1779 the army had been beaten. He then borrowed gunpowder and brandy from the forts, supplied his army afresh and sent them again to Aguna. On 24 January they came back to report victory, three days after the Mehu died. The raid was therefore not undertaken to satisfy the Oyo demands.

[2] A. Dalzel, *History*, p. 209.

[3] *Ibid.*

[4] 'Accounts and Daybooks for Whydah', 5 and 7 Feb. 1782 (T 70/1162); L. Abson to ?, 10 March 1782; John and Thomas Hodgson to R. Miles, 19 Jan 1782 (T 70/1545).

[5] 'An Account of vessels from Liverpool to the Coast of Africa since 1 January, 1783', Oct. 1783 (T 70/1549 (2)).

ber Abson, who had been at Whydah for the past sixteen years, wrote: 'Since I have been on the coast, I have never seen the quantity of Frenchmen arrive that has lately in so short a space of time, and more daily expected.'[1] In mid-October sixty French ships were reported to be at Angola alone.[2] In July 1783 Ollivier Montaguere complained that all the Yoruba-Aja ports were swarming with Portuguese ships which continued to come in still larger numbers.[3] So many in fact did they become that the Portuguese director later complained that the captains no longer obeyed the Portuguese law that enjoined them to trade one after another.[4]

This trend continued through 1784 and 1785, when many ships departed from the Cape Coast road for Whydah, Badagry, Lagos and other ports. Between January 1785 and January 1786 sixty-five ships were recorded as calling at Cape Coast Castle,[5] from where most of them took canoes and canoemen before departing to their different ports of trade. Between May 1786 and April 1787 fifty ships were recorded as calling at Cape Coast road.[5]

The fact that so many ships came out only signifies that the European conditions were once again favourable to the free movement of the ships from Europe. Before Dahomey could benefit from the situation, its rulers would have to draw these ships to the Whydah port. In this, developments in Oyo politics were helpful to Dahomey.

By 1781 the power of Oyo was on the wane. Abiodun's neglect of the army and his subordination of the other economic activities to the needs of the slave trade must have been among the important factors in this decline. In July 1783 the Bariba revolted against their tributary status and defeated an Oyo army sent against them to bring them back to their allegiance.[6]

---

[1] L. Abson to R. Miles, 2 Sept. 1783 (T 70/1545).
[2] L. Abson to R. Miles, 18 Oct. 1783 (T 70/1545).
[3] O. Montaguere to Ministre de Colonies, 12 July 1783 (AN. C. 6/26).
[4] F. Antonio de Fonseca e Aragão to King of Portugal, 25 June 1784 (AHU. S. Tome Caixa 10).
[5] 'Arrivals and Departures', May 1784–Sept. 1785 (T 70/1553); 16 Jan. 1785–31 Jan. 1786 (T 70/1554); May 1786–April 1787 (T 70/1555).
[6] L. Abson to R. Miles, 26 Sept. 1783 (T 70/1545). Abson, who had been commenting on the arbitrary way in which Kpengla raised the prices of the slaves, wrote: 'To this pitch is Whydah already arrived and the reason is simple: the Ihos (i.e. Oyo), the nation he pays tribute to have received two months ago a total overthrow from a country by name Barrabas (i.e.

Between 1781 and 1788 a series of quarrels broke out among the coastal kingdoms of the Oyo Empire which Abiodun could not effectively compose.[1] From August to November 1781 Gangan, the Akran of Badagry, in alliance with certain unspecified chiefs between Badagry and Lagos, attacked Porto Novo, the port of the Ajase Ipo.[2] The cause of the quarrel is completely obscure, but may have been that Gangan had not yet forgiven the king of Ajase Ipo for allowing Sessu to attack Badagry from his territory in 1776 and perhaps aiding him in the venture.

Because Porto Novo was regarded as vital to the economy of Oyo, an attack on it was sure to displease the Oyo authorities. Probably on Abiodun's orders, therefore, Gangan was deposed and deported to Brazil early in 1782, and Dovi, another Badagrian prince installed as Akran.[3] The disagreement between Ajase Ipo and Badagry, however, remained unresolved and about November 1782 Dovi, the new Akran, again attacked Porto Novo,[4] apparently without caring whether Oyo's interests were injured or not.

Abiodun therefore asked Kpengla to aid Ajase Ipo against Badagry, and Kpengla gladly accepted the duty because he knew that the ruin of the port of Badagry would be of some advantage to the trade of Whydah. Early in August 1783 the Dahomean army led by the Agau, the Ajase Ipo army and Sessu, the Badagrian pretender marched together against Badagry.[5] The allied army was, however, defeated and Kpengla had to confess that Badagry was too strong for the Dahomeans to attack.

This continued defiance and the recent failure of the Oyo army against the Bariba seem to have increased Abiodun's anger, and led him to order the complete destruction of Badagry.

Bariba) having lost in the battle II umbrellas and the generals under them...'; S. Johnson, *History*, p. 187. Contrary to Johnson, Bariba was lost in Abiodun's time.
[1] S. Johnson, *History*, p. 187, gives the impression that Abiodun's wars in the Popo country were wars of conquest. This is far from being so.
[2] L. Abson to R. Miles, 9 July (T 70/1545); O. Montaguere to Ministre de Colonies, 24 Nov. 1781 (AN. C. 6/26).
[3] A. Dalzel, *History*, p. 181.
[4] L. Abson to R. Miles, 14 Dec. 1782 (T 70/1545); O. Montaguere, 'Extrait du lettres', ? Jan.–? Feb. 1783 (AN. C. 6/26).
[5] L. Abson to R. Miles, 11 Aug. 1783, 4 Dec. 1783 (T 70/1545); 'Accounts and Daybooks for Whydah', 24 Aug., 28 Nov., 11 Dec. 1783 (T 70/1162); A. Dalzel, *History*, pp. 181–2.

To carry out Abiodun's order, a powerful army consisting of the Dahomeans, the Ketu, the Mahi and the Ajase, all under Oyo generals, started to assemble in April 1784.[1] The king of Lagos, hitherto an ally of Badagry, did not join the enemy forces, but agreed to prevent Badagry from getting any aid from the people of Lagos.

Responsible opinion appears to have regarded Abiodun's order as excessively harsh and the army generals adopted delaying tactics. The army which started to assemble in April was not ready until 23 August when the Dahomean contingent borrowed European boats to convey themselves.[2] Encamped before Badagry, they continued to delay the opening of hostilities. This delay ought to have given the Badagry a chance to sue for peace, but they chose rather to precipitate matters by themselves making the first attack, and were thoroughly worsted.

Dovi the Akran and some of his generals died fighting, the other leaders fled and their forces were dispersed. Badagry was completely razed to the ground. Some allied captains pitying the fleeing Badagrians, prevented them from being taken captives. The king of Lagos, probably Kutere, refused to enslave the refugees who came into his power and offered them a neutral place to settle near Lagos. The Dahomean contingent unceremoniously took their leave of their Oyo commanders on 23 September 1784.[3] The kingdom of Badagry, which had been founded or enlarged by the Allada and Whydah refugees and guaranteed by Ojigi in 1730, was no more.[4]

Although Abiodun's order was carried out, and Badagry destroyed, calm conditions did not return. For Abiodun took no measures to settle who should have authority over the abandoned territory or where the remnants of the Badagry people should live. Sessu, still determined to reign over the ruins, gathered the remnants of the Badagry people together under his own authority. Between 1784 and 1787 he established

---

[1] A. Dalzel, *History*, pp. 183–7; 'Accounts and Daybooks for Whydah', 23 Aug. 1784 (T 70/1162); 23 Sept. 1784 (T 70/1162). Dalzel notes Kpengla's actions without understanding, or at least explaining the politics behind them.

[2] 'Accounts and Daybooks for Whydah', 23 Aug. 1784 (T 70/1162).

[3] *Ibid.*

[4] This is worth noticing in view of the general opinion now current (for example, in C. W. Newbury, *The Western Slave Coast*, p. 30) that modern Badagry is the same ancient one founded in the 1730s by the dispersed Aja.

another Badagry, the origin of the present town, very near the coast. By January 1788 he had built two ports, one at his new Badagry and the other at a place called 'Cap Blanc',[1] and was determined to attract as many slaving ships as possible to his ports.

In August 1787 a son of Gangan who had accompanied his deported father to Brazil in 1782, returned and immediately sought to recover his patrimony. He asked the kings of Ajase Ipo and of Lagos to help him.[2] Whether the king of Ajase Ipo offered any help is unknown. The king of Lagos, however, took the opportunity to further his own expansionist ambition towards the west.

In March 1788 the Lagos naval army, consisting of about forty thousand men sent in two thousand boats, attacked a place called 'Peumeul', four miles east of the new Badagry. Sessu's brother, who had been installed chief of the town, fled and Sessu himself admitted that he had no forces with which to defend it.[3] The following month, Sessu rejected a Lagos demand for an annual tribute. Lagos thereupon again attacked the rest of Badagry, captured many of its citizens, but was still unable to enforce tribute.

Abiodun's action against Badagry had thus led to prolonged confusion and was therefore a sign of weakness rather than strength.

The same weakness was again demonstrated in Oyo's handling of an obscure quarrel which broke out between the kings of Weme and Ajase Ipo in 1786. Dalzel alleges that it was Kpengla who sowed dissension between them,[4] without saying how he did it. Oyo could not settle the quarrel peacefully and the king of Weme rashly attacked Ajase Ipo. His army was repulsed by the swivel guns of one Antonio Vaz, a Portuguese slave trader settled at Ajase Ipo.

Once again Abiodun was roused to action in defence of his 'calabash' and this time he decreed the destruction of Weme.

---

[1] Gourg to Ministre de Marine, 24 Jan. 1788 (AN. C. 6/26).

[2] Gourg to Ministre de Marine, 31 Aug. 1787 (AN. C. 6/26).

[3] A deposition by the 'Officers, Majors et mariners du Navire "le Solid" de La Rochelle...', 3 March 1788 (CCR. Cartoon xix); La Lugerne to Gourg, 25 Dec. 1788 (AN. C. 6/26). The size of the army seems an exaggeration.

[4] A. Dalzel, *History*, pp. 191–2; 'Accounts and Daybooks for Whydah', 3 April, 3 and 14 Dec. 1786 (T 70/1162).

In asking Kpengla to undertake the work, he said, Weme was 'too far to send any army for that purpose'.[1] This was a frank admission of the weakness of the Oyo army. Kpengla set out against Weme on 31 April 1786 and was there until November when the capital was finally taken and a large part of the population massacred.[1]

The king of Ajase Ipo, in defence of whose port the different campaigns had been undertaken, must have noticed that in the two destructive wars, the Dahomean army played the leading part. He must have reasoned also that if Weme was too far for the Oyo army, so surely was Ajase Ipo. He therefore concluded that the Oyo army was no longer a sufficient protection for his kingdom against any attack by his neighbours, and he started to look around for some other source of protection.

In June 1786 he talked to Senat, a French trader and the son-in-law of Ollivier Montaguere, about the possibility of the French establishing forts in his kingdom.[2] In July he formally invited 'the king of France to build three forts in my port, to guarantee commerce to his subjects and to fortify my own kingdom'.[3]

One of the forts was to be at Epe, to serve as a defence against any attack by Weme, the second was to be at Cotonou, to defend his kingdom against Dahomey and the third was to be at the beach at Porto Novo to serve as a general place of refuge for the king.[4]

For the privilege of building these forts, the French were to pay annually one hundred 'ounces' worth of goods in guns, gunpowder, brandy, cowries, hats and cloths of different types. French activities in Ajase Ipo were not to be centred in these forts, but would remain in 'Ardra', that is, the town of Ajase, twenty-five miles north of Porto Novo.[5]

---

[1] A. Dalzel, *History*, pp. 191–2; 'Accounts and Daybooks for Whydah', 3 April, 3 and 14 Dec. 1786 (T 70/1162).

[2] Senat to Ministre de Marine, 25 June 1786 (AN. C. 6/27).

[3] 'Copie (fidelle) de la permission qu'accorde le Roi d'Ardres aux Français de s'établir dans ses états', July 1786 (AN. C. 6/26).

[4] See note 5 below.

[5] 'Copie (fidelle) de la permission qu'accorde le Roi d'Ardres aux Français de s'établir dans ses états', July 1786 (AN. C. 6/26); Le Cte. de Flotte, 'Extrait du Journal...', 12 March 1787 (AN. C. 6/26). The mention of Cotonou here is interesting as it shows that the town was already in existence in the eighteenth century and was not founded in the 1830s as is generally supposed. See C. W. Newbury, *The Western Slave Coast*, p. 41. The

The disposition of these forts, the annual tributes demanded by the king of Ajase Ipo and the arrangement proposed for the French trade showed that security, not trade, was uppermost in the mind of the king of Ajase Ipo. The French traders, of course, saw this as a chance to extend French commerce in a port which seemed to them to promise an inexhaustible slave supply. For the next two years, until July 1788, French directors, traders, naval officers as well as the king of Ajase Ipo through his French-trained Hausa secretary, L. Pierre or Tamata,[1] continued to advocate the erection of, at least, one French fort in Ajase Ipo.[2]

The success of this plan would assure Porto Novo's lead in the export of slaves and its immunity from external attack. Dahomey would be deprived of any benefit accruing from the slow decline of Oyo and might in fact later be threatened by a powerful Ajase Ipo. The king of Ajase Ipo had no doubt that Kpengla would resent these implications and he therefore enjoined the greatest secrecy on all those who took part in the plans.

The weakening grasp of Oyo, however, ultimately made the execution of the project impossible. About the middle of 1787 Montaguere, recalled to France in disgrace, divulged the secret to Kpengla, who became incensed against all the European traders, particularly against the French, for what he regarded

paraphrase from de Flotte's account on this reads: 'Le Roi d'Ardra a envoyé un ministre à ce Commander pour le complimenter. Ce Noir a ouvert l'avis d'élever une redoute près du village de Cotony qui est le point où le Roi Dahomet pourvoit pénétrer dans le Royaume.' The difference between Porto Novo and Ardra was also clearly made by John Adams, the British slave trader, in J. Adams, *Sketches*, p. 16.

[1] This L. Pierre must not be confused with Pierre Hardy, as has been done by Akindele and Aguessy in *L'Ancien Royaume de Porto Novo*, p. 164. L. Pierre was a Hausa by birth, who was trained in Nantes and came back to Ajase Ipo as secretary of the king in the 1780s. How he got to Nantes and back is not known. Pierre Hardy was a French slave trader from La Rochelle, who frequently traded at Porto Novo and has written many rude things about Ajase Ipo people in his private letters now kept in the Chambre du Commerce de La Rochelle. He was a fervent advocate of the erection of a French fort at Porto Novo.

[2] Only a few examples of the voluminous correspondence on this subject can be quoted here; O. Montaguere, 'Project d'établissement à la Côte d'Afrique', 25 June 1786 (AN. C. 6/26); P. Hardie to Chambre du Commerce de La Rochelle, 16, 24 July, and 5 Sept. 1786 (CCR. Cartoon xix); Champagny, 'Mémoire...de la Côte de Guinée', 6 Sept. 1786 (AN. C. 6/26); 'Avis et certificat...à M. de Castries...', 25 Sept. 1787 (AN. C. 6/26); Gourg to Ministre de Marine, 6 July 1787 (AN. C. 6/26).

as a deliberate attempt to make war on him. He decided to prevent the erection of any fort at Porto Novo. Fully conscious that the Alafin would bluff and do nothing, he instructed the Yovogan to raid the Porto Novo beach whenever there was any large concentration of ships in that harbour, which the Yovogan successfully did at the beginning of July 1787 capturing four-teen French officers and crew, sixty-nine canoemen and thirty Ajase citizens.[1]

The attack naturally provoked widespread reactions. The king of Ajase Ipo complained to Abiodun and sent to Kpengla to find out why his army had behaved in such an unfriendly way. As expected Abiodun sent a threatening message to Kpengla but was placated with large presents as well as by the kind gestures made to Ajase Ipo. Kpengla denied having sent the Yovogan on such an errand, told the king of Ajase that he had no quarrel with him and released all the Ajase captives. The king of Ajase Ipo and the French traders also took the oppor-tunity to impress on the French government the urgent need to build a French fort at Porto Novo to prevent a recurrence of this raid.

However, on 8 July 1788 Kpengla sent a peremptory order to the king of Ajase Ipo and to Sessu of Badagry to forbid them any longer to allow ships to moor in their ports to trade. How Kpengla came to occupy such a strong position as to be able to order a virtual closure of Porto Novo, without any protest from Oyo, is unknown. The king of Ajase Ipo did not think it worth-while to appeal to Abiodun, who would not have easily agreed that his 'calabash' should thus be rendered useless if he had had the power to prevent it. Instead, he wrote to the French traders advising them very strongly not to come to his port or to Badagry any longer. He made it clear to them that if they did, their goods would be raided and he would not be able to give them any protection.[2] The project was therefore dropped.

The result of Oyo's weakness was to make Porto Novo, Whydah's chief rival, less attractive to the European traders.[3] From 1781 to the beginning of 1785, the trade of Dahomey

---

[1] 'Avis et Certificat...', 25 Sept. 1787 (AN. C. 6/26); A. Dalzel, *History*, pp. 195–6.

[2] L. Pierre to French Companies and to M. Gourg, 22 July 1788 (ADN. C. 738).

[3] Gourg to Chambre du Commerce de La Rochelle, 30 Sept. 1788 (CCR. Cartoon xix).

therefore revived a little. In January 1783 all the ships which had moored in Porto Novo before its troubles started, left there and came to Whydah harbour.[1] Around the end of November 1783, competition was so keen there that the six Portuguese ships then in harbour started trading together instead of one after another as their law had enjoined upon them.[2]

Kpengla immediately set about deriving as much advantage as possible from this boom. He asked Abopa, a Dahomean chief whose duty was apparently connected with trade, to make a comprehensive survey of the situation. The Abopa came to Igelefe on 20 April 1783[3] and soon after his return to Abomey two steps were taken, probably as a result of his recommendation.

On 4 July 1783 Don Jeronimo, 'Fruku', was sent to Igelefe[4] as the special representative of Kpengla. As a result of his twenty-four years in slavery in Brazil, he probably spoke Portuguese and knew something of the slave trade in Brazil. His duty would be to attract mainly the Portuguese ships to Whydah and advise Kpengla on their activities. There is, however, no record that he was able to do much. It was this post that Da Souza later occupied and made more memorable during the reign of Gezo.

Then on 30 August the Abopa again came to Igelefe accompanied by the Ajau, the first counsellor. In the name of the king he fixed new prices. He laid down the sizes, volumes and quantities of the European articles that would officially constitute the 'ounce' and be used in the Whydah trade. No Dahomean trader must take anything different on pain of death.[5] Some of these increases meant that the Europeans must henceforth pay double the price they used to pay for a single, slave but they could not protest because the competition was very keen.

It might thus appear that Dahomey's difficulties were over, but there remained the problem of finding sufficient slaves to meet the new increase in demand. Abson, Montaguere and the

---

[1] O. Montaguere, 'Extrait des Lettres', ? Jan.–Feb. 1783 (AN. C. 6/26); L. Abson to R. Miles, 3 April 1783 (T 70/1545); O. Montaguere to Ministre de Marine, 12 July 1783 (AN. C. 6/26).
[2] L. Abson to R. Miles, 30 July, 26 Sept., 1 Oct., 20 Nov. 1783 (T 70/1545).
[3] 'Accounts and Daybooks for Whydah', 20 April 1783 (T 70/1162).
[4] L. Abson to R. Miles, 26 Sept. 1783 (T 70/1545).
[5] *Ibid.*

Portuguese director continued to complain that the slaves were too few in Dahomey.[1] In October 1783 Kpengla himself noticed that the ships in his harbour were taking very long to get their cargo and he sent a public crier to Igelefe to urge all the traders to exert themselves to see that the ships in the harbour got their complete cargo as quickly as possible,[2] but the appeal produced no increase.

To get more slaves Kpengla had to raid, and that he soon planned to do on grand scale. His success, however, depended on the strength of his intended victims, but the fact that the ships then came in large numbers and brought munitions gave him an initial advantage. In April 1788 he asked all the European forts to supply him with all the guns and gunpowder in their forts.[3] Between the beginning of May and the end of November, he sent out three raiding parties.

The first, which consisted of a fairly large number of soldiers, departed in May and went against a Yoruba town called 'Crootoohoontoo' in Ketu kingdom.[4] It successfully surprised the town and made many captives, but on its return it was way-laid by the main Ketu army and almost all its soldiers were killed or captured. The second was despatched against the old Whydah in July but it achieved no greater success as the Whydah had fled. The Dahomean party returned with only 'a pitiful acquisition of a few baskets of salt'.[5]

The kingdom of Ketu in particular seems to have been marked down by Kpengla as the principal field for his raiding operations. Perhaps Aguna and Mahi, the ancient raiding grounds, had been almost denuded of their virile populations. The Ketu had followed up their success by sending a delega-tion to Abomey to seek a firm peace. Kpengla entertained it with insincere professions, and in October, soon after it had left,

---

[1] O. Montaguere, 'Extraits...', 2 March 1783 (AN. C. 6/26); L. Abson to R. Miles, 1 Oct. 1783 (T 70/1545); F. Antonio da Fonseca e Aragão to King of Portugal, 25 June 1784 (AHU. S. Tome Caixa x).

[2] 'Accounts and Daybooks for Whydah', 12 Oct. 1783 (T 70/1162).

[3] 'Accounts and Daybooks for Whydah', 17 Sept. 1788 (T 70/1163).

[4] A. Dalzel, *History*, p. 199; Gourg to Ministre de Marine, 16 July 1788 (AN. C. 6/26); E. Dunglas in *E.D.* vol. xx, p. 21. Dunglas calls the town 'Kroukrouhounto' but the place cannot now be identified. For the Ketu version of these attacks see E. G. Parrinder, *The Story of Ketu* (Ibadan, 1956), pp. 35 ff.

[5] A. Dalzel, *History*, p. 197; 'Accounts and Daybooks for Whydah', 27 July 1788 (T 70/1163).

he sent another raid into Ketu territory, but his army was again unsuccessful.[1]

Undaunted by his failures, Kpengla again prepared for a major attack on Ketu. During the *Anubomey* celebrations in December 1788 he announced that he would soon make an important war. In January 1789 he spread a false alarm that the Popo were coming to invade his kingdom,[2] and demanded guns and gunpowder on credit from the Europeans.

Early in February the expedition against Ketu set out, and returned towards the end of the month.[3] The details of this war are unknown. It is probable that Ketu city itself was not attacked and that the Dahomean success, if any, was limited. In fact the Dahomeans later discovered that the *Ifa* oracle had forecast that whenever they attacked Ketu, their king would die,[4] a convenient way of saying that for many years Ketu would remain too strong for Dahomey to attack.

It is impossible to say whether Kpengla would have been able finally to procure slaves, now that he had resumed the military initiative with a regular supply of firearms. For on 13 April 1789 he died of the smallpox at about the age of fifty-four, rather young for the kings of Dahomey.[5] Soon after, the internal conditions of Dahomey and the international conditions governing the slave trade deteriorated, plunging Dahomey back into depression and undoing whatever had been achieved in the last two decades.

For, in spite of the persisting depression, some advance had been made. In 1767 the Dahomean army had been weak and unable to protect the port or procure slaves for export. The

[1] A. Dalzel, *History*, p. 201.

[2] Gourg to Ministre de Marine, 27 Jan. 1789 (AN. C. 6/26).

[3] Gourg to Ministre de Marine, 2 and 28 Feb. 1789 (AN. C. 6/26); J. N. Inglefield to Philip Stephens, 20 June 1789 (Adm. 1/1988). The differences in the length of this campaign as given by the English and French sources could be due to the efficiency of the sources of information available to each of them.

[4] A. Dalzel, *History*, pp. 201–3; E. G. Parrinder, *The Story of Ketu*, pp. 35 ff.; F. E. Forbes, *Dahomey and the Dahomans* (London, 1851), p. 20.

[5] Gourg to Ministre de Marine, 25 April 1789 (AN. C. 6/26); 'Accounts and Daybooks for Whydah', 3, 5 and 20 May 1789 (T 70/1163); A Dalzel, *History*, p. 203; E. Dunglas in *E.D.* p. 25. Dalzel, followed by Dunglas, gives the date of Kpengla's death as 17 April 1789. Gourg, the French director who was on the spot when it happened, gives 13 April when he wrote less than two weeks after the event. He wrote: 'J'ai l'honneur de vous prévenir que le Roy Dahomet est mort le 13 de ce mois à 5 heures du matin de la petite verole...'

trade of Dahomey continued to diminish. The Dahomeans had been impoverished and had found it hard to pay the Oyo demands. There was a real possibility that the security of Dahomey might be jeopardised by the growing trade of the neighbouring ports.

In 1789 most of these dangers had disappeared. The Popo raids had stopped, Dahomey had resumed military initiative and there were hopeful signs that its trade might revive. No fundamental progress had, however, been made towards a solution of Dahomey's basic problem which was the kingdom's utter dependence upon an international economic system which Dahomey could not foster by itself. Tegbesu tried the peaceful method of an amicable settlement with the Popo and the old Whydah raiders, and Kpengla revived militarism, created a new port, made stringent laws, sent missions to the European directors and even threatened the Europeans in his kingdom, without achieving any substantial result. What finally helped Dahomey was the renewed enthusiasm for the slave trade that followed the end of the American war of independence, and the gradual decline of the power of Oyo.

# 6

## Threats to the new system, 1789-1818

When Agonglo ascended the throne in 1789 Dahomey had still not achieved its political independence or revived its declining economy. The successful solution of the economic problem was the more urgent task. The depression of the last twenty years affected all the citizens of Dahomey and was therefore potentially dangerous to the stability of the kingdom. Until conditions improved, projects for political independence would not evoke any general enthusiasm.

In one very important respect, local political conditions within the Oyo empire, of which Dahomey was a part, appeared favourable to the solution of both the economic and the political problems of Dahomey. The weakness of Oyo, which was first apparent in 1783, continued and intensified. Abiodun, the Alafin of Oyo since 1774, died in April 1789,[1] and was succeeded by Awole, who not only inherited the weakness left by Abiodun but also created new and insoluble problems for himself and the Oyo empire.

About the middle of 1790, a year after his accession, the Nupe (Tapa), hitherto a tributary people to Oyo, rebelled. The army which Awole despatched against them was defeated late in 1790 or early in 1791.[2] Nupe, like Bariba eight years earlier, thus achieved its independence from Oyo.

[1] Gourg to Ministre de Marine, 8 June 1789 (AN. C. 6/26). This is a very important date hitherto unknown. Gourg's exact words are: 'J'ai l'honneur de vous prévenir que le Roy des Alliots est mort presqu'en même tems [sic] que le roy Dahomet et même quelque tems avant, c'est à dire en Avril dernier.' I have taken into consideration all the events of this period, and have concluded that the 'Roy des Alliots' referred to here could be no other than the redoubtable Abiodun.

[2] About the middle of 1790 the Europeans were complaining that the slaves were getting scarce at Porto Novo and Badagry, which was always an indication that the Oyo, who wholly supplied those two ports, were experiencing some difficulties in making captives. In March 1791, around the same time that the defeat of Oyo was announced, there were no slaves at all to be had from Porto Novo. The Oyo were not at that time under the Nupe as Dalzel thought. Europeans on the coast were generally and quite

Soon after this, the decline of Oyo took a sudden and precipitate turn for the worse. A number of political mistakes brought the whole of its administration completely down within five years. The expedition which Awole ordered out about 1793 against Apomu did not leave Oyo. Another which he ordered against Iwere, a town not very far from Oyo, mutinied at the camp. All the king's supporters were massacred and the siege was raised without any attack having been made. Back at Oyo the rebel leaders demanded that Awole himself should abdicate, which he did by committing suicide about 1796.[1]

Before his death, the king's authority had vanished and Oyo was being deserted. The next two Alafin immediately after Awole reigned for less than eight months between them and were both forced to commit suicide. In fact it would appear that they had no authority whatever. Perhaps for more than twenty years after 1797, Oyo had no Alafin.

A detailed inquiry into the causes of such a quick and calamitous collapse of the mighty Oyo empire is beyond the scope of this work. The date of the death of Awole, which happened eight years before the first outbreak of the Fulani *Jihad* in far off Gobir, makes it unlikely that that event played any significant part in its collapse in the earlier stages. Since the rapid disintegration started immediately after Awole's order to attack Apomu, a partial explanation may be provided by a closer examination of that order and its implications for the Yoruba political system.

Apomu was a market town within the kingdom of Ife, to which the Oyo, the Ife, the Owu, the Ijebu and the Egba resorted for trade. To order the market to be destroyed merely out of a personal vengeance,[2] was to jeopardise the economic interest of all the other kingdoms concerned and incur their ill will.

More, however, was involved. As has already been noticed,

understandably prone to believe that one power in Africa was subject to yet another farther inland. Deniau de la Garenne to Ministre de Marine, 3 July 1790 (AN. C. 6/27); Hogg to T. Miles, 19 March 1791 (T 70/1560); S. Johnson, *History*, p. 187; A. Dalzel, *History*, p. 229.

[1] S. Johnson, *History*, pp. 189–2. Johnson says that Awole reigned for about seven years. Experience has shown that where he has been able to give a precise period, he is usually not far wrong.

[2] Awole's grievance against Apomu was that, before he ascended the throne, he had been ordered to be severely flogged by the Bale of Apomu for man-stealing and slave-trading. See S. Johnson, *History*, pp. 189–2.

the organisation of the Yoruba was based on the *Ebi* social theory, in which the Ooni (the king of Ife) was the 'father' who through various symbols sanctioned the appointment of every other important Yoruba oba (king). The symbol given by the Ooni to every Alafin elect was the *Ida Oranyan*, otherwise called the *Ida Ajase* (the sword of Oranyan or the sword of victory), without which no Alafin had any authority. Before obtaining it, every Alafin elect must promise on oath, through his accredited representatives, that he would never attack the kingdom of Ife.[1] It was on the sanctity of this oath, which rested on the analogy that a son must never strike his father, that the safety of the Ife kingdom and the tranquillity of the Yoruba country as a whole had depended for centuries. It was this same principle which the rulers of Oyo had defended between 1726 and 1730 when Agaja had broken it by invading Allada in 1724. By ordering an army against Apomu, therefore, Awole had broken his oath and the fundamental principles of the Yoruba 'constitution'. In doing so, he rendered himself and the Oyo generally odious in the whole Yoruba country and he automatically absolved all his subjects from their oaths to himself.

The result was an immediate and complete evaporation of the authority of the Alafin and an amazingly rapid collapse of the Oyo internal administration. Almost immediately, 'the king's messengers and *Ilaris* no longer carried that dread as before'. The Basorun refused to trace the theft of a koran when the Alafin ordered it. The army generals including Afonja at Ilorin and Edun at Gbodo, as well as Owota, the chief of the king's bodyguard, immediately renounced their allegiance.[2]

The only way by which authority could be restored in Oyo was by fresh rites being performed at Ile Ife. For some unknown reason, this proved immediately impossible. The powerful army leaders therefore started to assert their independence of the central authority and to create little kingdoms for themselves out of their local jurisdictions leaving Oyo itself to be ruled by a self-appointed junta. These rulers were not sufficiently well established until about 1805.

[1] This ceremony still goes on at the accession of every Alafin and was observed in great detail at the accession of the present one, though the oath is now politically meaningless.

[2] S. Johnson, *History*, pp. 189–194. Johnson's interpretation of these events is quite different but erroneous because he proceeded from the false premise that the whole of the Yoruba country was under the rule of Alafin.

These Oyo troubles might have eased Dahomey's attempts to solve its problems. If Agonglo had declared independence, the chances were that Oyo would be too divided to bring Dahomey back to allegiance. If he had occupied Porto Novo permanently, thereby preventing any trade from being carried on there and diverting its trade to Whydah, Oyo could hardly have offered any effective protest.

That Agonglo did not act effectively[1] can be accounted for by two main reasons. First, his own position at home was weak, and secondly, the European conditions and opinions were, by and large, increasingly unfavourable to the revival of trade in Whydah port.

The economic depression which had been going on for twenty years when Kpengla died in 1789 had started to cause a widespread discontent, particularly against the Tegbesu ruling line under whose regime the misfortune had occurred. In 1787 Gourg noticed a general restlessness among the Dahomeans and predicted a revolution.[2] In this atmosphere, the relatively mild succession contest which followed the death of Kpengla was significant and very ominous.

Four princes submitted their claims to the throne of Dahomey in April 1789. One was a son of Kpengla, a youth of about twenty-three. Two were Kpengla's brothers and therefore uncles of the youth, and the fourth was Don Jeronimo, otherwise known as Fruku.[3] Fruku's claim signifies that the descendants of the older sons of Agaja who had been excluded from the succession by Tegbesu now felt strong enough to challenge the Tegbesu line. Here indeed the danger lay, for the discontented elements in Dahomey now had a strong claimant to the throne who did not belong to the present ruling line.

The Migan and the Mehu, whose duty it was to elect a

---

[1] E. Dunglas in *E.D.* vol. xx, p. 32. Dunglas's colourful description of how Agonglo adopted the policy of independence from Oyo seems to be seriously confused. Considering Oyo's and Dahomey's conditions during these years it is unlikely that Agonglo refused to pay the annual tributes to Oyo at the opening of his reign, or that Oyo invaded Dahomey anew in the 1790s.

[2] Gourg to Ministre de Marine, 1 Aug. 1787 (AN. C. 6/26), 'De plus monseigneur, il ne tardera pas à y avoir une révolution...Il paroît qu'il y a un mécontentement général, et je crains bien que les forts ne soient obligés de se mettre en défense...'

[3] A. Dalzel, *History*, p. 223; Gourg to Ministre de Marine, 25 April 1789 (AN. C. 6/26); E. Dunglas in *E.D.* vol. xx, p. 27.

successor, backed Kpengla's young son, who took the name
Agonglo. It would seem, however, that public opinion, not least
among the influential chiefs, largely supported Fruku. For not
only were the losers not effectively silenced, Agonglo himself
was not crowned for a whole year, ostensibly because the Migan
was alleged to have been too ill to perform the traditional rites,[1]
but more probably because he was waiting for more public
support for his choice of candidate.

For a long time after Agonglo's election, no general support
was discernible. There was so much disagreement among the
chiefs, who were by no means unanimously happy at the election,
that for a whole year, state business was almost completely held
up. Abson, in disgust, complained on 20 April 1790 that he was

at a loss to know what we shall doe [*sic*] if things are here to be
decided by the king, for messengers sent to Dahomey never come
back. I have one there ever since the 5th February, the Portuguese
governor has one since January...and Deniau has a messenger ever
since January too with the king...We hear they are in pallavers
among themselves.[1]

The situation must have been fairly serious before the European directors could become aware of internal disagreements at
Abomey.

Agonglo only gained acceptance by his own very conciliatory
attitude. He made it a practice personally to visit the Migan in
his house, 'a mark of royal respect and condescension unknown
in former reigns'.[2] He promised publicly 'to indulge his subjects with many privileges'[2] as a result of which he abolished the
use of the gag. 'He redressed the grievances of the traders by
removing the oppressive restriction which had been laid upon
them by his father.'[3] Particularly he reduced taxes and incorporated into the army many of the tax collectors who must have
been a source of great and constant irritation to the impoverished
Dahomeans.

These actions and promises served to calm down the ruling
classes and to drive underground any manifestations of discontent by the general populace. In the middle of 1791 the

---

[1] L. Abson to Governor of Cape Coast Castle, 15 April 1790; L. Abson to
T. Miles, 20 April 1790 (T 70/1560).
[2] A. Dalzel, *History*, p. 223; Governor and Council, C.C.C., 20 Aug. 1789
(T 70/33 and T 70/1559).
[3] A. Dalzel, *History*, p. 223; E. Dunglas in *E.D.* vol. xx, pp. 27–8.

Migan and the Mehu, the two aged highest officers of the state, died within a week of each other.[1] This gave Agonglo the chance to nominate younger and more dynamic leaders to the state council and to bring that body fully over to his side. Despite this, Agonglo's position was never really strong. Although he realised that the only effective way by which popular discontent and opposition to himself could be completely removed was by an improvement in economic conditions of his people, to which problem he promptly addressed himself, all his efforts to improve the economy of Dahomey were rendered abortive largely by the lack of co-operation from his own subjects.

Immediately after his accession, he promised to follow the policies of his late father,[2] which meant procuring both slaves and ships for Whydah port. He was no sooner elected than he declared open all the trade routes leading to Whydah port, and reduced all the import duties to attract the non-Dahomean traders to Igelefe market.[3] It is not known whether this step met with any better success than Kpengla's method of driving away all the non-Dahomean traders, but the supply of slaves from outside was at best unreliable and the surest source continued to be raiding by the Dahomeans themselves.

On this method, Agonglo concentrated a great deal of his energy. Unfortunately owing to the prevailing disagreement among the chiefs, the first two raids, one against the old Whydah in 1789 and the other against an unnamed victim, probably the Mahi, in 1790,[4] were unsuccessful. Nor did the raids against the Mahi between 1791 and 1795 achieve much better results.

Only once during his short reign did Agonglo appear to have achieved any notable success against the Mahi. In May 1795 he despatched his army against the same Mahi province which had been continuously but unsuccessfully attacked since 1791.[5] This time, however, the army marched with a renewed enthusiasm, infused, according to the Dahomean oral traditions, by Agonglo

---

[1] Deniau de la Garenne to Ministre de Marine, 15 July 1791 (AN. C. 6/27).
[2] J. N. Inglefield to Philip Stephens, 30 May 1790 (Adm. I/1988); A. Dalzel, *History*, p. 224.
[3] J. N. Inglefield to Philip Stephens, 30 May 1790 (Adm. I/1988).
[4] 'Accounts and Daybooks for Whydah', 27 Oct. 1789, 15 Feb. 1790 (T 70/1163); L. Abson to R. Miles, 20 April 1790 (T 70/1560); A. Dalzel, *History*, p. 224.
[5] S. Mackenzie to Sec. of Admiralty, 15 Aug. 1795 (Adm. I/2131).

bestowing wives on the common soldiers. In the four engagements which took place between May and August, Agonglo's army was victorious and was confident of eventual success within the next month. It was probably on this occasion that they came back with 'upwards of one thousand prisoners'. Such a success was not repeated in Agonglo's reign, and the supply of slaves in Dahomey remained precarious and diminishing.

The only other way of bringing slaves to Whydah was by preventing trade in the nearby ports, which Agonglo also tried without much success. Towards the end of 1791 he sent raiding parties to Porto Novo and Badagry ports. In the former place, the crew and the canoemen of the three ships then in harbour were seized.[1] In the latter the Dahomeans were opposed by a Lagos army and they presumably withdrew.[2] In 1793 Agonglo again sent raiding parties against Badagry in the east and Little Popo in the west.[2] As in 1791 the party sent to Badagry came back empty handed and that sent against Little Popo found its victim too well prepared and had to divert its energy against Aguna, the old favourite slave-raiding ground north-west of Abomey.

Finally, at the beginning of 1795 the Dahomean army, in alliance with the Great Popo, came back against Little Popo.[3] A pitched battle ensued and went on for five days. At the end Agonglo's army was completely victorious. Three of the Little Popo generals were killed, the king and the chief next in rank to him, who was also the most important slave trader, were captured and presumably killed. The trade of Little Popo was disrupted for a short while, but it was already recovering towards the end of the year.

Whatever successes attended the raids on the nearby ports were therefore temporary and limited. They probably served to drive European slavers farther down the coast, well beyond the reach of Dahomean depredations, rather than to attract them back to Whydah.

In any case, European opinions and conditions were quite as unhelpful to Agonglo in the solution of his kingdom's economy

---

[1] Deniau de la Garenne to Ministre de Marine, 30 Sept. 1791, 4 March 1792 (AN. C. 6/27); T. Miles to A. Dalzel, 10 Oct. 1793 (T 70/1484).
[2] T. Miles to A. Dalzel, 10 Oct. 1793 (T 70/1483).
[3] T. Miles to A. Dalzel, 29 May 1795 (T 70/1571).

as his own position at home. In the last decade of the eighteenth century there seems to have been a growing conviction among the English traders that forts were indeed a hindrance rather than help to trade. Many of them therefore established their own private factories at Little Popo, Badagry and Lagos as well as farther away in Bonny and Calabar to which places they preferred to send their ships.[1]

In addition to this, Abson's management of the Whydah fort had become so inept as to undermine whatever little confidence was still placed in its usefulness. He had for long been inconveniently slow in sending his accounts to the headquarters at Cape Coast Castle, for which offence the Governor unsuccessfully recommended in January 1789 that Whydah fort be abandoned.[2] Worse was to come. As from 1790 Abson stopped all repair works on the fort which therefore started to fall down and to leak badly.[3] Moreover, he became increasingly subservient to the Dahomean authorities and less able to stand up for the rights of English traders.

For these reasons, Whydah port was unable to benefit from the steady flow of English ships which had continued since the end of the American war in 1783. Although the English captains continued to come to West Africa, unhindered by fears of French seizure, and unperturbed by arguments about the abolition of the slave trade,[4] only a few of them called at Whydah to trade. Indeed, by 1789 they had almost completely deserted Whydah.[5] Of the ninety-two ships which cleared in 1797 from Liverpool for Africa, only two went to Whydah as compared with thirty-six that went to Angola, thirty that went to Benin, Bonny, Old and New Calabar and four that went to Lagos.[6]

---

[1] R. Macaulay to T. Miles, 8 March 1791 (T 70/1560); L. Abson to Mann, 13 Aug. 1791 (T 70/1560).

[2] Governor and Council, Cape Coast Castle, to African Committee, 26 Jan. 1789 (T 70/33).

[3] E. William White to African Committee, 5 March 1809 (T 70/35); 'Remarks on Whydah fort', 1 Jan. 1804 (T 70/1163); Edmund Dodd and John Marshall, 'Observations on the state and condition of the fort and the trade thereof', 15 March 1793 (Adm. I/1714).

[4] 'Arrivals and Departures of Ships', Jan.–March 1789 (T 70/1559); Sept. 1789–Oct. 1790 (T 70/1561); Jan.–June 1791 (T 70/1564 (1)); July–Oct. 1791 (T 70/1564 (2)); Oct. 1791–Dec. 1792 (T 70/1565 (2)). Jan.–March 1793, Jan.–Nov. 1794 (T 70/1568); Nov. 1794–April 1795 (T 70/1570). 'Africa and the West India trade', 1805 (T 70/1585).

[5] J. N. Inglefield to Philip Stephens, 20 June 1789 (Adm. I/1988).

[6] 'Liverpool ships to Africa', 1797 (T 70/1575).

Much more serious than the effects of English attitude for the Whydah trade were those of the French Revolution, because they affected not only the French but also the Portuguese trade at Whydah. In 1794 the French, in a moment of Revolutionary fervour, abolished the slave trade as being incompatible with the principles of 'Liberty, Equality and Fraternity'[1] and although they later legalised it again on 20 May 1802,[2] French trade at Whydah did not revive during this period.

Soon the French decided to wage a war on the slave trade itself. In November 1794 a French squadron, falsely flying English colours, attacked and captured all the Portuguese ships trading in Whydah harbour. The Dahomeans protested very strongly, seized all the forts and confined all the directors and other tenants within the fort walls,[3] but none of these things discouraged the French.

In 1797 their squadron again seized the only two ships in Whydah harbour.[4] These French attacks on the slave trade went on intensively up to 1800, though they were not all directed at Whydah port.[5] Their general effect was nonetheless disadvantageous to its trade.

One by-product of these raids was the abandonment of the French fort at Whydah. Deniau de la Garenne, the director of the French fort, fearing the reaction of the Dahomean authorities after the French attack of 1797, the second in three years, escaped into one of the French ships, 'la Vengeur', and left Igelefe, leaving the fort in charge of a caretaker. Although he promised to come back, he never did, and the French fort was thus unceremoniously abandoned.

Another by-product of the French depredation was to dissipate Whydah's reputation as a safe anchorage. When the African Committee asked from their West African headquarters at Cape Coast in 1791 about which ports would be safe to trade in

---

[1] E. Dunglas, *E.D.* vol. xx, p. 33; Gaston-Martin, *Histoire de l'Esclavage dans les Colonies Françaises* (Paris, 1948), p. 228.

[2] 'Comptoir d'Amoukou et de Whydah', 25th Prairial, An 10 (i.e. 14 June 1802) (AN. C. 6/27).

[3] L. Abson to A. Dalzel, 14–22 Dec. 1794 (T 70/1570).

[4] L. Abson to A. Dalzel, 27 Aug. 1797 (T 70/1574); Citoyen Deniau to Pierre Bonon, 20 Aug. 1797 (AN. C. 6/27); P. Bonon to Cn. Ministre de la Marine et des Colonies, 10 Vendenaire, An 10 (AN. C. 6/27).

[5] Zachary Macaulay, Governor of Sierra Leone, to Captain Cornwallis, 2 May 1798 (Adm. I/1625); G. Nicholls to African Committee, 22 May 1798 (T 70/1575); James Digby to A. Dalzel, 8 Jan. 1800 (T 70/1576).

whatever the French decided to do, they were told that Whydah port was safe because 'the king of Dahomey is so absolute a monarch there as never to suffer Europeans settled in his dominions to have controversies of any hostile nature whatsoever'.[1]

The continued French attacks, which the Dahomean authorities could not effectively prevent, proved that assertion to be false. The Portuguese captains, the most constant traders at Whydah and therefore the greatest losers from those attacks, finding themselves defenceless against repeated French depredations, came only in small numbers in the 1790s.[2]

Agonglo was gravely concerned at the decreasing number of ships that visited his port, particularly as he must have realised that the supply of ships and arms formed part of the vicious chain that bound the economy of his kingdom, and he tried all he could to procure more. He, like his predecessor, held Abson responsible for the paucity of the English ships that called at Whydah, and he tried unsuccessfully to bully him into writing to England for more ships. For his failure, Abson was generally unpopular in Dahomey towards the end of his life. In May 1790 Agonglo sent two letters to the French government urging it to increase its trade to Whydah port but he got no reply.[3]

In 1795 the year which saw his army victorious both at the Mahi campaign and at Little Popo, he again made an effort to procure more Portuguese ships for Whydah. In March of that year he sent to the Queen of Portugal three ambassadors who carried a letter[4] in which Agonglo, after recalling the friendly relations that had existed between his ancestors and the kings of Portugal, talked about the sad state of the Portuguese trade in his kingdom, which he attributed to the then Portuguese director. He asked the Portuguese authorities to take steps to increase their trade to Whydah to which port he would like them to send all their ships. He also wanted them to send tobacco of the correct weight, as well as gold and silver to purchase slaves of better quality than those obtained for tobacco.

The ambassadors went to Lisbon by way of Brazil and re-

---

[1] Governor and Council, Cape Coast Castle, to African Committee, 1 March 1791 (T 70/1563).

[2] L. Abson to J. Ashley, 6 Sept. 1793 (T 70/1563).

[3] 'Colonies', 18 May 1790 (AN. C. 6/27).

[4] King of Dahomey to Queen Maria I of Portugal, 20 March 1795 (ABNJ. doc. 563); King of Dahomey to Governor of Bahia, 20 March 1795 (AHU. Bahia 16. 143).

turned to Dahomey in 1797, having been away for more than two years. Queen Maria sent two priests with them to convert Agonglo, but said nothing on the trade except that she would recall the Portuguese director against whom Agonglo had complained.[1]

The arrival of Agonglo's emissaries, bringing only spiritual consolation, brought to the surface the latent discontent in Dahomey. The Portuguese priests carried their altar pieces and their images with pomp from the beach to Igelefe,[2] a demonstration that impressed but did not please the Dahomeans. Agonglo's own misjudgement of the temper of his subjects cost him his life.

On 23 April 1797 Agonglo received in audience the Portuguese priests who outlined to him their mission. It would appear that he had been prepared for their message by his own ambassadors, and that he had made up his mind at least not to reject outright the invitation to embrace Christianity, probably because Queen Maria had stipulated that, unless he did, arms would not be forthcoming. He told the priests that he had been waiting for them and was ready to be instructed and baptised in the Catholic faith.[3] Whether he would in fact have gone through with it, we shall never know.

His apparent willingness to change the Dahomean religion immediately raised an urgent State emergency in which the defeated candidates or their descendants made themselves the defenders of the Dahomean 'Constitution'. A prince called Dogan at once put himself at the head of the disaffected. When the priests returned the second time to start to give instruction to the king, they were told that Agonglo was indisposed, suffering from the smallpox.[3] This was merely to send the priests away and keep them out of the intensive, but completely obscure, political activities that must have been going on inside

---

[1] Governor of Bahia to Secretary of State at Lisbon, 21 Oct. 1795 (AHU. Bahia 16. 143); Queen Maria to King of Dahomey, 16 Jan. 1796, 19 Feb. 1796; Queen Maria to Gov. of Bahia, 7 April 1796 (ABNJ. doc. 563).

[2] Dawson to Fitzgerald, 17 Nov. 1862 (CA. 2/016).

[3] Padre V. F. Pirez, *Viagem de Africá em o reino de Dahomé* (anno de 1800), pp. 59–76; Cn. Deniau to Cn. Bruix, 25 Noviose An 7 (AN. C. 6/27). The name of Dogan here should not be mixed up with another name 'Dekkon' (Dekan), whose pretension to the throne of Jena (Ijana) is said to have led to Adandozan's deposition in F. E. Forbes, *Dahomey and the Dahomans* (London, 1851), vol. II, pp. 24–5.

the palace walls. We shall never know whether a peaceful solution would have been reached if the arguments had gone on long enough.

On 1 May 1797 one of the women resident in the palace called 'Nai-Wangerie' (Na Wanjile) shot and killed Agonglo. There can hardly be any doubt that the persistent economic depression was already leading the kingdom to the verge of civil disobedience, and that the religious issue was no more than 'the last straw'. A dynastic war immediately ensued within the palace walls, in which Dogan and his faction were defeated and the supporters of Agonglo triumphed.[1]

Agonglo's second son, 'Ariconu', who must have been very young, was installed king of Dahomey under the title of Adandozan, in preference to his elder brother who had a defect in one foot.[1]

On 5 May Adandozan entered the Abomey palace and started to punish all those who had participated in, or in any way supported, his father's murder. Dogan and Na Wanjile were buried alive. Many princes, chiefs and war leaders who had supported the losing side must have been either executed or sold into slavery. It is probable that the mother of the future Gezo was among those sold at this time.[2]

Now that the dynastic rivalries had broken out into open violence, the chances of any peaceful succession in future became very dim. There were now two recognisable warring camps among the princes of Dahomey and the first step had been taken in what could become a prolonged civil conflict unless improved economic conditions rendered the king very popular and the claims of his descendants unassailable.

The accession of Adandozan meant that the Tegbesu line was once again triumphant and had a renewed opportunity to make good its claim to retain the throne of Dahomey. The circumstances of his accession, however, ensured that there could not immediately be a national united action to tackle the main economic problem. More than that, there was a lack of

---

[1] Padre V. F. Pirez, *Viagem de Africa*, pp. 59–76; M. J. Herskovits, *Dahomey*, vol. I, p. 14, records that certain Dahomean princes who had been sold into slavery during the crisis were still remembered in the 1930s during the celebration of the royal ancestral cult. J. Macleod, *Voyage to Africa*, p. 39.

[2] Le Herisse, *L'Ancien Royaume*, pp. 311–12; E. Dunglas in *E.D.* vol. xx, p. 35; M. J. Herskovits, *Dahomey*, vol. I, p. 12.

vigorous leadership as can be inferred from the installation of a minor. Adandozan had regents chosen for him for the first seven years of his reign and it was not until 1804 that he was old enough to rule on his own authority.[1] In fact for some time after that, European residents did not think he was entirely responsible for his actions. In 1806, nine years after his accession, a Frenchman, stranded in the French fort since 1803, said in a series of complaints, that 'the present king is very young and his word cannot be relied upon',[2] presumably because he changed his mind often according to the advice given to him by different elderly statesmen.

The composition of the regency which governed Dahomey during Adandozan's minority has not been preserved nor is it known how smoothly it worked. There is evidence that the regency council did not get on well with the Portuguese directors, four of whom were expelled in quick succession between 1797 and 1804. In addition, the lack of vigorous leadership meant that for many years the gallant attempt being made to improve the economy of Dahomey was slowed down or stopped. By the time Adandozan grew up, conditions were so changed for the worse that none of his measures brought any significant relief to Dahomey. Indeed it was during his reign that all the European forts were closed, which, to the ordinary Dahomean, was one more proof, if any more were needed, of the extraordinary 'bad luck' which the Tegbesu line had brought on Dahomey.

Nevertheless, when Adandozan took up the personal direction of his kingdom's affairs, he acted very vigorously to solve its economic problem. It was always his misfortune rather than his incompetence that all his measures were rendered useless by unfavourable external circumstances which he could not control.

Dahomean traditions, which are credible, relate that he conducted slave-raiding expeditions to the Mahi country which were probably unsuccessful, and that later he turned towards the Yoruba towns of Fita, Jaluku-Jalumo and Govie.[3] The diffi-

---

[1] Cn. Deniau to Cn. Bouix, 25 Noviose An 7 (AN. C. 6/27). Deniau said Adandozan was about twenty on his accession, but the chances are that Adandozan was not as old; King of Dahomey to King of Portugal, 20 Nov. 1804 (ABNJ. doc. 846).

[2] S. M. Goupil to ?, 1806 (AN. C. 6/27). Goupil was probably exaggerating because he was disgruntled.

[3] E. Dunglas in *E.D.* vol. xx, pp. 36–7, would imply that Adandozan's wars against the Mahi were successful, but he almost certainly has re-edited the traditions which he collected because of his conviction that Adandozan's

*Dahomey and its Neighbours*

culties confronting Oyo would completely isolate these towns and render them defenceless. In spite of that, the same Dahomean oral traditions relate that he was not any more successful than at Mahi. When that method failed, he tried disturbing the trade of the neighbouring ports. Partly as a result of the breakdown of authority in Oyo, the slave supply at Porto Novo had increased by 1803, and was soon to be further augmented by the outbreak of the Fulani *Jihad* in 1804.[1] In 1803 and again in 1805 Adandozan therefore sent raiders there to disturb its trading activities.[2] On the first occasion, all the Portuguese traders found there were seized and their boats and tents were burned. On the second occasion, the Dahomean army met and defeated the main army of Ajase Ipo. This was, however, a hollow and indeed an embarrassing success, for by 1805 the rulers of Oyo had sufficiently recovered at home to take up again a firm attitude. Adandozan received a stern warning to leave Porto Novo alone[3] which he never again dared to challenge.

To demonstrate still further the change in the local political atmosphere and Adandozan's utter helplessness, the rulers of Oyo sent to Adandozan in 1808 for the annual tributes which Adandozan was forced to pay in spite of his extreme poverty.[4] It is probable that the tributes were sent annually to Oyo until the deposition of Adandozan in 1818.

If Adandozan's local efforts to secure more slaves failed, still less successful were his diplomatic ones to secure an increase in the number of European ships that came to his port. In November 1804, soon after he was old enough to rule for himself, he sent two ambassadors to Portugal, accompanied by a Portuguese captured at Porto Novo the previous year.[5] His demands are of considerable interest as showing that he had learnt from the

achievements have been unnecessarily diminished. Considering the times and the circumstances, the army of Dahomey could not have had many successes.

[1] King of Ardra to King of Portugal, Ardra, 18 Nov. 1804 (ABNJ. doc. 846). The king said the trade of his port had been augmented by the *Male*, which means the Mohammedans.
[2] King of Dahomey to Governor of Bahia, 14 March 1804 (AHU. doc. Bahia 27.100); King of Dahomey to King of Portugal, 20 Nov. 1804 (ABNJ. doc. 846); 'Accounts and Daybooks for Whydah', 21 March 1805 (T 70/1163).      [3] S. M. Goupil to ?, 1806 (AN. C. 6/27).
[4] 'Accounts and Daybooks for Whydah', 10 March 1808 (T 70/1163).
[5] King of Dahomey to Governor of Bahia, 14 Nov. 1804 (AHU. Bahia 27. 100); King of Dahomey to King of Portugal, 20 Nov. 1804 (ABNJ. doc. 846).

abortive mission of 1797 and wanted to make Dahomey less dependent on European arms in future.

He emphasised that his own God was *Elegbara*[1] and by implication told the king of Portugal not to send missionaries to convert him. He wanted the Portuguese to send, not just ships and munitions, but persons who knew how to manufacture guns and gunpowder and who would be prepared to establish an arms factory in his kingdom. Moreover, he said he had gold mines in his kingdom which he would allow the Portuguese to work if they sent competent technicians. This was probably added merely to invite the Portuguese to prospect for gold in Dahomey.[2]

Like its immediate predecessor, the mission, although well received in Lisbon,[3] achieved no success. The Portuguese secretary of state decided that because the supply of slaves was greatly diminished in Dahomey, no friendship should be encouraged with Adandozan. He instructed the Governor of Brazil only to flatter or bully Adandozan into freeing the Portuguese prisoners in his court. He himself also wrote to Adandozan that the king of Portugal could not consider his request until those prisoners had been freed. The only benefit which Adandozan derived from his mission was six pieces of cloth sent to him by the Portuguese authorities. The attitudes of the Portuguese government indicate that Dahomey had no hope of a regular supply of ships from Portugal.

Behind this message lay Portugal's own internal difficulties as a result of increasing pressure by Napoleonic France. In 1805, the same year that saw the return of Dahomean ambassadors from Portugal, the Portuguese authorities were unable to send a successor to Jacinto Jose de Souza, the director of their fort, who died in that year. The storekeeper took over the direction, but for some unknown reasons the fort soon passed into private hands. The final blow was struck in 1807, when the Portuguese court itself was driven from Lisbon to Rio de Janeiro by Napoleon's invasion of Portugal.

[1] *Elegbara* is one of the Yoruba-Aja deities.
[2] Why both Agonglo and Adandozan should so much want a supply of gold is unknown, unless they needed it for trade with Ashanti or Dahomey's northern neighbours, for which there is no evidence.
[3] Governor of Bahia to King of Dahomey, 8 May 1805 (APB. Correspondence, vol. 15, f. 152); Secretary of State to Governor of Bahia, 30 July 1805 (ABNJ. doc. 846); Secretary of State for Portugal to King of Dahomey, 30 July 1805 (ABNJ. doc. 846).

From then on, all official contacts between the Portuguese court and their Whydah fort ceased for the rest of this period. Although Portugal continued stoutly to maintain its right of trade in 'Costa da Mina', in fact all Portuguese trade at Whydah appears to have stopped completely for a few years between 1807 and 1810. Officially or unofficially therefore, both the French and the Portuguese forts in Whydah were closed by 1807 and their trade there remained negligible or non-existent.

Meanwhile, the English trade in Whydah was also drying up. It had been expected that the death of Abson would end all the obstacles to the flow of the English ships to Whydah, but that did not occur after Abson's death on 27 June 1803.[1] Although Adandozan instructed the Yovogan to put the English fort in as good a state of repair as possible and wrote to the governor of Cape Coast Castle suggesting that James, Abson's assistant, be made director,[2] his letter was never replied to and misunderstandings and mutual suspicions quickly arose.

Some time after 1783, Abson seems to have assumed Dahomean citizenship. Moreover, he, like other directors of the forts, had the status of a chief under the Yovogan. After his death, therefore, Adandozan, in accordance with the Dahomean practices, seized Abson's property and four children from his marriage with a Dahomean woman,[3] as he would have done with any Dahomean chief after his death. James, the acting director, who did not fully understand the situation, reported Adandozan's 'tyrannical' measures to his superiors at the Cape Coast Castle, and all the officers qualified to take the directorship at Whydah fort were frightened away. It was not until March 1804 that Hamilton, who had refused it in 1803, agreed to become director at Whydah.[4]

[1] J. E. James to Jacob Mould, 28 June 1803 (T 70/1580); J. Macleod, *Voyage to Africa*, p. 79.
[2] 'Accounts and Daybooks for Whydah', 19 July, 1, 2 and 24 Aug. 1803 (T 70/1163).
[3] J. E. James to J. Mould, 15 July and 2 Aug. 1803 (T 70/1580); J. Macleod, *Voyage to Africa*, pp. 79–80. Macleod gives the impression that Sally's seizure was due to the king wanting to marry her contrary to her wishes. His explanation is probably wrong since that would not dispose of the seizure of Sally's elder brother George and her two younger brothers.
[4] J. Mould to J. E. James, 18 Aug. 1803 (T 70/1580); Minutes of the Council of Cape Coast Castle, 23 Dec. 1803 (T 70/1580); Minutes of the Council, 15 March 1804 (T 70/1581).

The governor of the Cape Coast Castle sent the report of Adandozan's action to the African Committee in London which in turn informed all the English traders to West Africa and communicated the information to the Board of Trade.[1]

The result of this unfavourable publicity was that Dahomey began to be very unpopular with the English, who were therefore henceforth very cautious in their dealings with Dahomey. Hamilton left Whydah in March 1805 under the pretext that he was going to welcome a new governor at Cape Coast Castle, but he did not return until January 1806, having been posted to another fort in the meanwhile. In November 1805, while he was still away, James, his assistant, died.[2] For a short while, the English fort had no officer. More than that, the fort contained absolutely nothing of value, the most valuable item in it being the flagstaff.[3]

This condition of the English fort aroused Adandozan's suspicion that the English might be planning to abandon their fort and he decided to prevent them. The only way open to him was to ensure that there was at least one Englishman left in the fort at any one time. Henceforth, no Englishman in Dahomey, whether he was an employee of the fort or not, was allowed to leave the country without a substitute.[4]

This desperate attempt to retain the English connection was interpreted by the English as a tyrannical measure taken by the king of Dahomey to restrict their freedom of movement and they became openly hostile. In May 1804 George Torrane, formerly an employee of the African committee, and later Governor of the Cape Coast Castle, visited Whydah as a naval officer and gratuitously gave a most unfavourable impression of the fort and of Adandozan:

[1] J. Mould to African Committee, 8 Sept. 1803 (T 70/34); Secretary, African Committee to Master of the Merchants Hall, Bristol, 23 Jan. 1804 (T 70/72). Sec. African Committee to W. Fawkener, 25 Jan. 1804 (T 70/72).

[2] 'Accounts and Daybooks for Whydah', 1 July and 12 Nov. 1805 (T 70/1163).

[3] Diggles Bayley to Capt. Malbon, 5 Jan. 1806 (Adm. I/2151).

[4] H. Hamilton to G. Torrane, 22 Feb. 1806 (T 70/1584); 'Accounts and Daybooks for Whydah', 10 Feb., 12, 20 and 25 March 1807, 10 Aug., 15, 29 Oct. 1807, 15 Jan. 1818 (T 70/1163). This policy was not given up throughout Adandozan's reign. In 1815, one Suett who came to trade at Whydah was detained though he was later released after good treatment. African Committee to Gov. and Council C.C.C., 15 Nov. 1815 (T 70/1599); the policy may have been behind the detention of every British explorer or agent sent to Dahomey later in the nineteenth century.

...it certainly is an object much to be desired that the fort at Why-dah may be abandoned. What is your governor there? A mere cypher to the king of Dahomey, who dare not leave the beach without his permission. Your list of slaves is said to be numerous...they are slaves only to the king and were you desirous of removing them or employing them, the event of the attempt would fully prove my assertion.[1]

When Bayley, the first victim of Adandozan's policy, was asked in 1806 by Captain Malbon of the Royal Navy ship then in Whydah harbour to give the state and condition of Whydah fort, he replied: 'with regard to the country, had you asked me the state of the worst country on earth, I could not give you a more vile description of it...'[2]

This was the state of the English opinion on Dahomey when in 1807 the British government abolished the slave trade. The question then was whether any form of British connection should be maintained with Dahomey. In November 1810 a Commission of Enquiry was appointed to recommend which of the British forts in West Africa should be retained and which abandoned.[3] The members of the commission visited West Africa but, because of Adandozan's notoriety, refused to visit Whydah fort.[3] They therefore collected all their information from the British officers in the Cape Coast Castle.

When the commission reported, it was quite emphatic that the British fort at Whydah

ought unquestionably to be given up; it is totally useless being without any trade and the ferocious king of Dahomey in whose territories it is situated so tyrannizes over the governor and the few people about him as to render such a subjection utterly disgraceful to the British flag.[3]

Almost everyone who commented on this report agreed with this recommendation.[4]

Only the African Committee, the body which had been entrusted with the care of all the English forts in West Africa,

---

[1] George Torrane to African Committee, May 1804 (T 70/34).
[2] Diggles Bayley to Capt. Malbon, 5 Jan. 1806 (Adm. I/2151).
[3] 'State and Condition of West African settlement', 15 Nov. 1810 (CO. 267/29).
[4] E. W. White to African Committee, 12 Oct. 1811 (T 70/1593); T. Norris to George Barnes, 20 Jan. 1812 (T 70/1594); Brown to Simon Cock, 10 March 1812 (T 70/1594).

opposed its abandonment. They argued that the country was populous and that the inhabitants showed 'a strong evidence of an advance in civilisation beyond what is apparent in other parts of the coast', that the land was fertile and produced indigo. They warned that its abandonment would only give advantage to the French and the Portuguese, who had not officially given up their forts, and would not mean a great deal of saving, since the cost of maintenance was not more than six hundred pounds a year.[1] Even the African Committee did not realise, however, that Adandozan very much wanted to retain the English connection.

Faced with the conflicting recommendations of two authoritative bodies, the Board of Trade took no decision and the fate of the English fort at Whydah was finally decided at Cape Coast Castle. On 26 July 1812 the Council there decided not to send any officer or provisions to the fort pending the pronouncement of the government, a decision which the African Committee later approved.[2] William's fort at Whydah was closed. This closure completed the process of abandonment of all the European forts at Whydah which had started in 1797. Indeed between 1807, when the Portuguese abandoned their fort and the English abolished the slave trade, and 1809, there seems to be practically no trade at all in Whydah port.

This terrible situation may have forced Adandozan and his advisers to think of an alternative basis of economy. In 1808 Adandozan actually tried to lead his people back to a love of agriculture, by inaugurating, in October of that year, the 'corn customs' or raising it from a private royal ceremony into a public celebration open to the masses.[3] He must no doubt have heard that the British had abolished the slave trade and were encouraging the people of the Gold Coast to take to agriculture and he probably hoped for some encouragement from them. Certainly without the help and co-operation of Dahomey's former European associates in the slave trade, such a project could not succeed. For the Dahomeans had been brought up for more than two centuries to extol the virtues of slave raiding. It would need an extraordinary effort, and a continuous demonstration of

---

[1] Secretary, African Committee to the Treasury, 9 April 1812 (T 70/73).

[2] Governor and Council, C.C.C. to African Committee, 26 Feb. 1812 (T 70/35); Sec. African Committee to Governor and Council, Cape Coast Castle, 11 May 1813 (T 70/73).

[3] 'Accounts and Daybooks for Whydah', 23 Oct. 1808 (T 70/1163).

practical necessity, to retrain them to have the same respect for agriculture as they had come to have for war.

Unfortunately, neither the co-operation nor the practical necessity was forthcoming, for Dahomey was soon internationally recognised as, or rather condemned to be, a slave-trading kingdom. After the British abolition of the slave trade in 1807, diplomatic negotiations were immediately opened to induce the other European powers to stop it likewise. In the note sent to the Portuguese government, the British government hoped that Portugal would not take the advantage of the British abolition to extend its own slave-trading operations, and specifically asked that Portuguese activities be limited 'to the territories in Africa which the Portuguese had till then been accustomed to frequent'.[1] The negotiations continued in 1808 after the court of Lisbon had removed to Rio de Janeiro. Finally in 1810, an Anglo-Portuguese treaty was signed, which permitted the continuation of the slave trade in Whydah port,[2] while denying such rights to any of the other neighbouring ports.

The first result was that the British squadron henceforth vigorously seized all the slaving ships found in the nearby ports of Porto Novo, Badagry, Little Popo and Lagos, the ports which had hitherto shared the trade with Whydah,[3] while leaving alone the ships found in Whydah harbour. This confirmed the Dahomeans in their belief that all they needed was, not agriculture, but increased raiding to procure more slaves. In this way, Adandozan's efforts to encourage agriculture was killed before it had any chance, and Adandozan's judgment may have been greatly discredited. In the long term, this British attitude towards the slave trade in Whydah after the 1810 treaty, which

[1] 'Abstract of Papers (selected for Lord Castlereagh in August 1814) on the subject of the steps which have successively been taken by the British Government...for abolishing the African slave trade, 1806–1814' (FO. 95/9). The relevant clause reads: ' It is however to be distinctly understood that the stipulations of the present article are not to be considered as invalidating or otherwise affecting the rights of the crown of Portugal to the territories of Cabinda and Molebo...nor as limiting or restraining the commerce of Ajuda and other ports in Africa (situated upon the coast commonly called in the Portuguese language the Costa da Mina), belonging to or claimed by the crown of Portugal.'
[2] See note 1, above.
[3] Cmdr. F. P. Irby to E. W. White, 5 Jan. 1812 (T 70/1594), to J. W. Croker, 9 Jan. and 4 March 1812 and 10 March 1812 (Adm. I/1966).

was in force throughout this period, and its later actions in sending missions to Abomey to persuade the king to abolish the slave trade, must have been difficult for the Dahomeans to reconcile.

The second result of the 1810 treaty was that, from about 1811 onwards, the slave trade started to revive in Dahomey. The report on the slave trade in 1811 recorded that the 'great scene of the slave trade is on the coast of Whydah, the Bight of Benin, Gaboon and the Portuguese settlements in the Congo and Angola'.[1] In 1812 it was reckoned that forty-five ships from Bahia traded at Whydah.[2] To these must be added the American privateers trading under the Spanish flag, who seem to have become predominant by 1816.[3] Even in the mid-eighteenth century, when the slave trade in Dahomey was at its peak, it is doubtful whether as many as forty-five ships called at Whydah port in any one year.

The revival, however, came too late to help Adandozan's position on the throne. In fact he could not take any credit for the revival after his recent advocacy of agriculture, and his opponents were likely to point out that he was not the best person to take the utmost advantage from the situation.

Moreover, by 1810, Dahomey had remained continuously in the grip of a depression that started about 1767. Forty years was an extremely long time, and the Dahomeans, who were proverbially loyal to their king, must have complained, however much in a muffled voice. Unfortunately for the historian, Dahomey is much more poorly served with documents in the first two decades of the nineteenth century than at any time since 1724, and we have no means of knowing exactly what happened and how the citizens reacted. There can be no doubt, however, that the first result of the commercial decline must have been widespread poverty.

The condition of the ordinary Dahomean was still further depressed by three years of natural disaster which started in 1809. In that year, a widespread famine occurred in Dahomey, followed in 1810 by an outbreak of an unfamiliar disease and an

---

[1] J. Higgins and Columbine, 'Report on the slave trade, 1811' (CO. 267/29).
[2] Cmdr. F. P. Irby to E. W. White, 5 Jan. 1812 (T 70/1594), to J. W. Croker, 9 Jan. and 4, 10 March 1812 (Adm. I/1996).
[3] J. Dawson to African Committee, 5 Nov. 1816 (T 70/1601); S. Cock to Viscount Castlereagh, 22 Dec. 1817 (FO. 95/9); J. Reid, J. Nicholls and others to African Committee, 27 April 1818 (T 70/1603 (i)).

unusually heavy rains which carried away half of the houses at Igelefe. In spite of this rain, however, the famine was still intense in December 1810.[1]

Like the bulk of the general populace, the monarchy was also impoverished. The *Anubomey* ceremonies in 1803, 1804 and 1805 were deferred late into the year instead of being held between December and March, and they were unimpressive when held.[2] In 1803 they were still on in June. In 1804 they did not start until August and in 1805 they started in April and went on for only a short time. The ceremonies may have been dispensed with altogether when conditions worsened, to the great discredit of Adandozan and the Tegbesu line.

In the same way, Adandozan found it increasingly difficult to pay the annual tributes to Oyo. The last recorded one sent in 1808 was obviously a heavy strain on the resources of the monarchy, and Adandozan did not hide his relief when at last the tributes proved acceptable.[3]

Because of the difficulties confronting Oyo, Dahomey stood in no real danger of Oyo invasion for non-payment of the annual tributes. Much more threatening was the danger of civil disturbance. As has been noticed, the Dahomeans blamed their misfortune, not on the slave trade but on the incompetence of the Tegbesu line in managing it. With an active hostile camp among the princes who opposed Adandozan, the situation would undoubtedly be exploited to Adandozan's disadvantage.

The events of the last six years of Adandozan's reign are shrouded in complete obscurity. There can be no doubt, however, that the failure of his policies and measures continued to be a source of widespread discontent, and that his opponents easily spread disaffection and planned rebellion without being detected. The Dahomean traditions recall the names of two princes, Tometin and Madogungun, who took the leading part in planning his overthrow.[4]

Perhaps the one man who gave the insurrection its greatest chance of success and who later supplied the means of bolstering

[1] 'Accounts and Daybooks for Whydah', 10 July 1809, 5 June, 22 Oct. and 31 Dec. 1810. (T 70/1163).
[2] J. E. James to J. Mould, 28 June 1803 (T 70/1580); 'Accounts and Daybooks for Whydah', 27 Aug., 27 Sept. and 15 Nov. 1804, 1, 4 and 5 April 1805 (T 70/1163).
[3] 'Accounts and Daybooks for Whydah', 10 March 1808 (T 70/1163).
[4] E. Dunglas in *E.D.* vol. xx, pp. 43–4.

up the new regime was Francisco Felix de Souza. His role in the history of Dahomey in the second and third decades of the nineteenth century must have been of decisive importance. Gezo himself never stopped saying that it was de Souza who made him king of Dahomey and he 'obeyed him on every point so far that he was considered the second king of Dahomey'. When he died on 8 May 1849 Gezo arranged his burial as he would that of a dead king, and only Isiodore, de Souza's eldest son, prevented human sacrifice being made at the funeral.[1]

Unfortunately, however, nothing much is known of this great man. Scraps of biographical information exist, from the hilariously funny account of Theodore Canot in 1836,[2] to the charitable ones of Thomas Birch Freeman in 1856 and the supercilious ones of Dawson in 1862. A pious attempt has also been made by Noberto, a descendant of de Souza, to record a life story of his great ancestor.[3] None of these is, however, completely reliable, mingling, as they do, much popular fantasy with little genuine reminiscence from de Souza's own mouth.

This is not surprising, for de Souza was a legendary figure even in his own lifetime. He was such a charming gentleman to all who came into contact with him, friends and foes alike, that he won their instinctive respect. A convinced opponent of the slave trade like Freeman wrote of him:

Whatever may have been his unhappy propensity as a slave dealer and however much that grave circumstance may have unhappily doomed his name and memory to censure and reprobation, yet as a man he was worthy of his position as a leading character among his fellow men and those who come in contact with him under circumstances calculated to draw out and bring into play his better feelings, as was my case, could not help cherishing towards him kindly and respectful feelings.[4]

It is probable that de Souza was a brother of Jacinto Jose de Souza, who succeeded to the directorship of the Portuguese fort at Whydah in 1804 and died in 1805. It is unknown exactly when he came to Dahomey, but it is extremely unlikely that he

---

[1] Dawson to Fitzgerald, Whydah, 17 Nov. 1862 (CMS. CA. 2/o16).
[2] The passage relevant to de Souza in Canot has been quoted extensively by Dunglas in *E.D.* vol. xx, pp. 39–41.
[3] Noberto Francisco de Souza in *E.D.* vol. xii (1955), pp. 17–21.
[4] T. B. Freeman, *Typescript of a Book*, p. 236 (MMA. B. West Africa, box 4).

was already there in 1788 as director of the Portuguese fort,[1] since Francisco Antonio de Fonseca e Aragão was the Portuguese director between 1782 and 1793.[2] De Souza told Freeman that he came to Whydah as a poor man who

used to watch the natives as they made certain offerings to fetish and notice where they threw the cowries offered on such occasions and watch his opportunity to gather them up to aid in furnishing the means for his daily subsistence.[3]

By 1803 he was a personal assistant to the storekeeper of the Portuguese fort because in that year he signed a document by which an army officer at Whydah arranged to have his salary paid in Portugal.[4] In 1806 he was the book-keeper of the Portuguese fort. When de Silva died or departed about 1807 de Souza probably became the director of the fort. By that time internal difficulties in Portugal prevented the Portuguese authorities from sending any provisions.

De Souza seems then to have withdrawn either to Badagry or to Little Popo (Anecho) where the slave trade was brisker than at Whydah only to be forced back to Igelefe when the news of the British abolition of the slave trade, the exertions of the resident Europeans to re-establish agriculture and the British naval squadron made the slave trade unprofitable anywhere else near Whydah. By 1810 he had probably become pre-eminently the richest Portuguese trader at Igelefe. His position would naturally have made him a creditor to Adandozan as all the directors of the forts had always been to the kings of Dahomey. What brought him in on the side of the plotters was Adandozan's inability to pay his debts. De Souza made an excessive demand to which Adandozan responded with public insult and an honourable confinement.[5] Annoyed and afraid for his personal safety, he fled to Little Popo where he remained until 1818.

The fact that de Souza, the richest resident Portuguese trader in the whole of the 'slave coast', joined the ranks of the dissident Dahomean princes, became the decisive factor in the

---

[1] N. F. de Souza in *E.D.* vol. XII, pp. 17–21.
[2] See Appendix 2, 'Directors of the Portuguese fort'.
[3] T. B. Freeman, *Typescript...*, p. 251 (MMA. BWA/4).
[4] Carlos Eugeni o Correa da Silva, *Uma Viagem ao estabelecimento Portugues de Sao João Baptista de Ajuda* (1865), p. 77. This would tend to disprove Canot's assertion that de Souza was illiterate.
[5] Dawson to Fitzgerald, 17 Nov. 1862 (CMS. CA. 2/016).

Dahomean dynastic struggle. Before he left Whydah he had already befriended Madogungun and from Little Popo he 'continued to send presents to Madogungun, advising him to win the heart of the people from the king'.[1] It was with these presents that the future Gezo secured enough support for his coup.

When the plan was ripe, Adandozan was deposed, during the *Anubomey* ceremony in 1818. The process was simple. The Mehu took off his shoes of office and the Migan told him that the ancient kings, Wegbaja and Agaja, rejected him. Without the support of these two officers, there was nothing that Adandozan could do. His supporters who tried to resist were easily overcome and a large number of them executed or enslaved and exported.[2]

Both the accession of Adandozan in 1797 and his deposition in 1818 have generally been explained without any references to the times. In the process, the facts have been completely forgotten and the character of Adandozan and his right to the throne have suffered unnecessarily. The Dahomean oral traditions, which everyone has hitherto believed, represent Agonglo as dying at a good old age. No one seems to remember that in fact he was shot at about the age of thirty-one. Adandozan and Gezo are now represented as half-brothers, while in fact they belonged to different families contending for the throne,[3] distant cousins who were both directly descended from Agaja.

Briefly the generally known story is that Adandozan and Gezo were brothers, the sons of Agonglo, and that Adandozan was the much older prince. Agonglo is said to have designated Gezo as his successor but, because of his age, Adandozan was asked to act as regent until Gezo was old enough. Adandozan refused to abdicate when the time came and had to be forcibly deposed.

Another version current in the middle of the nineteenth century was that Adandozan was in fact king but had to be deposed because of his excessive cruelties.[4] Sometimes these two

---

[1] Dawson to Fitzgerald, 17 Nov. 1862 (CMS. CA. 2/016).

[2] E. Dunglas in *E.D.* vol. xx, pp. 35–47. M. J. Herskovits, *Dahomey*, vol. 1, p. 14; E. Foa, *Le Dahomey* (Paris, 1895), pp. 18–21. As Herskovits had pointed out, the historical section of this book is absolutely untrustworthy. Great care must be taken not to believe every story told about the accession of Gezo.

[3] Le Herisse, *L'Ancien Royaume*, pp. 211–312; E. Dunglas in *E.D.* vol. xx, pp. 35–6.

[4] Dawson to Fitzgerald, 17 Nov. 1862 (CMS. C.A 2/016).

versions have been mixed together to produce the picture of Adandozan as a wicked regent, who loved power so much that he sold the mother of the rightful heir into slavery and who had to be forced to abdicate.[1]

These stories are totally misleading.[2] Foremost in the minds of Gezo's descendants who disseminated them was the desire to legitimise their line to the throne and preserve the appearance of continuity. Adandozan could not have been a regent for Gezo since, as we have noticed, he himself was too young to reign and had to have regents chosen for himself. Burton, who visited Dahomey in 1861, three years after the death of Gezo, heard privately that Adandozan was still alive, which may indicate that both Adandozan and Gezo were about the same age.[3]

The little that is known of Adandozan's personal character would imply that he was an imaginative and progressive young monarch, far ahead of his times.

Early in his reign he had tried to procure European education for Dahomean princes. In 1801 he sent two of them to be educated in England. The plan, however, miscarried and the children were sold into slavery instead in the West Indies. As soon as Adandozan heard it, he took vigorous steps to have them released and they were brought back to Dahomey in June 1803, after spending only a few days in England on their way back from the West Indies.[4] Adandozan's equally unsuccessful attempt in 1805 to have an ammunition factory built in Dahomey and to have the mining industry established by the Portuguese have been noted, as has his equally abortive attempt to lead Dahomey away from the slave trade to agriculture.

His deposition in 1818 was therefore not entirely as a result of his bad character. Rather it was the culmination of the dynastic struggle that had been going on in Dahomey since 1789 and which was brought about by the incurable economic depression of Dahomey. It was a proof that even Dahomey, which was built

[1] M. J. Herskovits, *Dahomey*, vol. 1, p. 12.
[2] This will be quite clear when the dynastic quarrels of 1789, the murder of Agonglo in 1797 and subsequent deportation of Gezo's mother are taken into account.
[3] Sir Richard Burton (ed. Isabella Burton), *A Mission to Gelele, King of Dahomey* (London, 1893, first published 1864), p. 293.
[4] J. Macleod, *Voyage to Africa*, pp. 103–6; Secretary, African Committee to Governor and Council, C.C.C., 6 April 1803 (T 70/72); J. Mould to African Committee, 8 Sept. 1803 (T 70/34).

to defeat the corrosive influences of the slave trade, was now helplessly trapped in the vicious circle imposed by the trade. Nothing that Agonglo and Adandozan had done between 1789 and 1818 had been able to prevent this threat to the stability of Dahomey.

The succession of a new line in the person of Gezo did not, however, herald a revolution in the national policy. The line of Tegbesu had been overthrown because it had failed to maintain a prosperous slave trade and to assert Dahomey's independence of Oyo. It was Gezo's declared objective to succeed where his predecessors had failed.

# Conclusion

The period covered in this work was one in which the slave trade was the most important economic activity affecting the lives of all Dahomeans, as indeed of all West Africans. From the introduction of the trans-Atlantic slave trade, every other productive activity was discouraged in various ways. In the old Aja country, anyone who had the brute force and lack of scruple to seize a fellow man could easily make money. In that way man-stealing became the most lucrative occupation. Agriculture and industrial pursuits became most unrewarding.

Because of this and because the Europeans wanted only young and healthy slaves industry was discouraged and agriculture deteriorated. The wealth that was so easily made through the sale of the slaves was put to no productive purpose, and was in fact easily lost. For life was too insecure. 'There was no point in expanding production, in planning and building for the future. Tomorrow all might be destroyed and the builders and planners might be enslaved or killed.'[1] The whole period was therefore one of general progressive decline, though a few individuals easily amassed momentary wealth.

Politically, the slave trade brought new notions and new means of power. A people who had reached political stability based on a set of beliefs, discovered that their practices and beliefs were not the only practicable or even the most efficient ones. A people who had believed that political authority ought to be based on natural allegiances like that between father and son, discovered that authority based on physical force could be quite as effective, or even more so. After all, it was not natural authority that made a man the slave of another. It was physical force obtained from the firearms supplied by the Europeans who imposed no rules or social responsibilities on its use. In this way, ancient precepts were first questioned and then disobeyed without any new ones being substituted in their place. The

[1] J. D. Fage, *History of West Africa*, pp. 86–7.

traditional political systems grew weak and no longer provided adequate security for individuals.

Progressive economic decline and the weakening of political bonds were dominant aspects of the situation in which the slave trade flourished. For the Aja in the early days of the slave trade, this meant the disappearance of their old solid world, and the growth of a new spirit of ruthless brutality and insecurity. There were not a few of them who welcomed this change, fed on it and wholeheartedly became 'partners in the trade'. However, the more responsible, 'the discerning natives', who must have been in a minority, resented the evil and tried, eventually unsuccessfully, to arrest the decline by stopping the slave trade.

Among those who tried to reform society in the Aja country were the founders of the kingdom of Dahomey. A little band of highly principled and far-seeing individuals, they withdrew themselves from Allada northwards, beyond the immediate reach of the slave raiders and of the slave trade influences.

In the face of the widespread instability and impermanence, the challenge facing them was to create a politically stable state. In a period when wealth could be easily amassed and equally easily lost, their problem was to make that state also economically viable.

To achieve political stability, they had to establish a state that would remedy the faults of the traditional system and resist the corrosive influences of the slave trade. In this they were largely successful. The state which they founded was not a development of the traditional organisation into feudal tyranny like that of medieval Europe. It was something more like a modern national state. Unlike the traditional system in which a kingdom was regarded as a family written large, and a country as a larger version of many families descended from the same ancestor, the founders of Dahomey saw a state as a power, in which citizenship was open to all and sundry, who were prepared to obey the king and serve him. Instead of authority being based on descent as in the traditional system, the founders of Dahomey based their authority on present force. In place of the decentralisation implied in the traditional system which weakened the central authority and rendered breakaways easy under the smallest kind of pressure, the founders of Dahomey concentrated all authority into the hands of the king. Seen in this light, the organisation of Dahomey was not 'traditional', in the same way as the old Aja kingdoms or the Yoruba kingdoms were. It was revolutionary, and so was the impact which it later made in the Yoruba-Aja country.

The king was the effective head of both the civil and the military arms of the state. He attended councils, personally reviewed cases from lower courts, and often went at the head of his army into war. All the chiefs were appointed by him and were directly responsible to him. He had power of life and death over everyone in the kingdom except the Migan whom he could only exile, and during the eighteenth century he did not hesitate to execute any of his officers for incompetence or disloyalty.

This effective centralisation, which enabled the kings of Dahomey to control all the means of physical force like firearms, cutlasses, bows and arrows, was the basis of the strength of Dahomey. This point is worth emphasising, for without it the firearms introduced during the slave trade would have been used for self-destruction as they had been used earlier by the Aja and would be used later by the Yoruba, who did not possess an equally strong political organisation at the centre. In other words, it was not the slave trade *per se* or even Dahomean patronage or strict control of it that strengthened Dahomey. Rather it was the fact that Dahomey was built, as the traditional Aja had not been built, to benefit from the most deadly weapons introduced by the slave trade. This is the fundamental similarity between Dahomey and Ashanti though their organisations were different in detail. It is also the fundamental difference between Dahomey and Oyo, which throughout the eighteenth century continued to base its political organisation on the *Ebi* social theory, and explains why in the nineteenth century the Yoruba country broke up while Dahomey remained united and strong.

Ironically, the submission to Oyo helped Dahomey to perfect its internal organisation. This was not simply because Dahomey was able to borrow useful Oyo institutions, which it did to advantage, but more because the submission forced Dahomey to avoid military adventures which might have led to its complete destruction, and to concentrate instead on perfecting its internal administration. In this way the period of Oyo rule over Dahomey was politically useful to the latter and gave it a long experience in internal administration which became invaluable in the nineteenth century.

Strange as it may sound, Dahomey was not a particularly

strong power for the greater part of the eighteenth century. After the brilliant successes of Agaja between 1724 and 1727, Dahomey almost disappeared under the successive Oyo raids and its own internal revolts.

In the two decades following the death of Agaja in 1740, the Oyo raids from the north and the old Whydah raids from the south-west, kept Dahomey pretty weak. The fate of the kingdom remained uncertain until the confirmation of the 1730 treaty in 1748. Even after that only the guns of the European forts, and particularly of the English fort under Goodson, prevented the old Whydah from regaining their old kingdom. In spite of these guns, however, Dahomey remained unable to hold the beach effectively and the old Whydah continued to molest all activities in the coastal belt of the kingdom until Abson helped Dahomey to conclude a treaty with the raiders in 1772.

The war which has generally been represented as having been fought between Ashanti and Dahomey in the mid-eighteenth century was in fact the drubbing which Ashanti received from the Oyo soldiers in 1764 around Atakpame area which appears to have been the boundary of the Oyo Empire in that direction. In 1776, when Dahomey wore its most prosperous look in the whole of the eighteenth century, an officer in the French fort said, as a matter of fact, that Dahomey was not a strong power and never had been. After that and until the end of the period covered here, Dahomey did not gain strength to any appreciable extent.

The significance and importance of Dahomey in the eighteenth century therefore did not lie in its military prowess, although it was a military state. Its greatest achievement and therefore its entitlement to fame lay in the ability of its rulers to keep its administration intact right through the period, in the face of all the fissiparous tendencies rampant during the age of the slave trade. This was not a small achievement.

The old Aja states had succumbed to the destructive forces of the slave trade. To the west of Dahomey, empires rose and fell. To the east, mighty Oyo crashed in an equally mighty fall, bringing the whole of the Yoruba country down with itself. But little, weak Dahomey kept its administration intact. It was this, rather than its strength, which enabled Dahomey to benefit from the chaos that followed the fall of the Oyo Empire.

The story of how Dahomey was able to keep its administration unimpaired is one of very great tenacity and endurance. The concentration of all authority in the hands of the king was not seriously challenged until the period between 1726 and 1730. Then the southern menace against which all the Dahomeans were united, appeared to most people as having been removed with the conquest of both Allada and Whydah. The Oyo invasions and the European obstructionist tactics which almost destroyed Dahomey could easily have diminished the authority of the king and weakened the administration. But although Agaja gave up all other policies he did not abandon the principle whereby all authority was retained by the king. Even when he had to disperse his subjects in the face of Oyo invasion, he retained that authority intact by sending an officer to accompany each group.

Whether by accident or by negotiation, the principle was conceded in the 1730 treaty which made Dahomey a tributary state of Oyo. After 1735 Agaja would rather have the state destroyed and himself buried under its ruin than concede an iota of the monarchical authority to those who wanted the slave trade thrown open to all and sundry. He continued to fight those of his subjects who wanted to diminish his authority though often without decisive victory. When he died in 1740 the only legacy which he left his son and successor, Tegbesu, was this principle of absolute monarchical authority.

Tegbesu defended the same principle with an almost ferocious rigour, even against his own brothers who sought to impair it. The early part of his reign was notorious for executions and sales into slavery in its defence. The Yovogans of Whydah, who by virtue of their position could easily become dangerous to the king's authority, bore the full force of this policy. The first nine of them were executed, sometimes on the faintest whisper of any allegation which tended to suggest a usurpation of the power of the king.

By 1751 all the Dahomeans, princes, nobles, soldiers and peasants had accepted the principle without question. Even the European directors grudgingly came to accept it and prefer it to lawlessness, though they later chafed under it. After that, the power of the king was never again questioned and the stability of the internal administration was assured. Even when discontent started in Dahomey, it was not against the authority of the monarchy, but against the person and family wielding that authority. In 1789 the Migan had no difficulty in foiling the plans of the Dahomean princes who wanted to seize the throne by force simply by challenging the insurgents to fire, if they dared, on the thrones of the ancient kings of Dahomey. It needed an unusually long economic depression to produce Agonglo's murder and Adandozan's deposition. Even then, Gezo was at pains to preserve the authority of the monarchy after his seizure of power, to the extent of protecting the sacred person of Adandozan whom he had deposed.

As a result of this administrative stability, two things stand out prominently in the history of Dahomey throughout the eighteenth century as indeed for the rest of its history until it was conquered by the French. The first was the longevity of its kings. Agaja reigned for at least thirty-two years. Tegbesu reigned for thirty-four, and both were said to be extremely old men before they died. Agonglo, the last king to die naturally during the period under survey, died at about the age of fifty-four, comparatively young. Adandozan, deposed in 1818, did not die until 1861, three years after the death of Gezo.

All the Dahomean kings in the eighteenth century, and later, were exceptionally gifted political leaders. Agaja was truly great, not only as a statesman, but also as a war general. His tremendous mental capacity and clear far-sightedness remained unimpaired almost until his death. Tegbesu was urbane, possessing the smooth manners and the ruthless calculations of a business executive. Kpengla was high-spirited, practical, rough and ready. Agonglo, despite his short and troubled reign, emerged as a clever tactician, and Adandozan, when he grew up, was 'progressive'. All of them showed themselves capable of sizing up the local political, if not, understandably, the international economic, situations.

The second prominent thing is the religious tenacity with which a policy adopted in one reign was carried on in the next and if necessary in the following one until the end sought was achieved. For example, it took three reigns and something around sixty to eighty years before Dahomey could conquer the whole of the Aja kingdoms and impose its own idea of a state on the Aja peoples. When Agaja finally decided to subscribe to the slave trade, all his successors became ardent slave traders. When Kpengla declared that his policy would be to seek independence from Oyo, all his successors faithfully followed the policy even though they all realised that they were too weak to achieve it. It was Gezo, the representative of the rival faction to the descendants of Kpengla, who finally carried out this policy. The stability created by the long reigns, and the continuity of policy, gave Dahomey many advantages. Policy makers could take a long-term view, knowing full well that if the end sought was not achieved in their own lifetimes, succeeding generations would work towards its achievement. Kpengla was expressing the general nature of the Dahomean policy when in 1783 he said that he was 'easy in pace but always pursuing'. So long as he kept the policy of his ancestors, no Dahomean king needed to take any precipitate actions. This made the men at the head of affairs think more of the interest of the kingdom than of their own individual names or memories.

That was a great contrast to the picture one has of contemporary Oyo, where only two kings, Ojigi and Abiodun, seem to have had fairly long reigns during the eighteenth century. Ojigi's reign probably did not exceed twenty years. Abiodun reigned effectively for only fifteen years and possibly for nineteen in all. All the others either died after a few years reign or were required to commit suicide by a usurper after only a few days as king.

When we come to consider the other objective which the founders of Dahomey set themselves, that of making their new state economically viable, it will be seen that the rulers of Dahomey were not as successful in that as in the first objective. The issue itself became dominant in the national life of Dahomey only from 1730 onwards. After the conquest of the coastal states, Agaja discovered that there just was no alternative to the slave trade if he wanted to maintain his country's link with Europe. But although he concluded the 1730 treaty with Brathwaite, he had lived too long to change his dislike of the trade and he spent the last years of his life containing slaving activities in his kingdom and its immediate environs.

Tegbesu took a less equivocal attitude and decided to base the economy of Dahomey wholly and solely on the slave trade. He seems to have believed that the trade could be peacefully pursued like any other business, and to have placed great confidence in the beneficial effects to be expected from it.

In spite of his exertions, however, it soon became clear that the slave trade, much less peaceful slave trade, was not a reliable basis for the economy. The brief period of commercial prosperity ended by 1767 and the last seven years of Tegbesu's reign witnessed the beginning of a depression that did not end until 1818, despite all the efforts of the rulers of Dahomey. In 1775, when peaceful slave trade had become obviously impracticable, Kpengla, Tegbesu's son and successor, started the slave raids, which were to be developed to such devastating extent by Gezo in the nineteenth century. Between 1775 and 1818, those raids were not spectacularly successful, and the slave trade in Dahomey continued to decline. First the American war of Independence, then the French Revolution and finally the abolition of the slave trade by the British government in 1807, all ensured that Dahomey did not prosper from the inhuman trade in the eighteenth century.

The resultant poverty caused widespread discontent which in turn adversely affected the political stability of Dahomey. Consequently, Agonglo was murdered in 1797 and Adandozan was chased from the throne in 1818. Unless the situation was firmly checked, the stage was set again for the political disorder so often the outcome of the slave trade.

Here then was a great paradox of the effect of the slave trade. At the beginning of the eighteenth century, Aja politics had become chaotic because of the increase in the trade. At the end of the century, instability was about to set into the kingdom of Dahomey because the trade was declining. Perhaps the rulers of Dahomey ought therefore to have concluded that once slave exporting became the major economic activity of a people, it was bound eventually to undermine the smooth running of the state whether it flourished or not.

As in the early years of the eighteenth century, they did not reach that conclusion. They continued to accept the slave trade even when everyone else concerned had started to reject or reconsider it. They laid the blame for their misfortunes on the mismanagement of their rulers, particularly the descendants of Tegbesu. These, rather than the slave trade, they were determined to change. After two unsuccessful attempts in 1789 and 1797, they finally succeeded when Adandozan was deposed in 1818.

Two sets of non-Dahomeans were intimately connected with the development of events in Dahomey in the eighteenth century. The first were the European factors and traders, who were mainly guided by their self interest which each pursued in his own way. By and large they can be said to have played no constructive role in either the political or economic development of Dahomey during the eighteenth century.

The English the French and the Dutch helped to break up the traditional Aja political system and to encourage Agaja's invasion of the coastal kingdoms in the hope of securing more slaves and greater influence. They discovered, however, that with Agaja's victory, they had exchanged incompetent allies for a stern taskmaster, who immediately ordered the Dutch out of the country. The English and the French later joined forces with either the Whydah or the Dahomeans whenever they thought it was in their interest. When order and regularity returned to Dahomey, they at first welcomed it but later chafed under it. The English, who had other establishments on the Gold Coast, progressively grew disinterested in Dahomey and their fort at Igelefe remained an out of the way post, reserved for punishing incompetent or offending officers from the Gold Coast.

The Portuguese pursued their self-interest differently. Officially established at Whydah in 1721, they were not greatly involved in all the pre-invasion political manoeuvres. They befriended Agaja immediately after his victory over the Whydah and were ready to mediate between all the contending parties during the troubled years immediately after 1727. Unlike the French and the English, they encouraged official contacts between the kings of Dahomey, the rulers of Brazil and the kings of Portugal. Nevertheless, they too wished to be regarded as above the law and complained bitterly when made to obey.

During the eighteenth century, all the European governments seem to have agreed that useful information should not be allowed to pass into the hands of the Africans. None of the Dahomean embassies to Portugal succeeded nor did they lead to an exchange of diplomatic representatives, though Agaja had proposed it. Throughout the eighteenth century, not one Dahomean was trained in Europe or even in São Tome. When Tegbesu wanted French education for his crown prince in 1751, it was denied him. When Adandozan sent two princes to be educated in England in 1801, they were sold into slavery instead.

Economically, the same self-interest governed their behaviour towards the commerce of Dahomey. Their friendship only lasted for as long as there was enough slave supply, and when that failed they would rather desert Dahomey than stay to help. The English did not really trade much or regularly at Whydah throughout the eighteenth century. The French and the Portuguese came to prefer Porto Novo towards the end of the century when Dahomey no longer furnished an abundance of slaves.

The other set of non-Dahomeans who were intimately connected with the events in Dahomey were the Oyo. As was to be expected, they played a very positive role both in the political and economic development of Dahomey, though only the unsavoury aspects of their century of imperial rule over Dahomey have usually been remembered by the Dahomeans.

Yet the rule of Oyo has its constructive aspects as well. As has already been noticed, the Dahomean submission to Oyo in 1748 and the peace imposed by the strong hands of the Basorun Gaha actually gave Dahomey a period of peace while Tegbesu reconstructed the foundations of the internal administration which stood Dahomey in such a good stead for the rest of its history. Without the administrative machinery, particularly the *Ilari* system, copied from Oyo by Tegbesu, the government of the enlarged kingdom of Dahomey would undoubtedly have been much less efficient. Economically, it was the Oyo who supplied Dahomey with the slaves which formed the foundation of its wealth and power during the reign of Tegbesu. Oyo's decision to develop its own port at Porto Novo started off the Dahomean depression which continued while Oyo had the power to maintain its port.

It was because Dahomey was largely successful in creating a politically stable state and largely unsuccessful in making it economically viable that it became the incorrigible slave trading kingdom in the nineteenth century. The incurable decline in Oyo had been aggravated by the outbreak of the Fulani *Jihad* and was just starting to engulf the rest of the Yoruba country in fratricidal wars in 1818. Thanks to the internal strength of Dahomey, Gezo had no difficulty in declaring Dahomey's independence of Oyo and benefiting, through the slave raids, from the Yoruba civil wars. Because of the economic depression of the previous reigns, Gezo argued, when asked to give up the slave trade, that he could not do so without losing his throne. By that he meant that it was the widespread economic depression that enabled him to depose Adandozan and unless he was more successful than Adandozan, he might equally be deposed. To retain the throne, he had to make the kingdom economically viable and that he proceeded to do through his unrelenting pursuit of the slave trade, the only economy that Dahomey had practised for almost a century. Even when the slave trade had finally ended, economic viability continued to engross the energy of the Dahomean rulers. It is not surprising that one of the main causes of the dispute between the French and the Dahomeans, which led to the French invasion of the kingdom in 1893, was the unwillingness of the Dahomean rulers to allow their sources of revenue to be curtailed.

# Appendix 1. Place-names

One problem that confronts a student of African history is that of identifying indigenous place-names in European documents. European writers not only gave European names to places in West Africa which had their own indigenous names (such as 'Slave Coast', 'Ivory Coast', Lagos, etc.), they also wrote African place-names as they sounded to them. Because of the wide phonetic variations between European languages, the number of ways in which an African name could be spelt was almost infinite. Thus Oyo was 'Io', 'Eyeo', 'Ayo', 'Ailleux', 'Alliots', etc. and Whydah was written 'Widah', 'Oueda', 'Juda', 'Fida', etc. Such well-known names as these, however, present little difficulty, particularly as they have continued to exist. When the places concerned have disappeared identification has remained impossible.

Sometimes, one place might be given two or more names, or two or more places might be given similar names because their original names sounded similar to European ears. In these two cases, the problem of unravelling which place was which can be very difficult.

Then there is the general West African system whereby a town shared the same name with its inhabitants. If, for certain reasons, the inhabitants were forced to abandon the town, they carried the name with themselves and gave it to any new settlement they might later found.

This was the case with modern Badagry. There was a town of the same name situated about twenty-four miles north of the present town, founded for, or augmented by, the Aja refugees after Agaja's invasion of the coast between 1724 and 1727. In 1785 it was destroyed and its inhabitants dispersed. Between 1785 and 1787 one Sessu gathered the remnants and settled them on the present site to which he gave the previous name Badagry.

The picture can become more complicated if, after a lapse of time, a group of people later settled in the previously deserted

213

town. They would then revive the old name without depriving the new settlement of the same name. This was how the several places called Ardra, Great Ardra, Little Ardra, etc., acquired their names.

Henri Labouret and Paul Rivet have concluded that modern Allada was the place which the Europeans called Great Ardra, and modern Godomey the place they called Little Ardra, or Offra.[1] This is correct if it is meant to identify the places called Great Ardra and Little Ardra before 1730. After 1730 and particularly from about 1760 onwards, the Europeans applied the names Great Ardra and Little Ardra to two other places. Little Ardra was applied to modern Porto Novo, and Great Adra to the town of Ajase, twenty-four miles north of Porto Novo.[2]

Again the situation developed as a result of Agaja's invasion of the coastal kingdoms. After the destruction of the old Allada kingdom, its rulers appealed to Oyo for help. In the 1730 settlement, the remnants of the conquered Allada people were resettled in another area, which the Oyo called Ajase Ipo, and its capital, Ajase. The Aja people who settled there, however, continued to call their new capital Allada, which the Europeans continued to spell Ardra or Ardres. The new Allada (Ajase) was situated east of the old one and was about twenty miles inland. In the meanwhile, Dahomey had taken over the capital of the old kingdom and continued to call it Allada.

The new kingdom later developed its own port, which was called Porto Novo by the Portuguese 'because it is the newest one known'.[3] This port became very popular from about the mid-1770s onwards and remained so until about the end of the slave trade. But it remained simply a port of disembarkation where a little town had grown up to offer facilities for the incoming ships or the outgoing slaves. The main trade itself continued to be transacted at the new Ardra (Ajase). For this reason the port, Porto Novo, was sometimes called 'Little Ardra' (the place of debarkation) to distinguish it from 'Great' Ardra (the place of trade). So that towards the end of the eighteenth century, Great Ardra was the new Ardra (Ajase) which the remnants of the Aja people from Allada had settled in 1730

[1] H. Labouret and P. Rivet, *Le Royaume d'Ardra*, p. 10.
[2] See map 4.
[3] Governor of Bahia to King of Portugal, 1775 (AHU. 8941 and 8942).

and Little Ardra was Porto Novo, its port. Porto Novo, however, remained a far more popular name than Little Ardra.

As could be seen from the map which Norris drew (map 4) the distinction was quite clear to contemporaries, who continued to write the old capital as 'Allada' and the new one as 'Great Ardra'. Porto Novo, however, increased in importance with the resumption of French contact with it in the fifth decade of the nineteenth century, and it subsequently gave its name to the whole kingdom of Ajase Ipo, at least in European literature.

# Appendix 2. Directors of the European forts at Whydah*

### Directors of St Louis Fort, Whydah (French)*

| | |
|---|---|
| Derigouyn | ? 1707–1710 |
| Chamois | 1710–1712 |
| du Coulombier | 1712–Nov. 1715 (ejected) |
| Bouchel | Nov. 1715–1722 |
| Levesque | ? 1722–? 1727 |
| Houdye Dupetitval | 1727–1729 (killed) |
| Gallot | 1730 (usurped the post) |
| Mallet de la Mine | 1730–1731 |
| Lavigne | 1732 (died) |
| Dubelay | 1733–1734 (died, suspected of poison by his fort doctor) |
| Delisle | 1734–1737 (died) |
| Laurent | 1737–1742 |
| Levens | 1742 (ejected) |
| Levet | 1742—21 Aug. 1747 (ejected) |
| Druno de la Court | Sept. 1747–March 1751 |
| Guestard | March 1751–1755 |
| Dubordieu | 1755–? |
| Pruneau de Pomegorge | 1763–1764 |
| Remillat | ? 1764–July 1764 (ejected) |
| Cuillie (ag.) | July 1764–Sept. 1765 |
| Guestard | 1765–1774 (died) |
| De Warel | 1774–1775 (ejected) |
| Olivier de Montagueret† | 1775–1786 |
| Gourg | 1786–1789 (ejected) |
| Deniau de la Garenne | 1789–1797 (absconded) |
| Pierre Bonon (ag.) | 1797–? |

* This list amends those given by Berbain and Dunglas whenever there is documentary evidence for so doing.
† Dunglas wrongly says Montaguere was obliged to leave.

*Fort of St John the Baptist* (*Portuguese*)

| | |
|---|---|
| Francisco Pereyra Mendes | 1721–July 1724 |
| F.P.R. | July 1724–1728 |
| João Bazilio | 1728–1743 (ejected) |
| R. P. Martinho da Cunha Barboza | 1743–1746 (died) |
| R. P. Francisco de Esperito Santo | 1746 (expelled) |
| Francisco Nunes Pereira (by usurpation) | 1746 |
| Felix Jose da Gouvea | 1747–1749 |
| ? | 1749–1751 |
| Luiz Coelho Brito | 1751 (died) |
| Theodozio Rodriges da Costa | 1751–1757 (ejected) |
| Antonio Nunes de Gouvea (ag.) | 1757–1759 (ejected) |
| Felix Jose de Gouvea | 1759–1762 (died) |
| Francisco Xavier da Silveira | 1762–1764 (died) |
| Jose Gomes Gomzaga | 1764–1765 |
| John Reveire | 1765–? |

Information on Portuguese activities ceased until 1778.

| | |
|---|---|
| Bernado Azevedo Coutinho | 1778–1782 |
| Francisco Antonio Fonseca e Aragão | 1782–1793 (expelled) |
| Manoel Lellis el Almeida (ag.) | 1793 |
| Francisco Xavier Alves | 1793–1796 |
| Manoel de Bastos Varella Pinto Pacheco | 1796–1799 (ejected) |
| Jose Ferreira de Araujo | 1799–1800 (ejected) |
| Jose Joaquim Marques da Graca | 1800–1804 (ejected) |
| Jacinto Jose de Souza | 1804–1805 (died) |
| Francisco Xavier Rodriges de Silva | 1805–? |

*Directors of William's Fort* (*English*)

| | |
|---|---|
| Captain Wilbourne | ? 1700–? |
| Peter Duffield | ? –Feb. 1704 |
| Richard Willis | Feb. 1704–1709 (died) |
| William Hicks | June 1709–April 1712 (died) |
| Hilliard and Green (ag.) | April 1712–May 1713 |
| Joseph Blaney | May 1713–March 1715 (ejected) |
| J. Errington and L. Green (ag.) | March–Aug. 1715 |
| R. Mason, D. Welsh and W. Bramston | Aug. 1715–April 1716 |
| W. Baillie | May 1716–Oct. 1720 |

Between 1717 and 1720, the fort was farmed out to private traders because the Company could not maintain it any more. The two people who combined to hire it were W. Baillieux and Johnson. The fort was handed back on 30 October 1720.

| | |
|---|---|
| John Stevenson | Oct.–Dec. 1720 |
| Ambrose Baldwyn | Jan. 1721–Feb. 1724 |
| Jeremiah Tinker | Feb. 1724–March 1727 |
| Abraham Duport | March 1727–Feb. 1728 |

Whydah fort became a dependency of Cape Coast Castle.

| | |
|---|---|
| Thomas Wilson | Feb. 1728–March 1729 |
| Charles Testefolle | April 1729–Nov. 1729 (executed) |
| Robert Urquhart (ag.) | Nov. 1729–Jan. 1730 |
| Edward Dean | Jan.–Dec. 1730 |

Between May and December 1730 John Brathwaite, one of the three joint governors at Cape Castle, came to Whydah.

| | |
|---|---|
| Robert Poulter | Jan.–June 1731 (died) |
| Edward Dean | June 1731–March 1733 |
| Charles Whitaker | March 1733–July 1734 (ran away) |
| John Wyat (ag.) | July–Oct. 1734 |
| Wm Whetstone Rogers | Nov. 1734–April 1735 |
| Alexander Spalding | Aug. 1735–1737 (? 1738) |
| Stephen Lushington | June 1738–March 1739 |
| Isaac Gregory | April 1739–1745 |

Whydah was made independent of Cape Coast Castle.

| | |
|---|---|
| Arthur Graham (ag.) | ? –Dec. 1745 |
| Henry Turner | Jan. 1746–Dec. 1746 (died) |
| William Devaynes (ag.) | 1747–July 1750 |
| Andrew Johnson | July 1750–Jan. 1751 (died) |
| Robert Livingstone | Jan.–Sept. 1751 |
| William Devaynes | Sept. 1751–Nov. 1752 |
| William Withers | Nov. 1752–Nov. 1753 |
| William Devaynes | Nov. 1753–Aug. 1762 |
| William Goodson | Aug. 1762–Feb. 1767 (died) |
| Richard Burgiss | Feb.–April 1767 |
| Archibald Dalzel | April 1767–1770 |
| Erasmus Williams | Aug.–Sept. 1770 (died) |
| Lionel Abson* | Oct. 1770–June 1803 (died) |
| Henry Edward James (ag.) | June 1803–March 1804 |
| Henry Hamilton | March 1804–June 1807 |
| Frederick James | July 1807–Feb. 1812 |

* Contrary to Dunglas's assertion, there was no English director called Sally in 1793. Sally was Abson's daughter.

# Appendix 3. Contemporary rulers in the Yoruba-Aja country

WHYDAH

Agbangla 1670 ?–1703
Aisan or Amat 1703–1708
Huffon 1708–1727 (died
  1733)

DAHOMEY

Wegbaja ?–? 1680
Akaba? 1680–? 1708
Agaja ? 1708–1740
Tegbesu 1740–1774
Kpengla 1774–1789
Agonglo 1789–1797 (murdered)
Adandozan 1797–1818 (deposed)

OYO

Ojigi ? –1736? (was definitely reigning between 1724 and 1730)

Gberu
Amuniwaiye } ? 1736–? 1746

Onisile     ? 1746–Aug. 1754

Labisi
Awonbioju }Aug.–Nov. 1754      } The usurpation of
                                  Basorun Gaha 1754–
Agboluaje                         1774
Majeogbe  }Nov. 1754–? 1770

Abiodun      ? 1770 (1774)–1789
Awole       1789–1796?
Adebo
Maku   } 1796 ?–1797 ?
Interregnum   ? 1797–1819 ?

# Bibliography

LIST OF PRIMARY SOURCES

1 (a) *Public Record Office* (*P.R.O.*) *T* 70: *African Companies*

T 70/1–7: Letter Books, from Africa and West Indies, 1678–1732.
T 70/13–14: Abstract for the Committee of Correspondence, 1703–6.
T 70/18–19: Abstract for the Committee of Accounts, 1704–19.
T 70/22–3: Abstract for the Committee of Goods, 1705–24.
T 70/26–7: Abstract for the Committee of Shipping, 1706–24.
T 70/28: Abstract for Various Committees, 1703–4.
T 70/29–36: Inward Letter Books, July 1751–March 1818.
T 70/39: Concerning the state of Trade in Africa in 1771.
T 70/52–4: Letters sent to Africa, 1703–40.
T 70/64: Instructions to Captains, 1719–44.
T 70/65: Instructions to Captains and Mates, 1737–44.
T 70/67: Instructions to chief Agents in Africa, 1737–50.
T 70/68: Letters between various servants of the Company in Africa
    and the Captains of certain ships, 1749–51.
T 70/70–4: Outward Letter Books, 1787–1818.
T 70/92–9: Royal Africa Company, Court of Assistants, 1723–52.
T 70/103–6: Minute Books, Committee of Seven, 1725–49.
T 70/143–50: Minute Books, Committee of Merchants Trading to
    Africa, 1750–1817.
T 70/155–62: Reports and orders, 1770–92.
T 70/176–7: Returns from the Commissioners for Trade and Planta-
    tions, also to the House of Commons...relating the general
    state of the trade to Africa, 1777.
T 70/378–426: Accounts and Journals, Cape Coast Castle, 1718–
    51.
T 70/584: Accounts and Journals for Popo, 1793–5.
T 70/592–8: Accounts and Journals for Whydah, 1718–27.
T 70/702–4: Journal and Ledger, 1745–6.
T 70/885–92: Accounts and Ledger for Whydah, 1718–39.
T 70/905–8: Accounts and Balance Sheets, 1751–86.
T 70/1158–63: Accounts and Daybooks for Whydah, 1751–1812.
T 70/1218: Ships Book, 1753, 1777.
T 70/1254: Trade, Gold Ledger at Whydah, 1724–6.
T 70/1454–6: Register of all servants and officers, 1750–1815.

Bibliography

T 70/1463–98: Private Books, 1704–94.
T 70/1515–1606: Detached Papers, 1750–1820.

(b) *Admiralty Records*
Adm. I/1516–2770: Captains' Letters, 1796–1816.

(c) *Foreign Office Records*
FO. 2/1: Slave Trade, Domestic and Various, 1825–38.
FO. 84/1–2: Slave Trade, Conference in London, 1816–19.
FO. 95/9: Miscellaneous, 1814–17.

(d) *Colonial Office Records*
CO. 267/29: State of West African Settlements, 1811.

2. *Parliamentary Papers*

Report of the Lords Committee of Council...concerning the present
state of trade to Africa and particularly trade in slaves, 1788.
Accounts and Papers (vol. 24), Minutes of Evidence taken in 1788 in
respect of the slave trade, 1789.
Accounts and Papers (vol. VII, 2), Minutes of Evidence on African
forts.

3. *Church Missionary Society Archives*

CA. 2/016: Miscellaneous.
CA. 2/021: James Barber.
CA. 2/028: Daniel Coker.
CA. 2/031: Bishop S. A. Crowther.
CA. 2/035: S. W. Doherty.

4. *Methodist Missionary Archives*

Box 4: West Africa, Biographical.

5. *Edinburgh University Library*

DK. 7/52: Letters of Archibald Dalzel.

6. *Archives Nationales, Paris: Colonies, C. 6. Sénégal Ancien*

C. 6/25: Mémoires sur la Guinée, Juda et Ardres; Divers, 1712–14.
Correspondence de M. Levet, Directeur à Juda, 1755; Corres-
pondence de Mr Guestard, directeur à Juda, 1755. Lettres du
Conseil Supérieur du Comptoir du Juda, 1752–63.
C. 6/26: Guinée, Juda, 1769–89; Royaume d'Ardres et fort d'Amou-
kou, 1787.
C. 6/27: Mémoires, non datés, antérieur à 1790; Royaume du Benin,
1785; Succession, Joseph le Beau; Juda, Divers, 1787–90,

1792–1806; Renseignements sur la Côte d'Afrique et le Sénégal,
1779–1801; Amoukou, 1802.

C. 6/27 *bis*: Mémoires et Carte de l'Abbé Bullet antérieur à 1785.

C. 6/30: Lettres entre les Compagnies françaises et anglaises, 1702–5;
Ordres donnés par les Compagnies françaises et anglaises à leur
commis, 1704–5; Mémoires et Projets, 1683–1802.

F. 2 A/2–6: Compagnies d'Afrique, 1681–1765.

F. 2 A/7–11: Compagnies de l'Assiente, 1701–70.

F. 2 A/13: Compagnie de Guinée.

### 7. *Archives Départementales, Nantes*

B. 5004/4, 5004/5, 16-J-9: Enregistrement des rapports.

B. 4570–4619: Enregistrement des rapports des capitaines au long
cours.

B. 4641–4664: Enregistrement des rapports de maîtres au cabotage.

C. 589: Les representations à faire au sujet de l'enlèvement d'un
navire par les Portugais sur la côte de Guinée.

C. 602: Les Armaments du port de Nantes pour la Guinée et le
nombre qu'on pourra introduire aux colonies, 1762–7.

C. 604: La préférence accordée aux Anglais par le Roi Dahomey qui
se plaignait des fusils qu'on lui avait envoyés, 1771–6.

C. 615: L'Opposition des Anglais au commerce des Français sur les
Côtes de Guinée, 1728–44.

C. 687: Lettres, requêtes, rapports, mémoires, addressés aux juges,
consuls et aux amirautés de Nantes, de Bordeaux, de La Rochelle
sur les hostilités commises par les Anglais contre le commerce
de France sur la côte de Guinée, 1737–52.

C. 727: Mémoire de M. Guestard, daté St Louis, contenant de
renseignement sur la trait des nègres et les objets d'échange
reclamés par le roi de Dahomey, 1773.

C. 738: Attestation de Ministres du Roi d'Ardres expliquant la
conduite des gens du roi de Dahomey, 1788, et avis addressé aux
capitaines françaises par Pierre, secrétaire du Roi d'Ardrés.

C. 739: Rapport sur la situation de Juda et le commerce de Guinée,
1732.

C. 740: Etats Généraux des Navires expédiés du Port de Nantes
pour la Guinée de 1748–75.

### 8. *Archives Départementales, La Rochelle*

B. 4570–4596: Enregistrement des rapports des capitaines au long
cours, 1693–1779.

B. 5590–5810: Amirauté de La Rochelle, Rapports, procès-verbaux,
déclarations, 1671–1792.

# Bibliography

9. *Chambre de Commerce et d'Industries de La Rochelle*
Carton XIX: Commerce d'Afrique—Traité des Noirs.

10. *Archivo Publico dos Bahia*
Ordens Regiais: 21–69, 1726–61.
Correspondence, 1805.

11. *Archivo Historico Ultramarino, Lisbon*
Codice 254, 1729.
Caixa 4–10, Sao Tome, 1732–84.
Caixa Bahia, 1795–97.

12. *Archivo Bibliotheca Nacional de Rio de Janeiro*
No. 563 (1795); No. 846 (1804).

SECONDARY SOURCES

The following list by no means exhausts the number of books that have been published on Dahomey. It is simply a selection of those that have been most useful to me in the preparation of this book. Works not mentioned here, but which have been used, are acknowledged in the footnotes.

Adams, Capt. John. *Sketches taken during ten Voyages to Africa between 1768 and 1800* (London, 1821).
—— *Remarks on the country extending from Cape Palmas to River Congo* (1823).
Agbo, Casimir, dit Alidji. *Histoire de Ouidah de XVIᵉ au XXᵉ siècle* (Avignon, 1959).
Akindele, A. and Aguessy, C. *Contribution à l'étude de l'ancien Royaume de Porto Novo* (IFAN, Dakar, 1953).
Astley, T. *A New and General Collection of Voyages and Travels*, 4 vols. (London, 1745–7).
Atkins, John. *A Voyage to Guinea, Brasil and the West Indies* (London, 1735).
Barbot, John. *A Description of the Coasts of North and South Guinea* (London, 1732).
Benezet, A. *Some Historical Accounts of Guinea* (Philadelphia, 1772).
Beraud. 'Notes sur le Dahomey', in *Bulletin de la Société de Géographie*, XII (1866), p. 371.
Berbain, Simone. *Le Comptoir Français de Juda au XVIIIᵉ siècle* (Paris, 1942).
Bertho, Jacques. 'La Parente des Yoruba aux peuplades de Dahomey et Togo', in *Africa* (1949), pp. 121–32.

Biobaku, S. O. *The Egba and their Neighbours, 1842–1872* (Oxford, 1957).

—— *Origins of the Yoruba* (Lugard Lectures, Lagos, 1959).

—— 'The Problem of Traditional History with special reference to Yoruba traditions', in *Journal of the Historical Society of Nigeria*, vol. II, no. 1, pp. 43–7.

Blake, J. W. *European Beginnings in West Africa, 1454–1578* (London, 1937).

Bosman, W. *A New and Accurate Description of the Coast of Guinea* (London, 1705).

Brunet and Giethlen. *Dahomey et Dépendances* (Paris, 1900).

Burton, Sir R. F. (ed. Isabella Burton). *A Mission to Gelele, King of Dahomey* (London, 1893, first published in 1864).

Clapperton, Hugh. *Journal of Second Expedition into the Interior of Africa* (London, 1829).

Cornevin, R. *Histoire des peuples de l'Afrique Noire* (Paris, 1960).

—— *Histoire de Togo* (Paris, 1959).

—— *Histoire du Dahomey* (Paris, 1962).

Coupland, R. *The British anti slavery Movement* (London, 1933).

Dalzel, A. *The History of Dahomey, An inland Kingdom of Africa* (London, 1793).

Davidson, Basil. *Black Mother* (London, 1961).

Davies, K. G. *The Royal African Company, 1672–1713* (London, 1957).

Donnan, Elizabeth. *Documents Illustrative of the history of the Slave Trade to America*, 4 vols. (Washington, D.C., 1930–4).

Duncan, John. *Travels in Western Africa in 1845 and 1846*, 2 vols. (London, 1847).

Dunglas, Edouard. 'Contribution à l'histoire du Moyen Dahomey', in *Etudes Dahoméennes*, vols. XIX, XX and XXI (1957–8).

Dupuis, Joseph. *Journal of a Residence in Ashantee* (London, 1824).

Edwards, Major T. 'Amazon—Mythology and Reality', in *West Africa Pamphlet*, no. 58.

Egharevba, Jacob. *A Short History of Benin* (Benin, 1953, first published in 1934).

Ellis, A. B. *The Ewe Speaking Peoples of West Africa* (London, 1890).

Fage, J. D. *An Introduction to the History of West Africa* (Cambridge, 1956).

Faux, Claude. 'Deux Anciens Comptoirs Françaises de la Côte de Guinée', in *BCHSAOF* (1922), pp. 122–37.

Gaston-Martin. *L'Ere des Negriers, 1714–1774* (Paris, 1931).

Geay, J. 'Origine, Formation et Histoire du Royaume de Porto Novo, d'après une légende orale des Porto Noviens', in (1924), pp. 619–34.

Hazoume, P. *Le Pact du sang au Dahomey* (Paris, 1937).

## Bibliography

Le Herisse. *L'Ancien Royaume du Dahomey* (Paris, 1911).

Herskovits, M. J. *Dahomey, An Ancient West African Kingdom*, 2 vols. (New York, 1938).

Johnson, Rev. S. (ed. O. Johnson). *The History of the Yorubas* (Lagos, 1956, first published 1921).

Labarthe, P. *Voyage à la Côte de Guinée* (Paris, 1803).

Labat, P. *Voyage du chevalier des marchais en Guinée, isles voisines, et à Cayenne, fait en 1725, 1726 et 1727*, 2 vols. (Paris, 1735).

Labouret, H. and Rivet, P. *Le Royaume d'Ardra et son Evangélisation au XVIIᵉ siècle* (Paris, 1929).

Landolphe, Captain (ed. J. S. Quesne). *Mémoire de Capitaine Landolphe* (Paris, 1823).

Lloyd, Christopher. *The Navy and the Slave Trade* (London, 1949).

MacInnes, G. M. *England and Slavery* (Bristol, 1934).

Macleod, John. *A Voyage to Africa, with some accounts of the Manners and customs of the Dahomian people* (London, 1820).

Marty, Paul. *Etudes sur Islam au Dahomey* (Paris, 1926).

Mathieson, W. L. *England in Transition, 1789–1832* (London, 1920).

Mercier, P. 'Notice sur le peuplement Yoruba au Dahomey-Togo', in *E.D.* vol IV (1950), pp. 29–40.

Newbury, C. W. *The Western Slave Coast and its Rulers* (Oxford, 1961).

Norris, R. *Memoirs of the Reign of Bossa Ahadee, King of Dahomey* (London, 1789).

Ogilby, John. *Africa, Being an Accurate Description of the Regions of the Aegypt, Barbary, Lybia, etc.* (London, 1670).

Parrinder, E. G. *The Story of Ketu* (Ibadan, 1956).

Piruz, Padre V. F. *Viagem de Africa em o Reino de Dahomé* (Brazil, 1800).

Richard-Mollard, J. *Afrique Occidentale Français* (Paris, 1949).

Roussier, P. *L'Etablissement d'Issigny, 1687–1702* (Paris, 1935).

Skertchly, J. Q. *Dahomey as It Is* (London, 1874).

Smith, William. *A New Voyage to Guinea* (London, 1744).

Snelgrave, William. *A New Account of Some Parts of Guinea and the Slave Trade* (London, 1734).

Ward, B. E. *Social Organisation of the Ewe-Speaking Peoples* (M.A. Thesis, London, 1949).

Whyndham, H. A. *The Atlantic and Slavery* (London, 1935).

Williams, Eric. *Capitalism and Slavery* (Virginia, 1945, first published in 1944).

# Index

Abiodun, Alafin of Oyo, 125, 145–6, 162–3, 164–8, 170, 175, 208
Abomey, capital of Dahomey, 22, 38, 95, 122, 125, 181; foundation of, 13, 21, 23; plateau of, 25, 62; population of, 26; under Agaja, 63, 88, 91; burnt by the Oyo (1726–30), 82, 90; evacuated by Agaja (1730), 89; court returns to (1743), 118; under Tegbesu, 117, 123, 133, 140, 143, 152–3; under Kpengla, 156, 159, 162, 171, 172; under Agonglo, 179; under Adandozan, 186, 195
Abomey-Calavi, slave market at (1776), 146
Abopa, Dahomean chief, 171
Abson, Lionel, director of English fort, 142, 143, 145, 149 n., 179; helps negotiate peace (1772), 153, 158, 205; and Dahomean decline in fortune, 160–2, 164, 171; ineptitude of, 182, 184; death (1803), 190
Accra, the, quarrel with Akwamu (1730), 92; Little Popo-, hired by Allada (1680), 33; army against Allada (1715), 49; attack Jakin (1726), 82; attack Dahomey (1737), 106
Adams, John, 160, 169 n.
Adamusu, 154; see also Kpengla
Adandozan, king of Dahomey, accession (1797), 186, 199; minority of, 187; economic measures, 187–8, 193–6; diplomacy, 188–93, 210; deposition of (1818), 111, 185 n., 198–201, 207, 209, 212; death (1861), 207; character, 200, 207
Afonja, Oyo general, 177
African Committee, in charge of English forts in West Africa, 5, 191–3
Africanus, Leo, 22

Agaja, king of Dahomey, 22, 131, 132, 137, 140, 147, 178, 199, 205; accession (1708), 39, 60–2; policies and administration, 63, 100–11 passim, 119, 121, 127, 128, 206; relations with Allada and Whydah, 23, 39, 63–5, 70–6 passim, 92–7 passim, 115, 177, 210, 213, 214; difficulties with Oyo, 68, 81–2, 95, 107; against the Mahi (1731), 98–9; against Jakin (1) 1732, 96, 99–100; (2) 1734, 105; (3) 1737, 106; attitude to Europeans and slave trade, 68, 74–81, 84–7, 94–8, 102–7 passim, 207, 208; against the Dutch, 5, 23–4, 106, 210; death (1740), 3, 107, 116 n.; physical characteristics, 62; character, 70, 107–9, 207
Agau, title of Dahomean General Commander, 65, 118, 119, 149, 153
Agazaye, 63
*Agbadjigbeto*, title of Agaja's spies, 63, 75
Agbangla, king of Whydah, 33, 35, 152
Agbo, Casimir, 39 n.
Agonglo, king of Dahomey, accession (1789), 175, 178–9; policies, 154 n., 178–9, 184–6, 189 n., 199; support of slave trade, 180–1; murder of (1797), 111, 186, 209; character, 207
Aguessy, 169 n.
Aguga, 53
Aguna, 155, 163, 172, 181
Ahangbe, twin sister of Akaba, 60–1
Aho, son of Dogbagri-Genu, 23, 37
Aho, Prince Justin, surviving head of Wegbaja family, 6, 25 n.
*Ahovi*, princes of Dahomey, 61
Aisan, ruler of Whydah, 35, 37, 38, 40
Ajara, ruler of, 133; slaves from, 128

227

# Index

Ajase, town of, 22, 168; see also Ardra(h)
Ajase Ipo, kingdom of, 21–2, 91–2, 139, 146, 165–70 passim, 188; ruler of, 167–70 passim, 214–15
Ajau, title of Dahomean Counsellor, 118, 171
*Ajele*, title of Oyo superintendent, 17, 125
Ajuda, 99
Akaba, king of Dahomey, 37–8, 60–2
Akindele, 169 n.
Akran, princes of Badagry, 156, 165–6
Akwamu, 33–4, 49–50, 81, 85, 90, 92; see also Ofori
Alafin, kings of Oyo, 81, 124–5, 146 n., 176–7; see also Abiodun, Awole, Obalokun, Ojigi
Albertus, Dutch factor, 56
Alege, Dahomean officer of French fort, 101–3
Alkomysh, language of the Olukumi, 13
Amat, ruler of Whydah, 35; see also Aisan
America, privateers from (1816), 195
American War of Independence (1776–83), 150–1, 174, 182, 209
Amissa, 129
Anago, Yoruba people, 134
Anecho, 198
Anglo-French War, 114, 127
Angola, 182, 195
Anomabu, 129
*Anubomey*, annual customs, 64, 102, 136, 161, 173, 196, 199
Aplogan, title of ruler of Gome, 41–2, 50, 68–9, 73, 86, 97, 105, 119
Apomu, Yoruba town, 176–7
Appah, 53, 104; see also Epe
Arabia, emigrants from, 11
Arda, 89
Ardra(h), (Ajase), town, 26, 57, 91 n., 168, 169 n., 214; king of, 45, 47, 188 n.
Ardra, Great, 214–15
Ardra, Little, 214–15
Ariconu, 186; see also Adandozan
Ashampo, army general, 105–6, 112, 120–1, 137–8
Ashanti, 81, 189 n., 204, 205; Odanquah of, 124
Aslo-Ouessa, 63
Assim, 26

Assu, chief, 40–1, 44–5, 49, 51, 97; island, 97, 98
Astley, T., 26, 37 n., 41 n.
Atakpame, 124
Atkins, John, 1
*Ato Anubomey* ceremony, 136; see also *Anubomey*
Avissu, 110; see also Tegbesu
Awole, Alafin of Oyo, 175–7
Awori, Yoruba kingdom, 9

Baagba, Dahomean officer, 101–2
*baba*, appellation given to Yoruba kings, 15
Badagry, kingdom of, 23, 91 n., 92, 111, 165–7; attacked by Agaja (1737), 107; trade at, 105, 115, 134, 139, 140, 146, 156, 198; Hertog's activities in, 24, 106; people of, 113, 166; port of, 164, 165, 167, 170, 175 n., 181, 182, 194; founding of old and new, 213
Bahia, 195
Baillie, William, director of English fort, 52–4, 56–8
Baldwyn, Ambrose, director of English fort, 58
Bans, 28
Barbot, John, 1
Bariba, the, 81, 164–5, 175
Basorun, title of leader of Oyo council of chiefs, 82, 145, 162, 177; see also Gaha
Bayley, Diggles, 192
Bayley, Paget, 142
Bazilio, J., director of Portuguese fort, 91, 96, 107, 112, 115, 121, 128
Benin, Yoruba kingdom, 9, 13 n., 21, 36, 182; Bight of, 195
Berbain, S., 121 n., 143 n., 151 n.
Blaney, J., director of English fort, 44–5, 48–9, 55
Bonny, 182
Borgu, 81, 164–5, 175
Bosman, William, 1
Bouchel, French resident agent at Allada, 40, 41 n., 54–5
Brandenburgers, European African Company of (established 1684), 5, 32
Brathwaite, J., director of Cape Coast Castle, 92, 94, 208
Brazil, Portuguese authorities in, 42, 130, 185, 210; slave trade to,

228

# Index

Ebi (cont.)
    24–5; inadequacies of, 33–5, 51,
        64, 68; end of system in Aja,
        66, 71; followed by Huffon, 69;
        followed in Yoruba country, 81,
        177, 204
Edun, army general, 177
Efon, Yoruba kingdom, 9
Egba, Yoruba kingdom, 9, 125,
        176
Egbado, Yoruba kingdom, 9
Egun, language of Allada, 23, 28
Ekiti, Yoruba kingdom, 9
Elbee, d', 28, 29
Elegbara, god of Adandozan, 189
Elmina, Dutch headquarters at, 54
English Royal African Company, ar-
        rival in West Africa (1553), 19;
        negotiations with Whydah, 5,
        42–3, 47, 48, 80, 92, 158; trade
        from Whydah, 32, 134, 143,
        147, 150, 163, 182, 194, 198,
        211; forts, 79, 113, 129, 138,
        145, 182, 190, 210; in debt,
        113–14; see also Abson, African
        Committee, Baillie, Baldwyn,
        Blaney, Cape Coast Castle,
        Dalzel, Deane, Devaynes, Duf-
        field, Goodson, Gregory, Hicks,
        Igelefe, James, Lambe, Rogers,
        Seven Years War, Testefolle,
        Turner, slave trade
Epe, kingdom of, 92, 99, 101, 111,
        113, 123, 128, 134; ruler of,
        59; port of, English plan fac-
        tory at (1714), 53–4, 55; Dutch
        withdraw to (1728), 80; trade
        at, 63, 75, 104, 105, 115, 139,
        140, 146
Ewe, Ghana people, 11

Fafore, chief, 97
Fanti, the, 96, 98
Favory, chief, 97
Fayrer, J., 145
Fita, Yoruba town, 187
Flotte, de, 169 n.
Fon, language of Dahomey, 87
Fon, the, 134
Fonseca e Aragão, de, Francisco
        Antonio, 198
Forbes, F. E., 185 n.
Freeman, Thomas Birch, 197
French, arrival in West Africa
        (c. 1530), 19, 26, 28; West

India Company (formed 1664),
        5–6; forts, 79, 84, 95, 112, 114,
        138, 168; factories, 29, 79;
        against the Dutch (1670), 29–
        30; Tezifon's embassy to (1670),
        30–1; relations with Whydah,
        35, 43, 48, 53, 58, 72, 96–7;
        negotiations with king of Allada
        (1715), 54–7, 75; against Agaja
        (1727), 79–80, 84–6; slave
        trade, 115, 139, 143, 147, 150,
        151, 159, 164, 169, 190, 193;
        trade affected (1794), by French
        Revolution, 183–4, 209; rela-
        tions with Tegbesu, 128, 129,
        134; excluded from Gold Coast
        by British (1749), 129; raided
        by old Whydah (1) 1767, 149,
        (2) 1770, 152; invasion of Daho-
        mey (1893), 212; see also
        Alege, Bouchel, D'Ayrie, de la
        Garenne, Delisle, Dubelay, Du
        Coulombier, Dupetitval, Gallot,
        Gourg, Guestard, Levens,
        Levet, Montaguere, Seven Years
        War, slave trade, Warell, de
Fruku, Dahomean prince, 116, 171,
        178–9
Fulani Jihad, outbreak of (1804),
        176, 188, 211
Fusupo, title of Dahomean army
        commander, 119

Gaboon, slave trade on coast of, 195
Gaha, Oyo Basorun, 125, 145,
        146 n., 162, 211
Gallot, Etienne, director of French
        fort, 87, 108, 216
Gangan, Akran of Badagry, 156, 165
Gaston-Martin, 143
Gbodo, 177
Gbonka, title of Oyo officer, 82
Gbowele, province of Mahi, 132
Gede, Yoruba people, 21
Gedevi, Yoruba people, 13 n.
Gezo, ruler of Dahomey, 171;
        mother sold into slavery, 186;
        seizure of power (1818), 154 n.,
        197, 199–201, 207; policy of
        independence from Oyo, 111,
        124, 201, 208, 211; death
        (1858), 207; support of slave
        trade, 209, 212
Glele, 100
Gobir, Fulani Jihad in, 176

230

# Index